Intermediate Spanish For Dummies

MW00999728

Regular Verb Conjugation

-ar Verbs (hablar [to speak])

Person	Present	Preterit	Imperfect	Future	Conditional	Present Subjunctive
yo	hablo	hablé	hablaba	hablaré	hablaría	hable
tú	hablas	hablaste	hablabas	hablarás	hablarías	hables
él, ella, Ud.	habla	habló	hablaba	hablará	hablaría	hable
nosotros	hablamos	hablamos	hablábamos	hablaremos	hablaríamos	hablemos
vosotros	habláis	hablasteis	hablábais	hablaréis	hablaríais	habléis
ellos, ellas, Uds.	hablan	hablaron	hablaban	hablarán	hablarían	hablen

-er and -ir Verbs (beber [to drink]; subir [to go up])

Person	Present	Preterit	Imperfect	Future	Conditional	Present Subjunctive
yo	bebo / subo	bebí / subí	bebía / subía	beberé / subiré	bebería / subiría	beba / suba
tú	bebes / subes	bebiste / subiste	bebías / subías	beberás / subirás	beberías / subirías	bebas / subas
él, ella, Ud.	bebe / sube	bebió / subió	bebía / subía	beberá / subirá	bebería / subiría	beba / suba
nosotros	bebemos / subimos	bebimos / subimos	bebíamos / subíamos	beberemos / subiremos	beberíamos / subiríamos	bebamos / subamos
vosotros	bebéis / subís	bebisteis / subisteis	bebíais / subíais	beberéis / subiréis	beberíais / subiríais	bebáis / subáis
ellos, ellas, Uds.	beben / suben	bebieron / subieron	bebían / subían	beberán / subirán	beberían / subirían	beban / suban

High-Frequency Irregular Verbs (Present Tense Only)

Irregular Verbs in the Present Tense

Infinitive	yo	tú	él, ella, Ud.	nosotros	vosotros	ellos, ellas, Uds.
dar (to give)	doy	das	da	damos	dáis	dan
decir (to say)	digo	dices	dice	decimos	decís	dicen
estar (to be)	estoy	estás	está	estamos	estáis	están
hacer (to do)	hago	haces	hace	hacemos	hacéis	hacen
ir (to go)	voy	vas	va	vamos	vais	van
poder (to be able to)	puedo	puedes	puede	podemos	podéis	pueden
poner (to put)	pongo	pones	pone	ponemos	ponéis	ponen
querer (to want)	quiero	quieres	quiere	queremos	queréis	quieren
saber (to know)	sé	sabes	sabe	sabemos	sabéis	saben
ser (to be)	soy	eres	es	somos	sois	son
tener (to have)	tengo	tienes	tiene	tenemos	tenéis	tienen
venir (to come)	vengo	vienes	viene	venimos	venís	vienen
ver (to see)	veo	ves	ve	vemos	veis	ven

BESTSELLING BOOK SERIES

Intermediate Spanish For Dummies®

Cheat Sheet

Parts of Speech

- A *noun* is a part of speech that refers to a person, place, thing, quality, idea, or action.
- A *verb* is a part of speech that shows action or a state of being. A *transitive verb* requires a direct object to complete its meaning. An *intransitive verb* doesn't have an object.
- A *pronoun* is a part of speech that replaces a noun.
- An *adjective* modifies a noun.
- An *adverb* modifies a verb, an adjective, or another adverb.
- A *preposition* shows the relation of a noun to some other word in the sentence.
- *Demonstrative pronouns* express "this," "that," "these," and "those."

- A *subject pronoun* is followed by the verb expressing the main action in the sentence. These pronouns include I, you, he, she, it, we, and they.
- *Possessive pronouns* indicate that something belongs to a specific person (my, your, his, her, its, our, their).
- *Interrogative pronouns* ask a question (who, which, what, and so on).
- *Direct object pronouns* replace direct object nouns and answer who or what the subject is acting upon.
- *Indirect object pronouns* replace indirect object nouns and explain to or for whom something is done.
- *Reflexive pronouns* show that the subject is acting upon itself.

Forming Gerunds

Forming Gerunds of Regular Verbs

Ending	Verb Example	Meaning	Gerund	Meaning
-ar	**bailar**	*to dance*	bail**ando**	*dancing*
-er	**comer**	*to eat*	com**iendo**	*eating*
-ir	**abrir**	*to open*	abr**iendo**	*opening*

Forming Gerunds of -er or -ir Verbs Ending in a Vowel

Verb Example	Meaning	Gerund	Meaning
caer	*to fall*	ca**yendo**	*dancing*
leer	*to read*	le**yendo**	*reading*
oír	*to hear*	o**yendo**	*hearing*
traer	*to bring*	tra**yendo**	*bringing*

Asking for Information

When you want to ask for information in Spanish, you'll more than likely use one of the following words/phrases:

¿cuánto(s)? ¿cuánta(s)?	*How much/many?*
¿cómo?	*How?*
¿cuándo?	*When?*
¿dónde?	*Where?*
¿adónde?	*(To) where?*
¿por qué?	*Why?* (for what reason)
¿para qué?	*Why?* (for what purpose)
¿quién(es)?	*Who?*
¿a quién?	*(To) whom?*
¿de quién?	*Whose?*
¿cuál(es)?	*What? Which one(s)?*
¿qué?	*What?*

Forming Commands (the Imperative) of Regular Verbs

Remember that the subject of a command is understood to be *you*.

The Imperative of Regular Verbs

Person	-ar Verbs	-er Verbs	-ir Verbs
	mirar (*to look [at], watch*)	**correr** (*to run*)	**partir** (*to leave*)
Ud.	**Mire.** (*Look.*) **No mire.** (*Don't look.*)	**Corra.** (*Run.*) **No corra.** (*Don't run.*)	**Parta.** (*Leave.*) **No parta.** (*Don't leave.*)
Uds.	**Miren.** (*Look.*) **No miren.** (*Don't look.*)	**Corran.** (*Run.*) **No corran.** (*Don't run.*)	**Partan.** (*Leave.*) **No partan.** (*Don't leave.*)
tú	**Mira.** (*Look.*) **No mires.** (*Don't look.*)	**Corre.** (*Run.*) **No corras.** (*Don't run.*)	**Parte.** (*Leave.*) **No partas.** (*Don't leave.*)
vosotros	**Mirad.** (*Look.*) **No miréis.** (*Don't look.*)	**Corred.** (*Run.*) **No corráis.** (*Don't run.*)	**Partid.** (*Leave.*) **No partáis.** (*Don't leave.*)

For Dummies: Bestselling Book Series for Beginners

Intermediate Spanish

FOR

DUMMIES®

by Gail Stein

WILEY
Wiley Publishing, Inc.

Intermediate Spanish For Dummies®

Published by
Wiley Publishing, Inc.
111 River St.
Hoboken, NJ 07030-5774
www.wiley.com

For general information on our other products and services, please contact our Customer Care Department within the U.S. at 800-762-2974, outside the U.S. at 317-572-3993, or fax 317-572-4002.

For technical support, please visit www.wiley.com/techsupport.

Wiley also publishes its books in a variety of electronic formats. Some content that appears in print may not be available in electronic books.

Library of Congress Control Number: 2007942524

ISBN: 978-0-470-18473-8

Manufactured in the United States of America

10 9 8 7 6 5 4 3 2 1

WILEY

About the Author

Gail Stein, MA, is a retired language instructor who taught in New York City public junior and senior high schools for more than 33 years. She has authored several French and Spanish books, including *CliffsQuickReview French I* and *II, CliffsStudySolver Spanish I* and *II, 575+ French Verbs,* and *Webster's Spanish Grammar Handbook.* Gail is a multiple-time honoree in Who's Who Among America's Teachers.

Dedication

This book is dedicated to the memory of my father, Jack Bernstein, who will always be there for me.

This book is also dedicated to my husband, Douglas, for his love and patience; to my wonderful children, Eric, Michael, and Katherine, for their encouragement and support; and to my mother, Sara Bernstein, for always rooting for me.

Author's Acknowledgments

Many thanks to Michael Lewis, my acquisitions editor, who was so helpful in getting this book off the ground. To Stephen R. Clark, my project editor, and Josh Dials, my copy editor, whose excellent editing skills and suggestions made this book a reality. To Dr. Victor E. Krebs, whose technical expertise and input were invaluable. And to all the other people at Wiley for their patience and help.

Publisher's Acknowledgments

We're proud of this book; please send us your comments through our Dummies online registration form located at www.dummies.com/register/.

Some of the people who helped bring this book to market include the following:

Acquisitions, Editorial, and Media Development

Project Editor: Stephen R. Clark

Acquisitions Editor: Michael Lewis

Copy Editor: Josh Dials

Technical Editor: Dr. Victor E. Krebs, Associate Professor of Spanish, Marian College

Editorial Manager: Christine Meloy Beck

Editorial Assistants: Erin Calligan Mooney, Joe Niesen, David Lutton

Cartoons: Rich Tennant (www.the5thwave.com)

Composition Services

Project Coordinator: Patrick Redmond

Layout and Graphics: Carrie A. Cesavice, Brooke Graczyk, Stephanie D. Jumper, Laura Pence

Proofreaders: Broccoli Information Mgt., Caitie Kelly

Indexer: Broccoli Information Mgt.

Publishing and Editorial for Consumer Dummies

    Diane Graves Steele, Vice President and Publisher, Consumer Dummies

    Joyce Pepple, Acquisitions Director, Consumer Dummies

    Kristin A. Cocks, Product Development Director, Consumer Dummies

    Michael Spring, Vice President and Publisher, Travel

    Kelly Regan, Editorial Director, Travel

Publishing for Technology Dummies

    Andy Cummings, Vice President and Publisher, Dummies Technology/General User

Composition Services

    Gerry Fahey, Vice President of Production Services

    Debbie Stailey, Director of Composition Services

Contents at a Glance

Table of Contents

Introduction

As someone who has surpassed the beginning level of Spanish, you consider yourself rather proficient in the language and want to discover more. So, here you are, eager to jump up to a higher level and perfect your skills. That's fantastic! Whether you're planning a trip, engaging in business with Spanish speakers, or are just a lover of languages, *Intermediate Spanish For Dummies* will help you reach your goals painlessly and effortlessly as you enhance your Spanish language writing skills.

When it comes to using a foreign language, you may be shy about speaking it, but I'm willing to bet that you're much more intimidated by writing it. Writing demands a bit more precision. My main goal is to help you become more comfortable with your Spanish language writing skills.

Intermediate Spanish For Dummies not only presents you with all the grammar you need to know to communicate on an intermediate level, but also provides you with clear examples and interesting and useful exercises that will help you hone your Spanish writing skills. I give you the opportunity to put what you've learned to work and to express your thoughts and ideas in writing. If you can finish the exercises in a flash, you know you've mastered the material well. Some exercises, of course, present more of a challenge and require additional attention and focus. That's to be expected. Just keep in mind that after you finish all the chapters, you'll be a full-fledged intermediate Spanish graduate! Feel free to brag to friends.

About This Book

Intermediate Spanish For Dummies is a refresher course, a reference book, and a workbook for people who have some experience with and knowledge of the fundamentals of Spanish and want to take their knowledge to the next level. It serves as a logical extension and complement to the ever-popular *Spanish For Dummies,* by Susana Wald (Wiley). If you want to get "up to speed" with language structures so that you can communicate comfortably and proficiently, especially with the written word, this book is for you.

Each chapter in this book presents a different topic that affords you the opportunity to practice your written communication skills by completing, or actually writing, e-mails, postcards, text messages, journal entries, and letters. I reinforce nuances of style, usage, and grammar rules every step of the way so that you learn and practice how native speakers and writers use the language. I also include plenty of examples to guide you through the rules and exercises and to expose you to colloquial, everyday, correct Spanish that native speakers expect to hear from someone using Spanish.

Before you move on, I must reiterate an important point: This is a workbook! Don't be afraid to write in it. Use your favorite pink highlighter or your trusty red pen to underline the points you want to remember. Don't recite the exercise answers in your head! That doesn't help you practice your writing skills. Put all the answers down on paper and commit to them before checking them in the Answer Key at the end of each chapter. This technique will help you get the most knowledge out of this book.

Conventions Used in This Book

In order to highlight the most important information and to help you navigate this book more easily, I've set up several conventions:

- Spanish terms and sentences, as well as endings or stems I want to highlight, are set in **boldface** to make them stand out.

- English equivalents, set in *italics,* follow the Spanish examples.

- An Answer Key appears at the end of every chapter. The key provides the correct answers to all practice activities within the chapter. The parts of the answers that you must provide appear in bold. In the more difficult activities, I include explanations for the correct answers.

- You'll see many abbreviations throughout the book. Don't let them throw you. For instance, you may find the following:

    - fem. (feminine)

    - fam. (familiar)

    - masc. (masculine)

    - pol. (polite)

    - sing. (singular)

    - pl. (plural)

Here's what you won't find in this book: Tons of translation exercises. Why not? Because you can't speak a foreign language colloquially or fluently if you try to translate your thoughts word for word from one language to the next. Language-acquisition experiments have proven that this learning method simply doesn't work, so translation exercises were long ago removed from textbooks across the country. To pick up a new language the way a child learns his or her first language, you must immerse yourself in the language so that you begin thinking in that language — and you can't do that by slowly and painfully translating one word at a time.

You will find some guided compositions that prompt you to express certain thoughts in this book. Don't, however, feel that you must translate the sentences given to you exactly as they appear. The Spanish language has its individual idioms and idiomatic expressions that give it color and flair. Here's a quick example: To say that it's sunny outside in Spanish, you remark: **Hace sol.** The literal English translation of this expression is *It is making sun.* Even my dear old grandma wouldn't have spoken English like that! Well, make sure you don't speak Spanish that way, either.

Foolish Assumptions

When writing this book, I made the following assumptions about you, my dear reader:

- You have some experience with and knowledge of the fundamentals of Spanish grammar. You're looking for the opportunity to review what you've already mastered and are intent on moving forward to new areas of knowledge.

✔ You can speak Spanish fairly well and are more interested in improving your writing skills.

✔ You want to perfect your Spanish because you're planning a trip, conducting business, or are a foreign-language student.

✔ You want to speak and write Spanish colloquially, like a native does, and you want to use Spanish in practical, everyday applications.

✔ You want a book that's complete but isn't so advanced that you get lost in the rules. I try to explain the rules as clearly as possible without using too many grammatical terms. I've left out the most advanced grammar because you simply don't need it to be understood in everyday situations. Keep it clean and simple and you'll do just fine, and others will appreciate your honest attempts at communicating in another language.

How This Book Is Organized

I've divided *Intermediate Spanish For Dummies* into six parts so that you can focus on whatever suits your fancy at the moment. Feel free to skip parts that you feel you already know or that are irrelevant to you. The following sections outline the focus of the six parts of this book.

Part 1: Reviewing the Basics

In this part, you review the vocabulary and knowledge of numbers that you need daily when using Spanish. Right from the first chapter, you're given a working vocabulary that will help you express yourself in most situations. I also give a quick grammar review as a refresher to what you've mastered on the elementary level. Finally, although you may think you're a pro at finding the right word in the dictionary, this part will show you how to avoid making common errors.

Part 11: Writing in the Present

This part shows you how to write in the present tense, using verbs that are regular and verbs that are really quite quirky. You practice asking and answering yes/no questions, as well as questions that ask for information. I also introduce the present progressive tense, which allows you to express actions that are taking place as we speak, and the mysteries of the present subjunctive — with clear explanations and examples.

Part 111: Writing for Specific Clarity

This part takes you on a tour of fundamental Spanish grammar: nouns, adjectives, adverbs, comparisons, direct and indirect object pronouns, commands, reflexive verbs, and prepositions. These topics reflect the building blocks of the language; you just can't write clearly without them. You discover how Spanish differs from English because of rules regarding gender (masculine or feminine forms of nouns and adjectives). You find out where to properly place the parts of speech in a sentence. And oddly enough, in this part, you learn things about English you never knew because no English teacher ever mentioned this grammar in any of your classes.

Part IV: Writing in the Past and in the Future

Part IV presents the two main past tenses in Spanish: the preterit and the imperfect. You find out how to form each of these tenses, and you review the conditions where they must be used. This exercise is particularly important because there's no English equivalent of the imperfect, making its use a bit strange to many people. You also see how to express what you're going to do in the future.

Part V: The Part of Tens

The three Tens chapters in this part will help you to improve your writing skills. I show you the ten most common writing mistakes people make in Spanish so that you can avoid them at all costs. You get ten tips that will show you how to write better sentences and steer clear of common grammar mistakes. Finally, you discover how to select which Spanish verb to use when two of them seem to have the same English definition.

Part VI: Appendixes

The final part is where you find the important reference material. Here you get multiple verb charts that give the conjugations for all types of verbs in all types of Spanish tenses and moods. This appendix will prove to be an invaluable tool when you need a quick reference guide. The other two appendixes in this part provide comprehensive Spanish to English and English to Spanish dictionaries, to which you can refer when you're doing chapter exercises.

Icons Used in This Book

Icons are those cute little drawings on the left side of the page that call out for your attention. They signal a particularly valuable piece of information, a rule that you should consider to avoid making an unnecessary error, or a list of exercises that you can complete. Here's a list of the icons in this book:

Remember icons call your attention to important information about the language — something you shouldn't neglect or something that's out of the ordinary. Don't ignore these paragraphs.

Tip icons are there to show you explicitly how to execute a task. Tips present time-saving tidbits that make communication quick and effective. If you want to know the proper way to do things, check out the Tip icons first.

The Differences icon points out certain differences between English and Spanish. If you want to know how Spanish constructions differ from those in English, these are the paragraphs you need to consult.

Practice icons flag exercises, which is where you need to go to put the grammar rules you read about into action. Language theory is grand, but if you can't apply it properly, it really isn't worth very much. The practice exercises are your golden opportunity to hone your Spanish skills.

Where to Go from Here

One great thing about this book (and all *For Dummies* books) is that you don't have to follow it chapter by chapter from the very beginning to the (not-so) bitter end. You can start where you like and jump all over the place if that is your pleasure. Each chapter stands on its own and doesn't require that you complete any of the other chapters in the book. This saves you a lot of time if you've mastered certain topics but feel a bit insecure or hesitant about others.

So, go ahead and jump right in. Get your feet wet. If you're not sure exactly where to begin, take a good look at the table of contents and select the topic that seems to best fit your abilities and needs. If you're concerned that your background may not be strong enough, you can start at the very beginning and slowly work your way through the book. If you feel confident and self-assured, skip right to the practice exercises and see how well you do. Because each lesson is an entity unto itself, you can hop around from the middle to the front to the back without missing a beat.

An important thing to keep in mind is that this isn't a race and it isn't a contest. Work at a pace that best suits your needs. Don't hesitate to read a chapter a second or third or even a fourth time several days later. You may even want to repeat some exercises. This is a book that you can easily adapt to your learning abilities. Remember, too, that you need to have a positive, confident attitude. Yes, you'll make mistakes. Everyone does — as a matter of fact, many native Spanish speakers do all the time. Your main goal should be to write and speak as well as you can; if you trip up and conjugate a verb incorrectly or use the feminine form of an adjective rather than the masculine form, it isn't the end of the world. If you can make yourself understood, you've won the greatest part of the battle.

Part I
Reviewing the Basics

In this part . . .

The easiest way to get some Spanish vocabulary under your belt and to feel like you're making immediate progress in your writing skills is to take a brief refresher course so you can review the basics. The chapters in Part I show you how much you already know.

I give you a rapid review of cardinal and ordinal numbers and how to use them when expressing the date and the time of day. I also present a quick grammar study. You're probably uttering a deep sigh at this moment, but this lesson will make the rules throughout the book easier to understand. Here you read all about nouns, pronouns, verbs, adjectives, and adverbs, and you get an explanation on how to use a bilingual dictionary so that you select the proper part of speech each and every time. With this strong foundation, you'll quickly gain the confidence you need to start jotting down your thoughts in Spanish.

Chapter 1

Looking at Some Everyday Basics

● ●

● ●

*W*hether you're a student, a traveler, a businessperson, or just someone interested in learning and using Spanish, knowing numbers, expressing dates, and relating the time of day are essential skills you'll need in everyday life. Students must follow a schedule, keep track of due dates, and be able to discuss the grades they receive. Travelers and many businesspeople must refer to flight numbers; departure and arrival times and dates; gate, pier, or track numbers; and currency exchange rates.

In addition, businesspeople must keep track of the dates and times of important appointments (this goes for students and travelers, too), the value of certain currencies, and interest rates. Surely, the ability to communicate numbers, times, and dates is completely indispensable to you no matter your background, concerns, or interests.

This chapter provides a review of everyday basics that you'll have to speak and write about. I review both cardinal numbers (the ones used to count) and ordinal numbers (the ones used to express numbers in a series), and I recap how you use these numbers to express dates and times of day (or night). By the time you review all the material in this chapter, you'll be a pro at doing the right thing at the right time — for the least amount of money!

Focusing on Spanish Numbers

I start off this chapter with numbers because you need them in order to express dates and tell time. And when I talk numbers, I'm talking cardinal and ordinal numbers. You use *cardinal numbers* (the more popular of the two) to count, to bargain with a merchant about a price, to express the temperature, or to write a check. You use *ordinal numbers* to express the number of a floor, the act of a play, or the order of a person in a race or competition.

Cardinal numbers

You use cardinal numbers many times every day. As a matter of fact, you probably use them at least once an hour in the course of normal conversation or in writing. The Spanish cardinal numbers are as follows:

Number	Spanish	Number	Spanish
0	cero	25	veinticinco (veinte y cinco)
1	uno	26	veintiséis (veinte y seis)
2	dos	27	veintisiete (veinte y siete)
3	tres	28	veintiocho (veinte y ocho)
4	cuatro	29	veintinueve (veinte y nueve)
5	cinco	30	treinta
6	seis	40	cuarenta
7	siete	50	cincuenta
8	ocho	60	sesenta
9	nueve	70	setenta
10	diez	80	ochenta
11	once	90	noventa
12	doce	100	cien (ciento)
13	trece	101	ciento uno
14	catorce	200	doscientos
15	quince	500	quinientos
16	dieciséis (diez y seis)	700	setecientos
17	diecisiete (diez y siete)	900	novecientos
18	dieciocho (diez y ocho)	1.000	mil
19	diecinueve (diez y nueve)	2.000	dos mil
20	veinte	100.000	cien mil
21	veintiuno (veinte y uno)	1.000.000	un millón
22	veintidós (veinte y dos)	2.000.000	dos millones
23	veintitrés (veinte y tres)	1.000.000.000	mil millones
24	veinticuatro (veinte y cuatro)	2.000.000.000	dos mil millones

English speakers generally write the number 1 in one short, downward stroke. In the Spanish-speaking world, however, the number 1 has a little hook on top, which makes it look like a 7. So, in order to distinguish a 1 from a 7, you put a line through the 7, which makes it look like this: 7̶.

You need to remember the following rules when using cardinal numbers in Spanish:

> ✔ **Uno** (*one*), used only when counting, becomes **un** before a masculine noun and **una** before a feminine noun, whether the noun is singular or plural:
>
> • **uno, dos, tres** (*one, two, three*)
>
> • **un niño y una niña** (*a boy and a girl*)
>
> • **sesenta y un dólares** (*61 dollars*)
>
> • **veintiuna (veinte y una) personas** (*21 people*)

✔ You use the conjunction **y** (*and*) only for numbers between 16 and 99. You don't use it directly after hundreds:

- **ochenta y ocho** (*88*)

- **doscientos treinta y siete** (*237*)

✔ You generally write the numbers 16–19 and 21–29 as one word. The numbers 16, 22, 23, and 26 have accents on the last syllable:

- 16: **dieciséis**

- 22: **veintidós**

- 23: **veintitrés**

- 26: **veintiséis**

✔ When used before a masculine noun, **veintiún** (*21*) has an accent on the last syllable:

- **veintiún días** (*21 days*)

- **veintiuna semanas** (*21 weeks*)

✔ **Ciento** (*100*) becomes **cien** before nouns of either gender and before the numbers **mil** and **millones.** Before all other numbers, you use **ciento.** **Un** (*one*), which you don't use before **cien(to)** or **mil,** comes before **millón.** When a noun follows **millón,** you put the preposition **de** between **millón** and the noun. **Millón** drops its accent in the plural (**millones**):

- **cien sombreros** (*100 hats*)

- **cien blusas** (*100 blouses*)

- **cien mil millas** (*100,000 miles*)

- **cien millones de dólares** (*100 million dollars*)

- **ciento noventa acres** (*190 acres*)

- **mil posibilidades** (*1,000 possibilities*)

- **un millón de razones** (*1,000,000 reasons*)

✔ In compounds of **ciento** (**doscientos, trescientos**), there must be agreement with a feminine noun:

- **cuatrocientos pesos** (*400 pesos*)

- **seisientas pesetas** (*600 pesetas*)

When it comes to numerals and decimals, Spanish uses commas where English uses periods, and vice versa:

English	*Spanish*
6,000	6.000
0.75	0,75
$14.99	$14,99

In most instances, people simply write numerals when they need to express numbers. However, when you write checks, the transactions won't take place unless you write out the amounts of the checks in words. For this exercise, fill in the incomplete checks with the written Spanish numbers.

Juan Gómez
1000 Calle Cruz
Madrid, España

Banco Nacional de España
1111 Avenida Cristóbal Colón
Madrid, España

101
00-000/000

(Fecha) _____ 20 ___

Páguese a
la orden de ___ Geraldo Nuñez _____ 79 ___ €

_____ EUROS

MEMORÁNDUM _____   _____
FIRMA AUTORIZADA

Juan Gómez
1000 Calle Cruz
Madrid, España

Banco Nacional de España
1111 Avenida Cristóbal Colón
Madrid, España

102
00-000/000

(Fecha) _____ 20 ___

Páguese a
la orden de ___ José Martín _____ 621 ___ €

_____ EUROS

MEMORÁNDUM _____   _____
FIRMA AUTORIZADA

Juan Gómez
1000 Calle Cruz
Madrid, España

Banco Nacional de España
1111 Avenida Cristóbal Colón
Madrid, España

103
00-000/000

(Fecha) _____ 20 ___

Páguese a
la orden de ___ Julia López _____ 1,595 ___ €

_____ EUROS

MEMORÁNDUM _____   _____
FIRMA AUTORIZADA

Juan Gómez	Banco Nacional de España	**104**
1000 Calle Cruz	1111 Avenida Cristóbal Colón	00-000/000
Madrid, España	Madrid, España	(Fecha) _____ 20 ___

Páguese a
la orden de _Luz Cabral_ _____ 42,717 €

_____ EUROS

MEMORÁNDUM _____ _____ FIRMA AUTORIZADA

Juan Gómez	Banco Nacional de España	**105**
1000 Calle Cruz	1111 Avenida Cristóbal Colón	00-000/000
Madrid, España	Madrid, España	(Fecha) _____ 20 ___

Páguese a
la orden de _Roberto Cádiz_ _____ 984,862 €

_____ EUROS

MEMORÁNDUM _____ _____ FIRMA AUTORIZADA

Ordinal numbers

You use *ordinal numbers* — those used to express numbers in a series — far less frequently than cardinal numbers, but they still have some very important applications in everyday life. Perhaps when you go to work, you must ask for your floor in an elevator. During a job interview or on a college application, you may have to express where you placed in your class standings. The following chart presents the Spanish ordinal numbers:

Ordinal	Spanish
1st	**primero**
2nd	**segundo**
3rd	**tercero**
4th	**cuarto**
5th	**quinto**
6th	**sexto**
7th	**séptimo**
8th	**octavo**
9th	**noveno**
10th	**décimo**

The following list outlines everything you must remember when using ordinal numbers in Spanish:

- Spanish speakers rarely use ordinal numbers after "10th." After that, they usually use cardinal numbers in both the spoken and written language:

    • **el séptimo mes** (*the seventh month*)

    • **el siglo quince** (*the 15th century*)

- Ordinal numbers must agree in gender (masculine or feminine) with the nouns they modify. You can make ordinal numbers feminine by changing the final **-o** of the masculine form to **-a:**

    • **el cuarto día** (*the fourth day*)

    • **la cuarta vez** (*the fourth time*)

    Primero and **tercero** drop the final **-o** before a masculine singular noun:

    • **el primer muchacho** (*the first boy*)

    • **el tercer hombre** (*the third man*)

- The Spanish ordinal numbers may be abbreviated. You use the superscript ^{o} for masculine nouns and the superscript ^{a} for feminine nouns. And you use ^{er} only for the abbreviations of **primer** and **tercer:**

    • **primero(a):** $1^{o(a)}$

    • **segundo(a):** $2^{o(a)}$

    • **tercero(a):** $3^{o(a)}$

    • **cuarto(a):** $4^{o(a)}$

    • **primer:** 1er

    • **tercer:** 3er

- A cardinal number that replaces an ordinal number above 10th is always masculine, because the masculine word **número** (*number*) is understood:

    la calle (número) ciento y dos (*102nd Street*)

- In dates, **primero** is the only ordinal number you use. All other dates call for the cardinal numbers:

    • **el primero de mayo** (*May 1st*)

    • **el doce de enero** (*January 12th*)

- In Spanish, cardinal numbers precede ordinal numbers:

    las dos primeras escenas (*the first two scenes*)

- You use cardinal numbers when expressing the first part of an address:

    mil seiscientos Avenida Pennsylvania (*1600 Pennsylvania Avenue*)

A business associate is visiting from Spain and needs some help. Respond to her e-mail by telling her which floor of the building will provide the assistance she needs. Write out the ordinal numbers. Consult the following directory of offices:

Edificio Cabeza de Vaca

Restaurante El Marino   10°

Cabrera y Cabrera, abogados   9°

Juan Cruz, contable   8°

Ana Vásquez, asesora fiscal   7°

Santiago López, reparaciones de computadores   6°

Rosita Rosario, sistemas de seguridad   5°

Carmen Sánchez, teléfonos celulares   4°

María Rodrigo, servicio de mensajero   3°

Alejandro Morales, rótulos y logos   2°

Tintorería Ruíz   1°

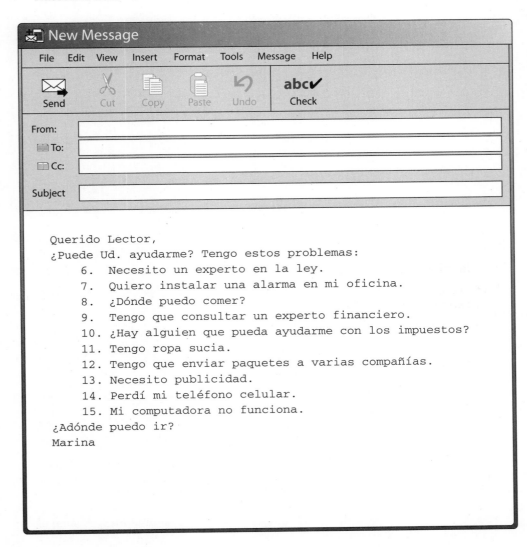

```
Querido Lector,
¿Puede Ud. ayudarme? Tengo estos problemas:
     6.  Necesito un experto en la ley.
     7.  Quiero instalar una alarma en mi oficina.
     8.  ¿Dónde puedo comer?
     9.  Tengo que consultar un experto financiero.
    10.  ¿Hay alguien que pueda ayudarme con los impuestos?
    11.  Tengo ropa sucia.
    12.  Tengo que enviar paquetes a varias compañías.
    13.  Necesito publicidad.
    14.  Perdí mi teléfono celular.
    15.  Mi computadora no funciona.
¿Adónde puedo ir?
Marina
```

```
New Message

File   Edit   View   Insert   Format   Tools   Message   Help

Send    Cut    Copy    Paste    Undo    abc✔
                                        Check

From:  [                                              ]
To:    [                                              ]
Cc:    [                                              ]
Subject [                                             ]


       Querida Marina,
            6.     Vaya al _____ piso.
            7.     Vaya al _____ piso.
            8.     Vaya al _____ piso.
            9.     Vaya al _____ piso.
           10.     Vaya al _____ piso.
           11.     Vaya al _____ piso.
           12.     Vaya al _____ piso.
           13.     Vaya al _____ piso.
           14.     Vaya al _____ piso.
           15.     Vaya al _____ piso.
```

Making Dates

Dates are important parts of everyday life (in more ways than one!). If you're writing a paper with a strict due date, leaving on vacation and need flight confirmations, or scheduling appointments for your clients and customers, you need to know how to express dates. To write out dates in Spanish, which I have you do later in this section, you have to practice the days of the week, the months of the year, and numbers (see the previous section).

Days

If you hear **¿Qué día es hoy?** someone must have forgotten what day of the week it is. You should respond with **Hoy es . . .** (*Today is . . .*) and then provide the name of one of the days I list here:

English	*Spanish*
Monday	**lunes**
Tuesday	**martes**
Wednesday	**miércoles**
Thursday	**jueves**
Friday	**viernes**
Saturday	**sábado**
Sunday	**domingo**

Unlike the English calendar, the Spanish calendar starts with Monday.

Here are two more guidelines for talking about days of the week in Spanish:

- ✔ Unless you use them at the beginning of a sentence, you don't capitalize the days of the week in Spanish:
  - **Lunes es un día de vacaciones.** (*Monday is a vacation day.*)
  - **Lunes y martes son días de vacaciones.** (*Monday and Tuesday are vacation days.*)
- ✔ You use **el** to express *on* when referring to a particular day of the week and **los** to express *on* when the action occurs repeatedly:
  - **No trabajo el sábado.** (*I'm not working on Saturday.*)
  - **No trabajo los sábados.** (*I don't work on Saturdays.*)

With the exception of **sábado** and **domingo,** the plural forms of the days of the week are the same as the singular forms:

Singular	*Plural*
lunes	**lunes**
martes	**martes**
miércoles	**miércoles**
jueves	**jueves**
viernes	**viernes**
sábado	**sábados**
domingo	**domingos**

Months

If you hear **¿En qué mes . . .?** someone is asking you in what month a certain event takes place. The curious person could be asking about the beginning or end of the school year, a special holiday celebration, the occurrence of a business meeting, or expected travel plans. I provide the names of the months in Spanish in the following table so that you can stay on top of all your important social and business obligations:

English	Spanish
January	**enero**
February	**febrero**
March	**marzo**
April	**abril**
May	**mayo**
June	**junio**
July	**julio**
August	**agosto**
September	**septiembre** (or **setiembre**)
October	**octubre**
November	**noviembre**
December	**diciembre**

Like days of the week, the months aren't capitalized in Spanish:

> **Junio es un mes agradable.** (*June is a nice month.*)
>
> **Junio y julio son meses agradables.** (*June and July are nice months.*)

In South American countries south of the equator, the seasons of the year are reversed. For example, when it's snowing in the United States, the sun is shining south of the equator.

In Spanish, the seasons are masculine except for **la primavera** (*the spring*):

> **el invierno** (*the winter*)
>
> **la primavera** (*the spring*)
>
> **el verano** (*the summer*)
>
> **el otoño** (*the autumn [fall]*)

Writing dates

If you want to ask a passerby or an acquaintance about the date, politely inquire **¿Cuál es la fecha de hoy?** (*What is today's date?*) The person should respond with **Hoy es . . .** (*Today is . . .*) and then use the following formula to express the correct date:

> day + (**el**) + cardinal number (except for **primero**) + **de** + month + **de** + year

The following is an example translation, using this formula:

> *Sunday, April 15, 2008:* **Hoy es domingo, el quince de abril de dos mil ocho.**

Now that you have a handy formula, you need to know a few more details about writing dates in Spanish:

✔ You express the first day of each month with **primero.** You use cardinal numbers for all other days:

- **el primero de enero** (*January 1st*)
- **el siete de enero** (*January 7th*)
- **el treinta de octubre** (*October 30th*)

✔ Use **el** to express *on* with Spanish dates:

Partimos el once de octubre. (*We are leaving on October 11th.*)

✔ In Spanish, you express years in thousands and hundreds, not only in hundreds:

1492: **mil cuatrocientos noventa y dos** (*fourteen hundred ninety-two*)

In Spanish, when dates are written as numbers, they follow the sequence day/month/year, which may prove confusing to English speakers — especially for dates below the 12th of the month:

You write *February 9th* as 2/9 in English, but in Spanish it's 9/2.

When speaking of dates in everyday language, the words and expressions that follow may come in handy:

English	Spanish	English	Spanish
a day	**un día**	*day before yesterday*	**anteayer**
a week	**una semana**	*yesterday*	**ayer**
a month	**un mes**	*today*	**hoy**
a year	**un año**	*tomorrow*	**mañana**
in	**en**	*tomorrow morning*	**mañana por la mañana**
ago	**hace**	*tomorrow afternoon*	**mañana por la tarde**
per	**por**	*tomorrow night*	**mañana por la noche**
during	**durante**	*day after tomorrow*	**pasado mañana**
next	**próximo(a)**	*from*	**desde**
last	**pasado(a)**	*a week from today*	**de hoy en una semana**
last (in a series)	**último(a)**	*two weeks from tomorrow*	**de mañana en dos semanas**
eve	**la víspera**	*within one (two) week(s)*	**dentro de una (dos) semana(s)**

You're writing a paper for your Spanish class on famous Hispanic men who fought for the independence of their country. Fill in the dates of their births and deaths in Spanish:

16. (August 20, 1778–October 24, 1842) Bernardo O'Higgins, hombre que luchó por la independencia de Chile, nació _____ y murió

    _____.

17. (May 8, 1753–July 30, 1811) Miguel Hidalgo, iniciador de la revolucion mexicana, nació _____ y murió _____.

18. (July 24, 1783–December 17, 1830) Simón Bolívar, libertador y hombre dominante de la independencia de Suramérica nació _____ y murió

    _____.

19. (January 28, 1853–May 19, 1895) José Martí, espíritu de la lucha por la independencia de Cuba, nació _____ y murió

    _____.

Telling Time

If you're anything like me, you consult your watch or a clock on a nearby wall several times a day. Knowing how to understand, speak, and write time-related words and phrases is a must for anyone who's studying a foreign language and planning to put these studies to use (to do some traveling one day, for instance).

If you hear **¿Qué hora es?** someone wants to know the time. You should start by responding with the following:

> **Es la una** + 1 o'clock hour or **Son las** + any time after 1

To express the time after the hour (but before half past the hour), use **y** (*and*) and the number of minutes. Use **menos** (*less*) + the number of the following hour to express the time before the next hour (after half past the hour).

You can also express time numerically (as shown in the third example here):

> **Es la una y media.** (*It's 1:30.*)
>
> **Son las cinco menos veinte.** (*It's 4:40.*)
>
> **Son las cuatro y cuarenta.** (*It's 4:40.*)

If you want to discuss *at* what time a particular event will occur, you can use a question — **¿A qué hora . . . ?** — or answer with **A la una** or **A las** + any time after 1:

> **¿A qué hora vienen?** (*At what time are they coming?*)
>
> **A la una.** (*At 1:00.*)
>
> **A las tres y cuarto.** (*At 3:15.*)

The following chart shows how to express time after and before the hour:

Time	Spanish
1:00	**la una**
2:05	**las dos y cinco**
3:10	**las tres y diez**
4:15	**las cuatro y cuarto** or **las cuatro y quince**
5:20	**las cinco y veinte**
6:25	**las seis y veinticinco**
7:30	**las siete y media** or **las siete y treinta**
7:35	**las ocho menos veinticinco** or **las siete y treinta y cinco**
8:40	**las nueve menos veinte** or **las ocho y cuarenta**
9:45	**las diez menos cuarto** or **las nueve y cuarenta y cinco**
10:50	**las once menos diez** or **las diez y cincuenta**
11:55	**las doce menos cinco** or **las once y cincuenta y cinco**
noon	**el mediodía**
midnight	**la medianoche**

When expressing time, the words and expressions I present in the following table may come in handy:

English Phrase	Spanish Equivalent	English Phrase	Spanish Equivalent
a second	**un segundo**	in an hour	**en una hora**
a minute	**un minuto**	in a while	**dentro de un rato**
a quarter of an hour	**un cuarto de hora**	until ten o'clock	**hasta las diez**
an hour	**una hora**	before nine o'clock	**antes de las nueve**
a half hour	**una media hora**	after seven o'clock	**después de las siete**
in the morning (a.m.)	**por la mañana**	since what time?	**¿desde qué hora?**
in the afternoon (p.m.)	**por la tarde**	since eight o'clock	**desde las ocho**
in the evening (p.m.)	**por la noche**	one hour ago	**hace una hora**
at what time?	**¿a qué hora?**	early	**temprano**
at exactly nine o'clock	**a las nueve en punto**	late	**tarde**
at about two o'clock	**a eso de las dos**	late (in arriving)	**de retraso**

One of your friends, Soledad, is very curious about your other friends' comings and goings. She wrote Marta an e-mail asking for information. Read the information provided by Soledad and then answer each question in her e-mail by giving the correct time in Spanish.

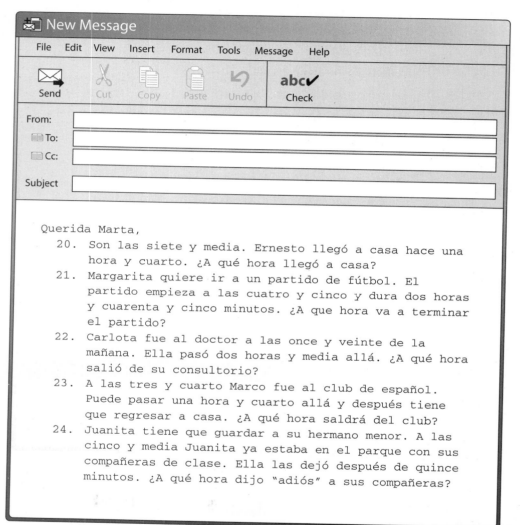

Querida Marta,

20. Son las siete y media. Ernesto llegó a casa hace una hora y cuarto. ¿A qué hora llegó a casa?

21. Margarita quiere ir a un partido de fútbol. El partido empieza a las cuatro y cinco y dura dos horas y cuarenta y cinco minutos. ¿A que hora va a terminar el partido?

22. Carlota fue al doctor a las once y veinte de la mañana. Ella pasó dos horas y media allá. ¿A qué hora salió de su consultorio?

23. A las tres y cuarto Marco fue al club de español. Puede pasar una hora y cuarto allá y después tiene que regresar a casa. ¿A qué hora saldrá del club?

24. Juanita tiene que guardar a su hermano menor. A las cinco y media Juanita ya estaba en el parque con sus compañeras de clase. Ella las dejó después de quince minutos. ¿A qué hora dijo "adiós" a sus compañeras?

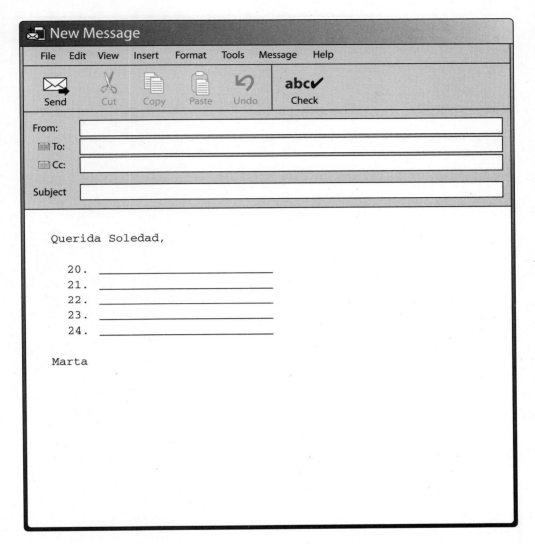

```
New Message

File   Edit   View   Insert   Format   Tools   Message   Help

  Send      Cut      Copy     Paste     Undo       Check

From:  [                                              ]
  To:  [                                              ]
  Cc:  [                                              ]

Subject [                                             ]


     Querida Soledad,

        20. _____
        21. _____
        22. _____
        23. _____
        24. _____


     Marta
```

You're traveling from Barcelona to Madrid; on your way, you must check the **Tren** (*train*) schedule. Write out all the numbers and times you see in Spanish.

Barcelona a Madrid

Número del tren	Salida	Llegada	Duración del viaje (1)	Cargo por ventas
01578	07:00	12:00	DIARIO del 19-03-2007 hasta el 31-05-2007	Turista: 65.30 Turista Niños: 39.20 Primera Clase: 101.20 Primera Clase Niños: 60.75

Barcelona a Madrid

Número del tren	Salida	Llegada	Duración del viaje (1)	Cargo por ventas
_____	_____	_____	DIARIO del _____ hasta que el_____	Turista: _____ Turista Niños: _____ Primera Clase: _____ Primera Clase Niños: _____

Answer Key

1 Check 101: **setenta y nueve**

2 Check 102: **seiscientos veintiuno**

3 Check 103: **mil quinientos noventa y cinco**

4 Check 104: **cuarenta y dos mil setecientos diecisiete**

5 Check 105: **novecientos ochenta y cuatro mil ochocientos sesenta y dos**

6 **noveno.** The lawyer is on the 9th floor.

7 **quinto.** The alarm company is on the 5th floor.

8 **décimo.** The restaurant is on the 10th floor.

9 **séptimo.** The financial consultant is on the 7th floor.

10 **octavo.** The accountant is on the 8th floor.

11 **primer.** The laundry service is on the 1st floor.

12 **tercer.** The delivery service is on the 3rd floor.

13 **segundo.** The sign company is on the 2nd floor.

14 **cuarto.** The cellphone company is on the 4th floor.

15 **sexto.** The computer-repair company is on the 6th floor.

16 **el veinte de agosto de mil setecientos setenta y ocho**

 el veinticuatro de octubre de mil ochocientos cuarenta y dos

17 **el ocho de mayo de mil setecientos cincuenta y tres**

 el treinta de julio de mil ochocientos once

18 **el veinticuatro de julio de mil setecientos ochenta y tres**

 el diecisiete de diciembre de mil ochocientos treinta

19 **el veintiocho de enero de mil ochocientos cincuenta y tres**

 el diecinueve de mayo de mil ochocientos noventa y cinco

20 **Ernesto llegó a casa a las seis y cuarto.** (*Ernesto arrived home at 6:15.*)

21 **El partido va a terminar a las siete menos diez.** (*The match is going to end at 6:50.*)

22 **Salió del consultorio del doctor a la una y cincuenta.** (*She left the doctor's office at 1:50.*)

23 **Marco saldrá del club a las cuatro y media.** (*Marco will leave the club at 4:30.*)

24 **Juanita dijo "adiós" a sus compañeras a las seis menos cuarto.** (*Juanita said "goodbye" to her friends at 5:45.*)

Barcelona a Madrid				
Número del tren	*Salida*	*Llegada*	*Duración del viaje (1)*	*Cargo por ventas*
mil quinientos	las siete	el mediodía	DIARIO **del diecinueve de marzo de mil novecientos siete hasta el treinta y uno de mayo de mil novecientos siete**	Turista: **sesenta y cinco euros treinta** Turista Niños: **treinta y nueve euros veinte** Primera Clase: **ciento uno euros veinte** Primera Clase Niños: **sesenta euros setenta y cinco**

Chapter 2

Selecting the Proper Part of Speech

. . . .

In This Chapter

▶ Differentiating between the various parts of speech

▶ Selecting the correct word for every situation

▶ Perfecting your use of a bilingual dictionary

. . . .

Years ago, diagramming sentences was an essential topic covered in English grammar class. Most students preferred to read the steamy, famous novel *du jour,* but they were forced to sit in class, pen (and sometimes ruler) in hand, figuring out where to place a noun, a verb, or an elusive direct or indirect object. Many old timers such as myself still remember this experience with a certain amount of distaste. Those tedious exercises, however, have served many of us very well in our careers; we're now tempted to mark up the grammar errors we see on signs, menus, and correspondences. For those who want to transfer that ability — the ability to understand, write, speak, and correct the "Queen's Spanish" — this chapter is essential reading.

In this chapter, I provide a quick course on identifying and using the parts of speech that make Spanish sentences grammatically correct. Specifically, you discover how to recognize verbs, nouns, adjectives, adverbs, and pronouns, and you get some practice in using them properly. Also, finding the correct word in a bilingual dictionary can be a tricky task. Don't worry, help is here! I show you how to navigate both sides of the vocabulary lists so that you don't make a mistake.

Identifying and Using Parts of Speech

You may be questioning why it's so important to know your Spanish grammar. Can't you just grab a dictionary when you want to find a word and move on? The answer would be "yes" if it were that simple a task. What many people fail to realize is that a Spanish word may have many applications depending on its usage in the sentence. In addition, many idiomatic phrases, when used properly, will distinguish a native speaker from someone who's unfamiliar with the language. (An *idiomatic phrase* is a phrase used in a particular language whose meaning can't easily be understood by a literal translation of its component words. An English example is *It's raining cats and dogs.*) As you browse through the following sections and do the exercises, you'll certainly realize the need to muscle up your grammar skills.

Nouns

A *noun* is the part of speech that refers to a person, place, thing, quality, idea, or action. Here are some examples of nouns in action:

- Person: The **boy** is friendly. (El **muchacho** es amable.)
- Place: I want to go **home.** (Quiero ir a **casa.**)
- Thing: I would like to see that **book.** (Quisiera ver ese **libro.**)
- Quality: I admire her **courage.** (Admiro su **coraje.**)
- Idea: **Communism** is a political theory. (El **comunismo** es una teoría política.)
- Action: The plane's **departure** is imminent. (La **partida** del avión es inminente.)

In everyday speaking/writing, you'll use nouns most often in the following forms:

- As the subject of a verb:

  Mary speaks Spanish. (**María** habla español.)
- As the direct object of a verb:

  I see **Mary.** (Yo veo a **María.**)
- As the indirect object of a verb:

  I speak to **Mary.** (Yo le hablo a **María.**)
- As the object of a preposition:

  I went out with **Mary.** (Yo salí con **María.**)

Unlike English nouns, all Spanish nouns have a gender: masculine or feminine. All words you use to qualify or describe a noun must agree with the noun with respect to gender. I discuss this in more detail in Chapter 3.

The Spanish language classifies nouns as common or proper, collective, or concrete or abstract. A *common noun* refers to a general class of persons, things, places, and so on:

El **hombre** es alto. (*The man is tall.*)

Los **edificios** son modernos. (*The buildings are modern.*)

Me gustan los **deportes.** (*I like sports.*)

A *proper noun* is the specific name of a person, thing, place, and so on:

George Washington fue un presidente. (*George Washington was a president.*)

Guernica es una pintura por Picasso. (*Guernica is a painting by Picasso.*)

España es un país en Europa. (*Spain is a country in Europe.*)

A *collective noun* is used singularly and refers to a group:

Mi **familia** es pequeña. (*My family is small.*)

A *concrete noun* refers to something that you can perceive with your senses; an *abstract noun* refers to an idea:

> Concrete: El **agua** es azul. (*The water is blue.*)

> Abstract: El **odio** es un vicio. (*Hate is a vice.*)

Pronouns

A *pronoun* is a part of speech used in place of a noun. The following list outlines the pronouns I discuss in this book:

- Demonstrative pronouns (see Chapter 3) express *this, that, these,* and *those:*

  Show me **that.** (Muéstreme **eso.**)

- Subject pronouns (see Chapter 4) are followed by the verb expressing the main action in the sentence (*I, you, he, she, it, we, they*):

  You are nice. (**Ud.** es simpático.)

- Possessive pronouns (see Chapter 3) indicate that something belongs to a specific person (*my, your, his, her, its, our, their*):

  That's **my** umbrella. (Es **mi** paraguas.)

- Interrogative pronouns (see Chapter 5) ask a question (*who, which, what,* and so on):

  Who is **that?** (¿**Quién** es?)

- Direct object pronouns (see Chapter 10) replace direct object nouns; they answer *who* or *what* the subject is acting upon. The direct object pronouns are **me, te, lo, la** (**le** in Spain), **nos,** (**os** in Spain), **los,** and **las** (**les** in Spain):

  I'll be seeing **you.** (**Te** veo.)

- Indirect object pronouns (see Chapter 10) replace indirect object nouns; they explain *to* or *for* whom something is done. They include **me, te, le, nos,** (**os** in Spain), and **les:**

  He wrote to **me.** (**Me** escribió.)

- Reflexive pronouns (see Chapter 11) show that the subject is acting upon itself (**me, te, se, nos,** [**os** in Spain]):

  They wake up early. (Ellos **se** despiertan temprano.)

- Prepositional pronouns (see Chapter 12) are used after prepositions (**mí, ti, él, ella, Ud., nosotros, vosotros** (in Spain), **ellos, ellas, Uds.**):

  They're going to the movies without **me.** (Van al cine sin **mí.**)

  The prepositional pronouns **mí** and **ti** become **migo** and **tigo,** respectively, after the preposition **con** (*with*):

  Is he going to school with **you?** (¿Va a la escuela **contigo?**)

Verbs

A *verb* is a part of speech that shows an action or a state of being. In Spanish, as in English, verbs change from their infinitive form (they're conjugated, in other words) as follows:

- ✔ To agree with the person performing the action (I, you, he, she, it, we, they)
- ✔ To indicate the time when the action was performed (past, present, future)
- ✔ To indicate the mood (subjunctive, imperative) of the action

The *infinitive* of the verb is its "raw" form — its "to" form before it's conjugated. Infinitives in Spanish have three different endings, and you conjugate them according to these endings: **-ar, -er,** and **-ir** when a subject is present or is implied. The following presents a sample conjugation of *to swim:*

nadar (*to swim*)	
He likes **to swim.**	Le gusta **nadar.**
He **swims** rather well.	Él **nada** bastante bien.
We **swim** well, too.	Nosotros **nadamos** bien también.

Verbs are classified as transitive or intransitive. A *transitive verb* must be followed by a direct object to complete its meaning:

> I opened **the door.** (Yo abrí **la puerta.**)

An *intransitive verb* doesn't require an object:

> I understand. (Yo comprendo.)

You can use some verbs both transitively and intransitively:

> She **speaks** Spanish. (Ella **habla** español.)

> She **speaks** well. (Ella **habla** bien.)

Also, a verb may be used reflexively or reciprocally to show that the subject is acting upon itself (see Chapter 11):

> I **washed myself.** (Yo **me lavé.**)

> They **love each other.** (Ellos **se aman.**)

Adjectives

An *adjective* is a part of speech that describes a noun:

> The house is **white.** (La casa es **blanca.**)

A Spanish adjective can have other applications, too, which I outline in the following list:

- ✔ A possessive adjective tells to whom the noun belongs:

  It's **my** book. (Es **mi** libro.)

- ✔ A demonstrative adjective shows *this, that, these,* or *those:*

  That film is good. (**Esa** película es buena.)

- ✔ An interrogative adjective asks the question *whose, which,* or *what:*

  Whose car is that? (**¿De quién** es ese coche?)

- ✔ An indefinite adjective shows an indefinite amount:

  He has **many** friends. (Él tiene **muchos** amigos.)

- ✔ A number (cardinal or ordinal; see Chapter 1) is an adjective that gives a specific amount:

  I need **a** pen. (Necesito **un** bolígrafo.)

  It's his **tenth** birthday. (Es su **décimo** cumpleaños.)

Adverbs

An *adverb* is a part of speech that modifies a verb, an adjective, or another adverb (all of which are underlined in the following list):

- ✔ Modifying a verb: You <u>speak</u> **quickly.** (Ud. <u>habla</u> **rápidamente.**)
- ✔ Modifying an adjective: Her grandmother is **very** <u>old</u>. (Su abuela es **muy** <u>vieja</u>.)
- ✔ Modifying an adverb: They eat **too** <u>slowly</u>. (Ellos comen **demasiado** <u>despacio</u>.)

In English, many adverbs end in *-ly:* calmly, certainly, and so on. In Spanish, many adverbs end in **-mente: tranquilamente** (*calmly*), **ciertamente** (*certainly*), and so on.

Read each sentence very carefully and determine the part of speech that's missing: noun, verb, adjective, or adverb. Select the answer that best completes the sentence. Here's an example:

Q. When will the <u>play</u> begin? ¿Cuándo va a empezar _____?

    a. el jugo

    b. jugar

    c. tocar

    d. la obra

A. **d.** ¿Cuándo va a empezar **la obra?**

1. It's time to <u>act</u>. Hay que _____.
   a. acto
   b. comportarse
   c. ponerse en acción
   d. representarse

2. My <u>back</u> hurts. Me duele _____.
   a. la espalda
   b. el apoyo
   c. el trasero
   d. de atrás

3. Is he going to <u>break</u> his promise? ¿Va a _____ su promesa?
   a. romper con
   b. descansar
   c. faltar a
   d. cambiar

4. She lives <u>close</u>. Ella vive _____.
   a. sofocante
   b. cercana
   c. cerrada
   d. cerca

5. The mechanic is going <u>to fix</u> my car. El mecánico va a _____ mi coche.
   a. preparar
   b. arreglar
   c. fijar
   d. estar en un apuro

6. This car <u>handles</u> like a dream. Este coche _____ de maravilla.
   a. va
   b. procesa
   c. hace
   d. toca

7. The <u>match</u> was exciting. El _____ era interesante.
   a. combinado
   b. fósforo
   c. emparejar
   d. partido

8. The museum is <u>on the right</u>. El museo está _____.

    a. a la razón

    b. a la derecha

    c. al derecho

    d. justo

Utilizing a Bilingual Dictionary

A *bilingual* Spanish dictionary is one with a Spanish to English section and an English to Spanish section (complete with idiomatic words and expressions). A good dictionary also will have Spanish pronunciation and spelling rules. Using a bilingual Spanish dictionary may sound easy, but it requires a lot of finesse and patience. Finding the exact word you want to use forces you to read carefully, to know your parts of speech, and to double check your findings.

 In the front of every bilingual dictionary you'll find a list of abbreviations, identifying the parts of speech and gender of a noun. This list is invaluable in determining if the word you're looking for is a noun, pronoun, verb, adjective, adverb, and so on. Table 2-1 gives you a quick look at the most useful abbreviations you can expect to find.

Table 2-1	Useful Abbreviations		
Abbreviation	*Full Word*	*Abbreviation*	*Full Word*
adj	adjective	nm (sometimes sm)	masculine noun
adv	adverb	neg	negative
conj	conjunction	p. ej.	for example
EEUU	United States	pl	plural
excl	exclamation	pp	past participle
f.	feminine	pref	prefix
infin	infinitive	prep	preposition
inv	invariable	pron	pronoun
irr	irregular	sing	singular
liter	literary	v (sometimes vb)	verb
m.	masculine	vi	intransitive verb
mf	masculine and feminine	vr	reflexive verb
n (or sometimes s for substantive)	noun	vt	transitive verb
nf (sometimes sf)	feminine noun		

To understand how a person may be confused by what he or she finds in a bilingual dictionary, it helps to look at an example of a dictionary entry. Focusing on the word "well," here's what you should find:

well

n	**pozo** (m.)
vi (*to well up*)	**brotar, manar**
adv (*in a good way*)	**bien**
adj (*healthy*)	**bien**
excl	**bueno, pues**

Perhaps you can see how confusing an entry can be: One word has five different applications. When looking at the Spanish equivalents for the English word "well," you have to make sure you select the proper word. Allow me to include some sample sentences to give you some practice. In the following, select the word that you think fits:

1. I am **well**, thank you. Estoy _____ gracias.

2. There is no water in the **well**. No hay agua en _____.

3. You speak Spanish **well**. Ud. habla _____ el español.

4. Tears will **well** up in my eyes. Las lágrimas van a _____ en mis ojos.

5. **Well**, that story is interesting! _____, esa historia es interesante.

How do you check yourself to make sure you chose properly? It takes your left hand. That's right! You must always keep fingers from both hands on both sides of the dictionary. Search for the word using your right hand, and then check the Spanish section with your left hand to make sure you used the correct part of speech. Generally, the dictionary will contain examples to help you. So, if you picked **pozo** for the first example, for instance, when you look on the Spanish side, you'll see *n.* (or *s.*) and [**de agua**] after the word **pozo,** which indicates that you've made a mistake. This method may be tricky and time-consuming, but it certainly helps you select the word you need.

So, how did you do? Check your answers:

1. **bien** 2. **el pozo** 3. **bien** 4. **brotar** 5. **bueno**

Using your bilingual dictionary, try your hand at the following sentences to see how many you can complete properly.

9. He has a **cold.** Tiene _____. I'm **cold.** Tengo _____.

10. What was the **end** result? ¿Qué fue el resultado _____? The match is going **to end** at 10 o'clock. El partido va a _____ a las diez.

11. She is going to **play** the piano. Ella va a _____ el piano. He likes **to play** golf. Le gusta _____ al golf.

12. Is that book **good?** ¿Es _____ ese libro? He works for the common **good.** Trabaja por _____ común.

13. Please **hand** a towel to Julia. Favor de _____ una servilleta a Julia. I hurt my **hand.** Me daño _____.

14. Are they going **to fire** many workers? ¿Van a _____ a muchos obreros? Did you see the **fire?** ¿Ha visto el _____?

15. You aren't going **to miss** the train. Ud. no va a _____ el tren. Excuse me, **miss.** Perdón, _____.

16. It's one of a **kind.** Es _____. You are very **kind.** Ud. es muy _____.

17. Our plane is going **to land.** Nuestro avión va a _____. They live off the **land.** Viven de la _____.

18. At what time are you going **to leave** the house? ¿A qué hora va a _____ de casa? You must **leave** the keys in the office. Ud. tiene que _____ las llaves en la oficina.

19. What is your **net** profit? ¿Qué es su beneficio _____? The fish is in the **net.** El pez está en _____.

20. Let's go to the **park.** Vamos al _____. She is going **to park** the car. Ella va a _____ el coche.

21. Are you going **to pass** the test? ¿Vas a _____ el examen? Are they going **to pass** by your house? ¿Van a _____ por su casa?

22. It's not a **question** of money. No es _____ de dinero. I have a **question.** Tengo _____.

23. Who won the **race?** ¿Quién ganó _____? What is her **race?** ¿Cuál es su _____?

24. Is the child **safe?** ¿Está _____ el niño? Put your money in the **safe.** Ponga su dinero en la _____.

25. They are going **to train** their dog. Van a _____ a su perro. I missed the **train.** Perdí el _____.

26. Let's go for a **walk.** Vamos a dar _____. We are going **to walk** through the park. Vamos a _____ por el parque.

Answer Key

1 c. "Act" is used as a verb in the sense of putting oneself into action.

2 a. "Back " is used as a noun. **Espalda** refers to that part of the body.

3 c. "Break" is used as a verb. **Faltar** means *to lack* and **cambiar** means *to change*.

4 d. "Close" is used as an adverb.

5 b. "Fix" is used as a verb in the sense of *to repair.*

6 a. "Handles" is used as a verb. The idiomatic expression **ir de** means *to handle.*

7 d. "Match" is used as a noun referring to a game.

8 b. "Right" is used as an adverb.

9 Use the noun **un resfriado,** which refers to an illness. Use the noun **frío** in this idiomatic expression, which refers to body temperature.

10 Use **final** as an adjective. Use **terminar** as a verb.

11 **Tocar** means *to play an instrument.* **Jugar** means *to play a sport.*

12 **Bueno** is used as an adjective describing the book. **El bien** is used as a noun.

13 Use **pasar** as a verb meaning *to pass something over.* **La mano** is a noun.

14 **Despedir** is the verb you use to fire someone. **El fuego** refers to the noun.

15 **Perder** is the verb meaning *to miss a train.* **Señorita** is a noun.

16 Use **único** as an adverb to represent something unique. Use **amable** as an adjective to describe someone who's nice.

17 **Aterrizar** is a verb. **La tierra** is a noun.

18 **Salir** is a verb that means *to leave a place.* **Dejar** is a verb that means *to leave something behind.*

19 You use **neto** as an adjective. **La red** is a noun.

20 **Parque** is a noun. **Apacar** is a verb.

21 **Aprobar** is the verb that means *to pass an exam.* **Pasar** is the verb that means *to pass by a place.*

22 **Cuestión** is the noun you use when referring to an issue. Use **una pregunta** when the subject is asking a specific question.

23 **La carrera** is the noun for a race that's a contest. **Raza** is the noun for a person's race.

24 **Seguro** is an adjective. **La caja fuerte** is a noun.

25 **Adiestrar** is the verb that means *to train an animal.* **El tren** is a noun.

26 **Un paseo** is a noun. **Andar** is a verb.

Part II
Writing in the Present

The 5th Wave   By Rich Tennant

In this part . . .

1 try not to dwell on the past; as for the future, well, who knows what's in store for each and every one of us? So, the perfect place to start after dealing with the basics is the here and now — the present. After you master the art of conjugating present-tense verbs, you'll find the other tenses to be less of a challenge.

In this part, you deal with all things present. You find out why masculine and feminine genders are important in Spanish, how to identify them, and how to make sure that all the words in your sentences agree in gender (and in number [singular or plural]). I introduce you to articles (the, a, an), demonstrative adjectives and pronouns (this, that, these, those), and possessive adjectives and pronouns (my, mine, and so on). You also discover how to make nouns plural.

Wait, there's more! I explain how to form the present tense of regular verbs, verbs with spelling and stem changes, and those elusive irregular verbs. Are you the curious type? You also find out how to ask and answer yes/no questions and questions that pry much deeper. Finally, I explain the formation and use of the present progressive and give you a thorough explanation of how to use the present subjunctive.

Chapter 3

Sorting Out Word Gender

. . . .

In This Chapter

▶ Getting gender specific with definite articles

▶ Keeping it general with indefinite articles

▶ Applying demonstrative adjectives and pronouns correctly

▶ Determining the gender of nouns

▶ Forming the plural of nouns

▶ Showing possession

. . . .

*L*et the battle of the sexes begin! Gender is a battle that English speakers don't fight. In English, a noun is simply a noun; you don't have to worry about a noun having a gender (a masculine or feminine designation). In Spanish, however, a noun has a gender, and the gender of a noun very often determines the spelling of other words in the sentence. What determines this gender? Certainly not what we perceive to be masculine or feminine. Don't assume anything. For instance, a tie (**una corbata**) is feminine in Spanish, while lipstick (**un lápiz de labios**) is masculine! Don't ask me why. I can't explain it. Gender in language is one of those things you have to accept. Take heart, though, because in Spanish, many word endings will help you to determine the gender of certain nouns.

In this chapter, I help you to correctly mark the gender of a noun by using definite articles (which express *the*), indefinite articles (which express *a, an,* or *some*), or demonstrative adjectives (which express *this, that, these,* or *those*). You find out how you can avoid repetition of the noun by using demonstrative pronouns. I demystify the gender of nouns by showing you noun endings that tend to be masculine or feminine. You discover the tricks to making nouns plural. Finally, after you've built some confidence with nouns, you can read up on the three different ways to show possession of things.

Marking Gender with Definite Articles

A *definite article* expresses the English word *the* and indicates a specific person or thing, such as "the boy" or "the book." If you know whether a noun is masculine or feminine in Spanish (or singular or plural), you must choose the correct definite article to "mark" that noun in order to say *the*. Using definite articles is easy after you determine the noun's gender (see the sections on gender later in this chapter).

 The definite article precedes the noun it modifies and agrees with that noun in number and gender. For example, **El muchacho es rubio y las muchachas son morenas.** (*The boy is blond and the girls are brunette.*)

Identifying the definite articles

Spanish features four distinct definite articles that correspond to *the* in English. The following table lists these articles:

	Masculine	*Feminine*
Singular	el	la
Plural	los	las

Here are some examples of these definitive articles in action:

El muchacho es grande. (*The boy is big.*)

Los libros son interesantes. (*The books are interesting.*)

La muchacha es alta. (*The girl is tall.*)

Las casas son blancas. (*The houses are white.*)

Using the definite articles

You'll come across many instances in Spanish where you'll use the definite article even though you may or may not use it in English. Study the rules in the following list; they show how you use the definite articles in Spanish in many different situations:

- With nouns in a general or abstract sense:

  El amor es divino. (*Love is divine.*)

- With nouns in a specific sense:

  La tía María trae regalos. (*Aunt Maria brings gifts.*)

- With names of languages (except after the verb **hablar** and after the prepositions **de** and **en**):

  Me gusta el español. (*I like Spanish.*)

  ¿Dónde está mi libro de español? (*Where's my Spanish book?*)

  Escríbame en español. (*Write to me in Spanish.*)

- With parts of the body (when the possessor is clear) in place of the possessive adjective:

  Me duelen los pies. (*My feet hurt.*)

- With titles and ranks when you aren't addressing the person:

  La señora Rivera está aquí. (*Mrs. Rivera is here.*)

  Siéntase, Señora Rivera. (*Have a seat, Mrs. Rivera.*)

- With last names:

  Los Gómez viven en Colombia. (*The Gómez's live in Colombia.*)

- With days of the week (except after the verb **ser**):

  El domingo voy a México. (*On Sunday I'm going to Mexico.*)

  Hoy es miércoles. (*Today is Wednesday.*)

- With seasons (you may omit the article after **en**):

  No trabajo en (el) verano. (*I don't work in the summer.*)

- With dates:

  Es el cinco de mayo. (*It's May 5th.*)

- With the hour of the day and other time expressions:

  Son las once y media. (*It's 11:30.*)

  Salgo por la tarde. (*I'm going out in the afternoon.*)

- With the names of many cities and countries (there's a tendency to omit the article in current usage):

  el Brasil, el Canadá, el Ecuador, el Japón, el Paraguay, el Perú, El Salvador, el Uruguay, la Argentina, la China, La Habana, la India, los Estados Unidos

  Visitamos (el) Brasil. (*We visited Brazil.*)

  Vivo en los Estados Unidos. (*I live in the United States.*)

   Capitalized articles are actually parts of the names of the countries, whereas articles in lowercase are not. For example, **Yo nací en El Salvador pero pasé muchos años en la Argentina.** (*I was born in El Salvador but I spent many years in Argentina.*)

- With rivers, seas, and other geographical locations:

  El Orinoco es un río. (*The Orinoco is a river.*)

- With the names of boats or ships:

  El Titanic se hundió. (*The Titanic sank.*)

- With adverbs and infinitives used as nouns (this is optional when the infinitive serves as the subject of the sentence):

  Lo hizó por el bien commún. (*He did it for the common good.*)

  (El) decir la verdad es una virtud. (*Telling the truth is a virtue.*)

- With weights and measures to express *a, an,* and *per:*

  Cuestan seis dólares la media docena. (*They cost $6 per half dozen.*)

- With clothing used in a general sense:

  Al entrar él se quitó el sombrero. (*Upon entering he removed his hat.*)

Omission of the definite articles

You omit the definite articles in the following situations in Spanish:

- Before nouns in apposition (when one noun explains another):

  Madrid, capital de España, es una ciudad popular. (*Madrid, the capital of Spain, is a popular city.*)

- Before numerals that express the title of rulers:

  Carlos Quinto (*Charles the Fifth*)

Contractions with the definite articles

Spanish features only two contractions. They occur when the definite article **el** is joined with the preposition **a** (**a** + **el** = **al**) or **de** (**de** + **el** = **del**). The only exception to the rule is when the definite article is part of the title or name. Here are some examples of this construction:

> **Vamos al Uruguay.** (*I'm going to Uruguay.*) **Voy a El Salvador.** (*I'm going to El Salvador.*)
>
> **Soy del Uruguay.** (*I'm from Uruguay.*) **Soy de El Salvador.** (*I'm from El Salvador.*)

The neuter lo

Neuter, in language, means that a word has no gender. You can identify a few neuter words in Spanish. One of them is the article **lo,** which you use only in the singular. The following list presents some examples of how you use **lo:**

- Before an adjective used as a noun to express an abstract idea or a quality:

   Lo normal es dormir de noche. (*It is normal to sleep at night.*)

- **Lo** + an adjective (or adverb) + **que,** which means *how:*

   ¿Ves lo serio que es? (*Do you see how serious it is?*)

   Es increíble lo rápidamente que él corre. (*It's incredible how fast he runs.*)

- **Lo** preceded by **a,** which means *in the manner of* or *like:*

   Ella habla a lo loco. (*She talks like crazy.*)

Marking Gender with Indefinite Articles

An *indefinite article,* which expresses the English words *a, an,* or *some,* refers to persons or objects not specifically identified (such as "a boy" or "some books"). Just like with definite articles, when you know whether a noun is masculine or feminine (and singular or plural), you can choose the correct indefinite article to "mark" that noun.

As with definite articles, the indefinite article precedes the noun it modifies and agrees with that noun in number and gender.

Identifying the indefinite articles

Four Spanish indefinite articles correspond to *a, an,* and *one* in the singular and to *some* in the plural. The following table presents these articles:

	Masculine	*Feminine*
Singular	un	una
Plural	unos	unas

Here are some examples of the indefinite articles in action:

Compró un abrigo. (*She bought an [one] overcoat.*)

Es una mujer muy astuta. (*She is a very astute woman.*)

Necesito unos limones y unas limas. (*I need some lemons and some limes.*)

Omission of the indefinite articles

You omit the indefinite article from your Spanish constructions in the following situations:

✔ Before unmodified nouns that express nationality, profession, or religious or political affiliation:

El señor Robles es professor. (*Mr. Robles is a teacher.*)

When the noun is modified, you use the indefinite article, however:

El señor Robles es un profesor liberal. (*Mr. Robles is a liberal teacher.*)

✔ Before unmodified nouns in apposition (unless you're referring to a family or business relationship):

Cervantes, escritor español, escribió Don Quijote. (*Cervantes, a Spanish writer, wrote Don Quixote.*)

✔ Before the following nouns:

- **cien** (*one hundred*) — **cien niños** (*one hundred children*)
- **cierto** (*certain*) — **ciertos idiomas** (*certain languages*)
- **mil** (*one thousand*) — **mil dólares** (*one thousand dollars*)
- **otro** (*other*) — **otra clase** (*another class*)
- **qué** (*what a*) — **qué lástima** (*what a pity*)
- **semejante** (*similar*) — **problema semejante** (*a similar problem*)
- **tal** (*such a*) — **tal cosa** (*such a thing*)

It's a rainy day in paradise! You're on a cruise, and you've finally found the time to write a letter to your pen pal in Mexico. Complete the letter in Figure 3-1 by filling in the correct definite article, indefinite article, or nothing at all. Use one of the following choices: **el, la, los, las, lo, al, del, un, una, unos,** or **unas.**

Querido Juan,

Hoy es (1)_____ lunes pero no trabajo en (2)_____

oficina. Estoy de (3)_____ vacaciones con mi primo, Ernesto, y

con (4)_____ compañero mío, Carlos. Ernesto es (5)_____

programador y Carlos es (6)_____ artista serio. Nos llevamos bien.

Mis amigos y yo hacemos (7)_____ crucero. Tenemos

(8)_____ camarote magnífico a bordo (9)_____ barco

grande que se llama (10)_____ Reina María (11)_____

Sexta. Nos levantamos temprano por (12)_____ mañana porque

hay (13)_____ mil cosas que hacer. (14)_____ Primero

tomamos (15)_____ desayuno enorme. Comemos (16)_____

más posible porque todo es muy delicioso. Entonces siempre queremos

participar en todas (17)_____ actividades a bordo

(18)_____ barco. Vamos (19)_____ gimnasio todos

(20)_____ días. Nadamos en (21)_____ piscina.

Jugamos (22)_____ golf miniatura, (23)_____ volíbol, y a

(24)_____ naipes. Generalmente tomamos (25)_____

almuerzo a (26)_____ una con tres muchahas inglesas y nos

divertimos muchísimo. Durante (27)_____ día, cuando llega

(28)_____ barco a (29)_____ puerto interesante,

salimos para hacer (30)_____ visita (31)_____ país o de

(32)_____ isla. (33)_____ semana pasada Ernesto

compró (34)_____ discos compactos para sus hermanos y Carlos

compró (35)_____ camisetas. Yo tenía (36)_____ mucha

suerte. Yo compré (37)_____ reloj de oro en (38)_____

tienda libre de impuestos. Yo pagué solamente (39)_____ cien

dólares. ¡Qué ganga! Por (40)_____ noche, siempre hay

(41)_____ bailes y (42)_____ espectáculos. De vez en

cuando pasan (43)_____ película reciente. Una vez vimos

(44)_____ desfile de modas. Ernesto y Carlos piensan que

(45)_____ crucero es estupendo. Yo pienso (46)_____ mismo.

Su amigo,

José

Person, Place, or Thing for $200: Using Demonstrative Adjectives and Pronouns

Personally, I'm not content with just "anything" or "anyone;" I like to make my requirements and needs known! I do so by specifically referring to *this, that, these,* or *those* things or people. If you're like me, you need to make use of the Spanish demonstrative adjectives (placed before nouns) that enable you to express exactly what or whom you're seeking.

And when my mind is made up, it's often easier to point and ask someone to please give me or direct me to *this [one], that [one], these [ones],* or *those [ones].* In these instances, Spanish demonstrative pronouns (which replace the demonstrative adjectives and their nouns) come in very handy.

Dealing with demonstrative adjectives

Demonstrative adjectives indicate or point out the person, place, or thing to which a speaker is referring. For instance, "this shirt" or "that pair of pants." Demonstrative adjectives precede and agree in number and gender with the nouns they modify. In Spanish, you select the demonstrative adjective according to the distance of the noun from the speaker. Table 3-1 presents demonstrative adjectives and addresses this distance issue.

Table 3-1		Demonstrative Adjectives		
Number	*Masculine*	*Feminine*	*Meaning*	*Distance*
Singular	**este**	**esta**	*this*	Near to or directly concerned
Plural	**estos**	**estas**	*these*	with speaker
Singular	**ese**	**esa**	*that*	Not particularly near to or
Plural	**esos**	**esas**	*those*	directly concerned with speaker
Singular	**aquel**	**aquella**	*that*	Far from and not directly
Plural	**aquellos**	**aquellas**	*those*	concerned with speaker

The following list shows these demonstrative adjectives in action:

- **Estos pantalones son cortos y esta camisa es larga.** (*These pants are short and this shirt is large.*)

- **Tengo que hablar con esa muchacha y esos muchachos ahí.** (*I have to speak to that girl and those boys there.*)

- **Aquellos países son grandes y aquellas ciudades son pequeñas.** (*Those countries are large and those cities are small.*)

Here's what you need to know about demonstrative adjectives in Spanish:

✔ You use them before each noun:

este abogado y ese cliente (*this lawyer and that client*)

✔ You can use adverbs to reinforce location:

esta casa aquí (*this house here*)

esas casas ahí (*those houses there*)

aquella casa allá (*that house over there*)

Forming sentences with demonstrative pronouns

A *demonstrative pronoun* replaces a demonstrative adjective and it's noun. You use it to make the language flow more naturally in writing and in conversation. Demonstrative pronouns express *this (one), that (one), these (ones),* or *those (ones).* The only difference between a demonstrative adjective and a demonstrative pronoun in terms of writing is the addition of an accent to the pronoun. You can see these accents in Table 3-2.

Table 3-2			Demonstrative Pronouns	
Number	**Masculine**	**Feminine**	**Meaning**	**Distance**
Singular	**éste**	**ésta**	*this (one)*	Near to or directly concerned
Plural	**éstos**	**éstas**	*these (ones)*	with speaker
Singular	**ése**	**ésa**	*that (one)*	Not particularly near to or
Plural	**ésos**	**ésas**	*those (ones)*	directly concerned with speaker
Singular	**aquél**	**aquélla**	*that (one)*	Far from and not directly
Plural	**aquéllos**	**aquéllas**	*those (ones)*	concerned with speaker

The following list presents some examples of these demonstrative pronouns in action:

✔ **Mire éstos y ésta también.** (*Look at these and this one, too.*)

✔ **Quiero ése y ésas.** (*I want that and those.*)

✔ **Aquél es viejo y aquélla es moderno.** (*That one is old and that one is modern.*)

Here's what you need to know about demonstrative pronouns in Spanish:

✔ They agree in number and gender with the nouns they replace:

Me gusta este coche y ésos . (*I like this car and those.*)

✔ You use a form of **aquél** to express *the former* and a form of **éste** to express *the latter:*

Patricia es la hermana de Francisco; éste es rubio y aquélla es morena.
(*Patricia is the sister of Francisco; Francisco* [the latter] *is blond and Patricia* [the former] *is brunette.*)

You're walking through your place of business with your boss while hastily taking notes about the attitudes of the workers. Write out full sentences from your notes by combining the elements I provide with demonstrative adjectives and pronouns. Follow the examples provided, where I list all the elements. First you have the demonstrative adjective, then the noun, then the adverb, then the demonstrative pronoun, then lo, then **es** for singular or **son** for plural, and finally **también,** which means *also.*

Q. abogado/aquí/fiel

A. **Este** abogado aquí **es** fiel **y éste lo es también.** (*This lawyer is proud and so is this one.*)

Q. vendedoras/ahí/habladores

A. **Esas** vendedoras ahí **son** habladoras **y ésas lo son también.** (*Those saleswomen are talkative and so are those.*)

47. programadora/ahí/inteligente

_____

48. ingeniero/allá/razonable

_____

49. técnicos/aquí/simpáticos

_____

50. banqueros/ahí/honrados

_____

51. secretarias/ahí/amables

_____

52. obreros/allá/ambiciosos

_____

53. directora/allá/sincera

_____

54. científicas/aquí/serias

_____

55. hombre de negocios/aquí/optimista

_____

56. empleadas/allá/agresivas

_____

57. investigador/ahí/trabajador

_____

58. traductora/aquí/concienzuda

_____

Pitting Masculine versus Feminine in the World of Spanish Singular Nouns

Spanish nouns are either masculine or feminine. Nouns that refer to males are always masculine, and nouns that refer to females are feminine, no matter their endings. You can't always be sure when it comes to places or things, though. In Spanish, certain endings are good indications as to the gender (masculine or feminine designation) of nouns. For instance, nouns that end in **-o** (except **la mano** [*the hand*] and **la radio** [*the radio*]) often are masculine. Nouns that end in **-a, -ad** (**la ciudad** [*city*]), **-ie** (**la serie** [*the series*]), **-ción** (**la canción** [*the song*]), **-sión** (**la discusión** [*discussion*]), **-ud** (**la salud** [*health*]), and **-umbre** (**la costumbre** [*custom*]) generally are feminine.

Here are more rules that deal with gender in Spanish:

✔ Certain nouns belonging to a theme are masculine. These include

- Numbers (**el cuatro** [*four*])
- Days of the week (**el jueves** [*Thursday*])
- Compass points (**el norte** [*north*])
- Names of trees (**el manzano** [*apple tree*])
- Compound nouns (**el mediodía** [*noon*])
- Names of rivers, lakes, mountains, straits, and seas (**el Mediterráneo** [*the Mediterranean*])

✔ Certain nouns belonging to a theme are feminine. These include

- Many illnesses (**la gripe** [*the flu*], **la apendicitis** [*appendicitis*])
- Islands and provinces (**la Córsega** [*Corsica*])

The following sections dive into some more detail with respect to noun gender in Spanish, including some special cases you must consider.

Reverse-gender nouns

Some Spanish nouns are tricky because they end in **-a** but are masculine, while others end in **-o** but are feminine. These nouns may be referred to as *reverse-gender nouns*. For instance, some nouns that end in **-ma** and **-eta** (words that are derived from the Greek language) are masculine, as are the words **el día** (*the day*) and **el mapa** (*the map*). The following table outlines these masculine words:

-ma	*-eta*
el clima (*the climate*)	**el planeta** (*the planet*)
el drama (*the drama*)	
el idioma (*the language*)	
el poema (*the poem*)	
el problema (*the problem*)	
el programa (*the program*)	
el sistema (*the system*)	
el telegrama (*the telegram*)	
el tema (*the theme*)	

Here are a couple of nouns that end in **-o** and are feminine:

- **la mano** (*the hand*)
- **la radio** (*the radio*)

Note that **la foto** is the abbreviation for **la fotografía** (*the photgraph*) and **la moto** is the abbreviation for **la motocicleta** (*the motorcycle*).

Nouns that are the same for both genders

Some nouns have the same spelling for both genders. For these nouns, all you have to do is change the definitive article to reflect whether the person in question is male or female. The following table presents the most common of these nouns:

Masculine	*Feminine*	*Translation*
el artista	**la artista**	*the artist*
el dentista	**la dentista**	*the dentist*
el periodista	**la periodista**	*the journalist*
el telefonista	**la telefonista**	*the operator*
el modelo	**la modelo**	*the model*
el joven	**la joven**	*the youth*
el estudiante	**la estudiante**	*the student*

The following nouns, however, always remain feminine, regardless of the gender of the person being described:

la persona (*the person*)

la víctima (*the victim*)

Nouns whose meanings change

Some nouns change meaning according to their gender. In the masculine form, a noun in this category can mean one thing, and in the feminine form, it has a totally different meaning. Knowing the proper usage is the difference between praying to the Pope or to a potato! You simply must memorize nouns in this category. The following table presents some of the high-frequency Spanish words whose meanings change according to gender:

Masculine	Meaning	Feminine	Meaning
el capital	the capital (money)	la capital	the capital (country)
el cura	the priest	la cura	the cure
el frente	the front	la frente	the forehead
el guía	the male guide	la guía	the female guide; the guidebook
el Papa	the Pope	la papa	the potato
el policía	the police officer	la policía	the police force; the police woman

Special cases

When it comes to languages, you can always find some exceptions to the rule. In Spanish, for instance, masculine nouns that refer to people and end in **-or, -és,** or **-n** require the addition of a final **-a** to get the female equivalent. And if the masculine noun has an accented final syllable, you drop that accent in the feminine form. Here are some examples:

el professor → **la profesora** (*the teacher*)

el francés → **la francesa** (*the French person*)

el alemán → **la alemana** (*the German person*)

Of course, you must watch out for two exceptions to this rule:

el actor (*the actor*) → **la actriz** (*the actress*)

el emperador (*the emperor*) → **la emperatriz** (*the empress*)

Some nouns have distinct masculine and feminine forms. The following table presents a list of these nouns, which you simply must memorize:

Masculine	Meaning	Feminine	Meaning
el duque	the duke	la duquesa	the duchess
el héroe	the hero	la heroína	the heroine

el hombre	the man	la mujer	the woman
el marido	the husband	la esposa	the wife
el príncipe	the prince	la princesa	the princess
el rey	the king	la reina	the queen
el yerno	the son-in-law	la nuera	the daughter-in-law

To prevent the clash of two vowel sounds, the Spanish language uses the masculine singular article **el** (**un**) with feminine singular nouns that begin with a stressed *a* sound (**a-** or **ha-**). In the plural, you use **las** (**unas**) for these nouns. Here are some commonly used words with this designation:

el agua (*the water*); **las aguas** (*the waters*)

un alma (*a soul*); **unas almas** (*some souls*)

el ave (*the bird*); **las aves** (*the birds*)

un hacha (*an ax*); **unas hachas** (*some axes*)

el hambre (*the hunger*); **las hambres** (*the hungers*)

You're studying for a vocabulary test in your Spanish class. Use the following words to complete the definitions described by the clues. You must add the appropriate definite article. The following example gets you started:

agua	avión	capital
yerno	lección	llave
mano	mapa	muchedumbre
pez	planeta	poeta
rey	serie	verdad

Q. sinónimo por una lengua

A. **el idioma** (*the language*)

59. grupo de muchas personas — _____

60. líquido incoloro e inodoro compuesto por oxígeno e hidrógeno — _____

61. esposo de la hija — _____

62. hombre o mujer que escribe versos — _____

63. parte del cuerpo entre la muñeca y la punta de los dedos — _____

64. hombre soberano de un reino — _____

65. animal vertebrado acuático — _____

66. principio aceptado como cierto — _____

67. cosas relacionadas que se suceden — _____

68. materia que se aprende o estudia — _____

69. cuerpo celeste — _____

70. aparato de navegación aérea — _____

71. representación, sobre un plano, de la Tierra o de una ciudad — _____

72. ciudad donde reside el gobierno — _____

73. instrumento que sirve para abrir o cerrar una puerta — _____

Adding to Your Knowledge with Noun Plurals

You use *noun plurals* to refer to more than one person, place, thing, quality, idea, or action. Not surprisingly, just as you do in English, you use the letters **-s** and **-es** to form the plurals of Spanish nouns. The following list outlines the many plural variations you see in Spanish nouns and the rules for forming plurals:

✔ You add **-s** to form the plural of nouns ending in a vowel:

el mango (*the mango*); **los mangos** (*the mangoes*)

la manzana (*the apple*); **las manzanas** (*the apples*)

✔ You add **-es** to form the plural of nouns ending in a consonant (including **-y**):

el emperador (*the emperor*); **los emperadores** (*the emperors*)

el rey (*the king*); **los reyes** (*the kings*)

✔ You add or delete an accent mark in some nouns ending in **-n** or **-s** to maintain the original stress:

el joven; los jóvenes (*the youths*)

el examen; los exámenes (*the tests*)

la canción; las canciones (*the songs*)

el francés; los franceses (*the Frenchmen*)

el ingles; los ingleses (*the Englishmen*)

el limón; los limones (*the lemons*)

el melón; los melones (*the melons*)

el melocotón; los melocotones (*the peaches*)

✔ Nouns that end in **-z** change **z** to **-c** before you add **-es:**

la luz (*the light*); **las luces** (*the lights*)

✔ Nouns that end in **-es** or **-is** don't change in the plural, except for **el mes** (*the month*), which becomes **los meses** (*the months*):

el lunes (*Monday*); **los lunes** (*Mondays*)

la crisis (*the crisis*); **las crisis** (*the crises*)

- ✔ Compound nouns (nouns composed of two nouns that join together to make one) don't change in the plural:

  el abrelatas (*can opener*); **los abrelatas** (*can openers*)

- ✔ You express the plural of nouns of different genders (where one noun is masculine and the other[s] is feminine) with the masculine plural:

  el rey y la reina (*the king and queen*); **los reyes** (*the kings* or *the king[s] and the queen[s]*)

  el muchacho y la muchacha (*the boy and the girl*); **los muchachos** (*the boys* or *the boy[s] and the girl[s]*)

- ✔ Some nouns are always plural, such as

  las gafas/los espejuelos (*eyeglasses*)

  las matemáticas (*mathematics*)

  las vacaciones (*vacation*)

You're looking out your hotel window into the street. Note your observations of the street scene below in your travel journal. Write all the English words in parentheses in their Spanish plural equivalents. Here's an example to get you started:

Q. Dos _____ tocan _____. (*people, guitars*)

A. Dos **personas** tocan **guitarras**.

74. Dos_____ hablan de sus _____. (Frenchmen, vacation)

75. Dos_____ venden _____, _____

    _____ y _____. (men, peaches, lemons,

    melons)

76. Dos_____ cantan bellas _____. (young people, songs)

77. Dos_____ tienen dos_____ en las _____.

    (boys, fish, hands)

78. Dos_____ buscan sus _____. (women, eyeglasses)

79. Dos_____ miran los _____. (tourists, skyscrapers)

80. Dos_____ hablan de las _____. (judges, laws)

81. Dos_____ indican que hay dos_____ de fútbol los

    _____. (signs, matches, Mondays)

82. Dos_____ llevan _____. (Germans, umbrellas)

83. Dos_____ hablan de los _____ españoles.

    (students, kings)

These Are My Things! Expressing Possession

The majority of people in the world are possessive of their loved ones and their things. You have several ways to express possession in Spanish: by using the preposition **de** (*of*), by using possessive adjectives before the persons or things, or by using possessive pronouns to take the place of possessive adjectives and their nouns. The sections that follow guide you through the ways you can stake your claims.

Using de

Expressing possession by using the preposition **de** (*of*) is quite unlike what people are accustomed to in English. English speakers put an apostrophe + s after the noun representing the possessor: John's family, for instance. Spanish nouns have no apostrophe s; you must use a reverse word order joined by the preposition **de.** The following list presents the rules of using **de:**

- ✔ You use the preposition **de** between a noun that's possessed and a proper noun representing the possessor:

  Es el coche de Julio. (*It's Julio's car.*)

- ✔ You use **de** + a definite article between the noun that's possessed and a common noun representing the possessor:

  Tengo el abrigo de la muchacha. (*I have the girl's coat.*)

- ✔ **De** contracts with the definite article **el** to form **del** (*of the*) before a masculine singular common noun:

  Necesito el libro del profesor. (*I need the teacher's book.*)

- ✔ If the sentence contains more than one possessor, you need to repeat **de** before each noun:

  Voy a la casa de Roberto y de Marta. (*I'm going to Robert and Marta's house.*)

- ✔ You use a construction that's the reverse of English to answer the question "**¿De quién es . . .?**":

  ¿De quién(es) es la idea? (*Whose idea is it?*)

  Es la idea de Julia y del hermano de Julia. (*It is Julia's and her brother's idea.*)

Utilizing possessive adjectives

You use a *possessive adjective* before the noun that's possessed in order to express *my, your, his, her, its, our,* or *their.* Possessive adjectives must agree in gender and number (singular or plural) with the objects that are possessed; they never agree with the possessors. Table 3-3 outlines the possessive adjectives, and the following examples illustrate the previous points:

Julia escribe a sus amigas. (*Julia writes to her friends.*)

Yo perdí mis gafas. (*I lost my glasses.*)

Nosotros escuchamos a nuestro profesor. (*We listen to our teacher.*)

Table 3-3	Possessive Adjectives			
English word	*Masculine singular*	*Masculine plural*	*Feminine singular*	*Feminine plural*
my	mi	mis	mi	mis
your	tu	tus	tu	tus
his/her/your	su	sus	su	sus
our	nuestro	nuestros	nuestra	nuestras
your	vuestro	vuestros	vuestra	vuestras
their/your	su	sus	su	sus

Because **su** can mean his, her, or their, you can clarify who the possessor really is by replacing the possessive adjective (**su**) with the corresponding definite article (**el, la, los,** or **las**) + noun + **de** + **él** (**ellos, ella, ellas, Ud., Uds.**):

> *I need his (her) help.*
>
> **Necesito su ayuda.**
>
> **Necesito la ayuda de ella (él).**

With parts of the body or clothing, when the possessor is clear, you replace the possessive adjective with the correct definite article:

> **Me cepillo los dientes dos veces al día.** (*I brush my teeth twice a day.*)

Replacing nouns with possessive pronouns

A *possessive pronoun* replaces a noun. For instance, **Tu coche y el mío son deportivos.** (*Your car and mine are sporty.*) To form a possessive pronoun, you select the definite article corresponding in number and gender to the noun being possessed and then add the corresponding possessive pronoun (see Table 3-4). Here are some examples:

> **Tu hermana y la mía son pelirrojas.** (*Your sister and mine are redheads.*)
>
> **A tu hermano le encanta la ópera; al mío también.** (*Your brother likes the opera; mine, too.*)

Note the contraction with **a** and **él**.

> **El coche de tu primo es viejo; el del mío es nuevo.** (*Your cousin's car is old; my cousin's is new.*)

Table 3-4	Possessive pronouns			
English word	*Masculine singular*	*Masculine plural*	*Feminine singular*	*Feminine plural*
mine	**mío**	**míos**	**mía**	**mías**
yours (fam. sing.)	**tuyo**	**tuyos**	**tuya**	**tuyas**
his, hers, its, yours	**suyo**	**suyos**	**suya**	**suyas**
ours	**nuestro**	**nuestros**	**nuestra**	**nuestras**
yours (fam. pl.)	**vuestro**	**vuestros**	**vuestra**	**vuestras**
theirs	**suyo**	**suyos**	**suya**	**suyas**

After the verb **ser** (*to be*), you generally omit the definite article:

    Este asiento es mío, no es suyo. (*This seat is mine, not yours.*)

You're having a business lunch with colleagues. Write down notes expressing possession by filling in the missing words. Here's an example:

Q. (Her) _____ trabajo es bueno. El trabajo (Mrs. Rivera's) _____ es mejor pero (yours [familiar]) _____ es excelente.

A. **su/de la Señora Rivera/el tuyo**

84. (My) _____ oficina es lujosa. La oficina (Mr. Gómez's) _____ es grande pero (yours [formal]) _____ es pequeña.

85. Los empleados (Mrs. López's) _____ son simpáticos. (Theirs) _____ son amables pero (our) _____ empleados son concienzudos.

86. (His) _____ contrato es importante. El contrato (Juan's) _____ lo es también. (Yours [informal]) _____ es más importante.

87. (Their) _____ ventas son elevadas. Las ventas (Roberto's and María's) _____ son bajadas. (Mine) _____ son buenas.

88. (Your [formal]) _____ beneficios son excelentes. (Mine) _____ son estupendos. ¿Cómo son (hers) _____ ?

89. (Your [informal]) _____ secretaria es prudente. (Theirs) _____ es amable. (Ours) _____ es sagaz.

Answer Key

1 You generally don't use the definite article before the name of the day of the week.

2 **la**

3 You don't need the definite article after the preposition **de** and before the noun **vacaciones.**

4 **un**

5 You omit the indefinite article before an unmodified profession.

6 **un**

7 **un**

8 **un**

9 **un**

10 **La**

11 You omit the definite article before numerals expressing the titles of rulers.

12 **la**

13 You omit the indefinite article before the number **mil.**

14 You don't use the definite article before the **primero.**

15 **un**

16 **lo**

17 **las**

18 **del**

19 **al**

20 **los**

21 **la**

22 **al**

23 **al**

24 **los**

25 **el**

26 **la**

27 el

28 el

29 un

30 una

31 del

32 la

33 la

34 unos

35 unas

36 You don't need to include an article in the idiomatic expression **tener suerte.**

37 un

38 una

39 You omit the indefinite article before the number **cien.**

40 la

41 No article is needed after the word **hay** (*there is/are*).

42 See Answer 41.

43 una

44 un

45 el

46 lo

47 **Esa** programadora ahí **es** inteligente **y ésa lo es también.**

48 **Aquel** ingeniero allá **es** razonable **y aquél lo es también.**

49 **Estos** técnicos aquí **son** simpáticos **y éstos lo son también.**

50 **Esos** banqueros ahí **son** honrados **y ésos lo son también.**

51 **Esas** secretarias ahí **son** amables **y ésas lo son también.**

52 **Aquellos** obreros allá **son** ambiciosos **y aquéllos lo son también.**

53 **Aquella** directora allá **es** sincera **y aquélla lo es también.**

54 **Estas** científicas aquí **son** serias **y éstas lo son también.**

55 **Este** hombre de negocios aquí **es** optimista **y éste lo es también.**

56 **Aquellas** empleadas allá **son** agresivas **y aquéllas lo son también.**

57 **Ese** investigador ahí **es** trabajador **y ése lo es también.**

58 **Esta** traductora aquí **es** concienzuda **y ésta lo es también.**

59 **la muchedumbre** (*crowd*)

60 **el agua** (*water*)

61 **el yerno** (*son-in-law*)

62 **el poeta** (*poet*)

63 **la mano** (*hand*)

64 **el rey** (*king*)

65 **el pez** (*fish*)

66 **la verdad** (*truth*)

67 **la serie** (*series*)

68 **la lección** (*lesson*)

69 **el planeta** (*planet*)

70 **el avión** (*airplane*)

71 **el mapa** (*map*)

72 **la capital** (*capital*)

73 **la llave** (*key*)

74 **franceses/vacaciones**

75 **hombres/melocotones/limones/melones**

76 **jóvenes/canciones**

77 **muchachos/peces/manos**

78 **mujeres/gafas**

The Spanish word for *eyeglasses* is always plural.

79 **turistas/rascacielos**

The Spanish word for the compound noun *skyscraper* is always plural.

80 **jueces/leyes**

81 **carteles (letreros)/partidos/lunes**

82 **alemanes/paraguas**

83 **estudiantes/reyes**

84 **Mi/del señor Gómez/la suya**

85 **de la señora López/Los suyos/los nuestros**

86 **Su/de Juan/El tuyo**

87 **Sus/de Roberto y de María/Las mías**

88 **Sus/Los míos/los suyos**

89 **Tu/La suya/La nuestra**

Chapter 4

Writing in the Present with Action

. . . .

In This Chapter

▶ Determining when to use subject pronouns

▶ Corresponding in the present tense

▶ Utilizing common verbal expressions in Spanish

. . . .

*I*n Spanish, when you write or speak, you have to be careful to use verbs properly so that you can get your meaning across. Whereas English comes to many speakers naturally because they've been immersed in the language since birth, people have to internalize the rules, expressions, idioms, and idiosyncrasies of a foreign language. This requires a bit of effort and some practice until you can achieve a good comfort level with new vocabulary and a different way to express yourself.

It greatly helps to start by writing in the present tense, because for most people, that's where the action and interest is — in the here and now. Truth be told, although English has the reputation of being a very difficult language to learn, its present-tense verbs are rather easy to use because almost all of them follow the same set of rules. In Spanish, you'll discover that the overwhelming majority of present-tense verbs are very simple to use because they're very predictable. However, you'll also find out that some verbs walk to the beat of a different drummer; for these verbs, you have to learn or memorize their patterns or irregularities.

In this chapter, I start you off with subject pronouns, because they come first in the sentence. After you successfully navigate the Spanish subject pronouns, you're going to form the present tense with many types of verbs that enable you to talk and write about events and situations that occur now. Finally, I present some high-frequency expressions that will help your Spanish sound more colloquial and more natural.

Using Subject Pronouns

A *subject pronoun* is a word used in place of a subject noun. This pronoun identifies who or what is performing the action of the verb. In this chapter, Spanish subject pronouns may be used before verbs in the present tense to express who or what is acting.

In English, you use subject pronouns all the time in place of, or to avoid, repeating subject nouns. It's much simpler to write "They left" rather than "Mr. Anthony Bolavolunta and Miss Cleopatra Johnson left." The subject pronouns *I, you, he, she, we,* and *they* enable you to write clear, concise sentences. Subject nouns and pronouns alike are followed by the appropriate forms of the verbs expressing particular actions.

You don't use Spanish subject pronouns as frequently as their English counterparts, because a Spanish verb ending generally indicates the subject. You use Spanish subject pronouns, therefore, mainly to be polite, to emphasize or stress the subject, or to be perfectly clear as to whom the subject is.

Just like in English, Spanish subject pronouns have a person (first, second, or third) and a number (singular or plural), as you can see in Table 4-1.

Table 4-1		Spanish Subject Pronouns		
Person	*Singular*	*Meaning*	*Plural*	*Meaning*
1st person	**yo**	*I*	**nosotros (nosotras)**	*we*
2nd person informal (familiar)	**tú**	*you*	**vosotros (vosotras)**	*you*
2nd person formal (polite)	**usted (Ud.)**	*you*	**ustedes (Uds.)**	*you*
3rd person	**él**	*he*	**ellos**	*they*
	ella	*she*	**ellas**	*they*

Unlike the English subject pronoun *I,* which is always capitalized, the Spanish pronoun **yo** is capitalized only at the beginning of a sentence. You always write the abbreviations **Ud.** and **Uds.** with capital letters, even though you write the English equivalent *you* with a lowercase letter, unless it appears at the beginning of a sentence. When **usted** and **ustedes** aren't abbreviated, they're capitalized only at the beginning of a sentence. Here are some examples:

> **Yo me voy.** (*I'm leaving.*)
>
> **Eduardo y yo salimos.** (*Edward and I are going out.*)
>
> **¿Busca Ud. (usted) algo?** (*Are you looking for something?*)
>
> **¿Uds. (ustedes) necesitan ayuda?** (*Do you need help?*)

Applying subject pronouns

The use of certain subject pronouns can be confusing for many reasons. Two different Spanish pronouns may have the same English meaning. Some Spanish subject pronouns are used primarily in Spain or in Latin America. Finally, some Spanish subject pronouns refer only to females and others refer to males or to a mixed group of males and females. The following sections help you select the correct subject pronouns for all circumstances in all parts of the Spanish-speaking world.

Tú versus Ud.

You use the informal (familiar) subject pronoun **tú** to address one friend, relative, child, or pet, because it is the informal, singular form of *you.* Basically, you use **tú** to express *you* when you really like the person or pet:

> **Tú eres mi mejor amigo.** (*You're my best friend.*)

You use **Ud.** to show respect to an older person or when speaking to a stranger or someone you don't know well, because **Ud.** is the formal, singular form of *you*. You may also use **Ud.** when you want to get to know the person better:

> **¿Es Ud. español?** (*Are you Spanish?*)

Vosotros (vosotras) versus Uds.

Vosotros and **vosotras** are informal (familiar) plural subject pronouns expressing *you*. The **vosotros** (**vosotras**) form is used primarily in Spain to address more than one friend, relative, child, or pet — the informal, plural form of *you*. You use **vosotros** when speaking to a group of males or to a combined group of males and females. You use **vosotras** only when speaking to a group of females. Basically, you only use **vosotros** (**vosotras**) in Spain when speaking to a group of people you really like!

> **¿Vosotros me comprendís?** (*Do you understand me?*)

Uds. is a plural subject pronoun that also expresses *you*. **Uds.** is used throughout the Spanish-speaking world to show respect to more than one older person or when speaking to multiple strangers or people you don't know well. **Uds.** is the formal, plural form of "you" and replaces **vosotros** (**vosotras**) in Spanish (Latin, Central, and South) America. Basically, you're playing it safe if you use **Uds.** when speaking to a group of people:

> **Uds. son muy simpáticos.** (*You are very nice.*)

You don't express the English pronoun *it* as a subject in Spanish; it can be understood from the meaning of the sentence:

> **¿Qué es?** (*What is it?*)
>
> **Es una herramienta.** (*It's a tool.*)

Él versus ella

Él refers to one male person (*he*); **ella** (*she*) refers to one female person:

> **Él toca la guitarra mientras ella baila.** (*He plays the guitar while she dances.*)

Ellos versus ellas

Ellos (*they*) refers to more than one male or to a combined group of males and females, no matter the number of each gender present. **Ellas** refers to a group of females only:

> **Juan y Jorge (Ellos) escuchan.** (*Juan and Jorge [They] listen.*)
>
> **Luz y Susana (Ellas) escuchan.** (*Luz and Susana [They] listen.*)
>
> **Juan y Luz (Ellos) escuchan.** (*Juan and Luz [They] listen.*)
>
> **El niño y mil niñas (Ellos) escuchan.** (*The boy and 1,000 girls [They] listen.*)

Nosotros (nosotras)

When you're talking about someone else and yourself at the same time, you must use the "we" (**nosotros/nosotras**) form of the verb. **Nosotros** refers to more than one male or to a combined group of males and females, no matter the number of each gender present. **Nosotras** refers to a group of females only:

> **Jorge y yo (Nosotros) jugamos al tenis.** (*George and I [We] play tennis.*)
>
> **Luz y yo (Nosotras) jugamos al tenis.** (*Luz and I [We] play tennis.*)

Omitting subject pronouns

In English, you use subject pronouns all the time to explain who's doing what. In Spanish, however, you use subject pronouns a lot less frequently because the verb ending generally indicates the subject. If you look ahead to the section that follows, you'll notice that, no matter the infinitive ending of the verb (**-ar, -er, -ir**), if the verb form ends in **-o**, the subject must be **yo** because no other verb has an **-o** ending. **Hablo español,** for instance, can only mean *I speak Spanish.*

If, on the other hand, you see **Habla español,** it's unclear whether the subject is **él** (*he*), **ella** (*she*), or **Ud.** (*you*) if the sentence is taken out of context. When given the context, you usually omit the subject pronoun **él** or **ella**: **Le presento a mi amiga, Marta. Habla español.** (*Let me introduce you to my friend, Marta. She speaks Spanish.*)

To avoid confusion, you regularly use the subject pronoun **Ud.** to differentiate between *he, she,* and *you:*

> **¿Habla español?** (*Do you [he, she] speak Spanish?*)
>
> **Mi novio habla español. Habla bien.** (*My boyfriend speaks Spanish. He speaks well.*)
>
> **¿Habla Ud. español?** (*Do you speak Spanish?*)

You regularly use the subject pronoun **Uds.** for sentences in the plural to differentiate between *they* and *you:*

> **Cantan bien.** (*They [You] sing well.*)
>
> **Mis primos están en el coro. Cantan bien.** (*My cousins are in the chorus. They sing well.*)
>
> **Uds. cantan bien también.** (*You sing well, too.*)

Writing (and Talking) in the Present

It must seem rather silly that I want you to read a paragraph about using the present tense. Obviously, you use the present tense to indicate what a subject is doing or does customarily:

> **Nosotros miramos la televisión cada día.** (*We watch television every day.*)
>
> **Ana trabaja en la ciudad.** (*Ana works in the city.*)

But I'll bet you didn't know that in Spanish, you can also use the present to ask for instructions or to discuss an action that will take place in the future:

> **¿Preparo la cena ahora?** (*Shall I prepare dinner now?*)
>
> **Te veo más tarde.** (*I'll see you later.*)

You also use the present tense with the verb **hacer** (*to make, do*) + **que** to show that an action started in the past and is continuing into the present:

>**¿Cuánto tiempo hace que Ud. estudia el español?** (*How long have you been studying Spanish?*)

>**Hace dos años (que estudio el español).** (*I've been studying Spanish for two years.*)

In the following sections, I help you identify the regular verbs in Spanish, and then I show you their present-tense conjugations. I also go through the many changes that verbs may experience when used in the present tense.

When two consecutive verbs follow a subject noun or pronoun, you conjugate the first verb and leave the second verb in its infinitive form:

>**Yo prefiero ir de compras.** (*I prefer to go shopping.*)

Regular verbs

If you want to use the present tense in Spanish, you have to figure out how to conjugate verbs. You probably haven't heard the word "conjugation" in any of your English classes, even when you had those pesky grammar lessons, because people automatically conjugate verbs in their native language without even thinking about it. So, what exactly do I mean by conjugation? Plain and simple, *conjugation* refers to changing the infinitive of a verb (the "to" form — *to smile,* for example) to a form that agrees with the subject. "I **smile** and he **smiles,** too." "You **stretch** and he **stretches,** too." "We **worry** and she **worries,** too."

In Spanish, all verbs end in **-ar, -er,** or **-ir.** Most verbs are *regular,* which means that all verbs with the same infinitive ending follow the same rules of conjugation. If you memorize the endings for one regular **-ar, -er,** or **-ir** infinitive, you'll be able to conjugate all the other regular verbs within that "family." Here's how it works: Take the infinitive and drop its ending (**-ar, -er,** or **-ir**), and then add the endings for the subject pronouns as indicated in Table 4-2.

Table 4-2	Regular Verb Conjugation in the Present		
Subject	*-ar Verbs*	*-er Verbs*	*-ir Verbs*
	ganar (*to earn, to win*)	**beber** (*to drink*)	**decidir** (*to decide*)
yo	gan**o**	beb**o**	decid**o**
tú	gan**as**	beb**es**	decid**es**
él, ella, Ud.	gan**a**	beb**e**	decid**e**
nosotros	gan**amos**	beb**emos**	decid**imos**
vosotros	gan**áis**	beb**éis**	decid**ís**
ellos, ellas, Uds.	gan**an**	beb**en**	decid**en**

Here are some examples of regular verbs in the present tense:

> **¿Gana Ud. bastante dinero?** (*Do you earn enough money?*)
>
> **No bebo café.** (*I don't drink coffee.*)
>
> **Ellos deciden quedarse en casa.** (*They decide to stay home.*)

English verbs have only two different verb forms in the present tense: the first- and second-person singular and all plural forms — I (You, We, They) **work** hard — and the third-person singular form — He (She) **works** hard.

For your reference, the following tables list many regular verbs that follow this easy conjugation in the present. Common regular **-ar** verbs include

-ar Verb	Meaning	-ar Verb	Meaning
ayudar	to help	mirar	to look at
buscar	to look for	necesitar	to need
caminar	to walk	olvidar	to forget
comprar	to buy	organizar	to organize
desear	to desire	pagar	to pay
escuchar	to listen (*to*)	preguntar	to ask
estudiar	to study	regresar	to return
firmar	to sign	telefonear	to phone
gastar	to spend (*money*)	tomar	to take
hablar	to speak, to talk	viajar	to travel
llegar	to arrive	visitar	to visit

Common **-er** verbs include

-er Verb	Meaning
aprender	to learn
beber	to drink
comer	to eat
correr	to run
creer	to believe
deber	to have to, to owe
leer	to read
prometer	to promise

Common **-ir** verbs include

-ir Verb	Meaning
abrir	to open
asistir	to attend

decidir	to decide
descubrir	to discover
escribir	to write
partir	to divide, to share
subir	to go up, to climb
vivir	to live

Your Spanish class is going on a trip to see a Spanish movie. Write notes in your journal to express what each person does on the trip by giving the correct present form of the verb I provide in parentheses. Here's an example:

Q. (practicar) Los muchachos _____ el español.

A. Los muchachos **practican** el español. (*The boys practice Spanish.*)

1. (tomar) Nosotros _____ el autobús para ir al cine.

2. (partir) Todos los estudiantes _____ de la escuela a las tres.

3. (esperar) Uds. _____ el autobús delante de la escuela.

4. (correr) Vosotros _____ para tomar el autobús.

5. (llegar) El autobús _____ al cine a las tres y media.

6. (asistir) La clase _____ al primer pase de la película.

7. (comprar) Vosotros _____ billetes para la clase.

8. (deber) Nosotros _____ practicar el español.

9. (hablar) Tú _____ español conmigo.

10. (mirar) Entonces yo _____ la película.

11. (leer) Todo el mundo _____ los subtítulos.

12. (describir) Yo _____ bien la película en español.

13. (beber) Uds. _____ demasiado refrescos.

14. (compartir) Nosotros _____ un saco de dulces.

15. (comer) Yo _____ también palomitas.

16. (aprender) Tú _____ mucho.

17. (decidir) Vosotros _____ que es una buena película.

18. (aplaudir) Tú _____ la película.

Verbs with spelling changes

Some Spanish verbs undergo spelling changes in order to preserve the original sound of the verbs after you add a new ending. This is nothing to be overly concerned about, because the change occurs only in the first-person singular (**yo**) form of the verb. In the present tense, verbs with the endings I list in Table 4-3 undergo spelling changes.

Table 4-3	Spelling Changes in the Present Tense		
Infinitive Ending	**Spelling Change**	**Verb Examples**	**Present Conjugation**
vowel + **-cer/-cir**	c → zc	ofre**cer** (*to offer*); tradu**cir** (*to translate*)	yo ofre**zco**; yo tradu**zco**
consonant + **-cer/-cir**	c → z	conven**cer** (*to convince*); espar**cir** (*to spread out*)	yo conven**zo**; yo espar**zo**
-ger/-gir	g → j	esco**ger** (*to choose*); exi**gir** (*to demand*)	yo esco**jo**; yo exi**jo**
-guir	gu → g	distin**guir** (*to distinguish*)	yo distin**go**

The majority of the verbs that undergo spelling changes in the present tense end in vowel + **-cer** or vowel + **-cir**. Only a few high-frequency verbs fall under the other categories (**-ger, -gir, -guir**); in all likelihood, you'll see them rarely, if at all.

Here are the verbs with spelling changes in the present tense that you can expect to encounter most often:

Spanish Verb	*Meaning*
aparecer	*to appear*
conocer	*to know* (*to be acquainted with*)
merecer	*to deserve, merit*
nacer	*to be born*
obedecer	*to obey*
parecer	*to seem*
producir	*to produce*
reconocer	*to recognize*
reducir	*to reduce*
reproducir	*to reproduce*

Verbs with stem changes

Some Spanish verbs undergo stem changes — internal changes to a vowel in order to preserve the original sound of the verbs after you add a new ending. In the present tense, all stem changes for these verbs occur in the **yo, tú, él** (**ella, Ud.**) and **ellos** (**ellas, Uds.**) forms. You conjugate the **nosotros** and **vosotros** forms in the normal fashion (their stems resemble the infinitive).

-ar stem changes

Many Spanish verbs with an **-ar** ending undergo stem changes in all forms except **nosotros** and **vosotros.** The following list details these changes:

✔ e → ie: For instance, empezar (*to begin*) changes to yo emp**ie**zo (nosotros emp**e**zamos). Here are the most frequently used Spanish verbs that fit into this category:

- cerrar (*to close*)

- comenzar (*to begin*)

- despertar (*to wake up*)

- negar (*to deny*)

- nevar (*to snow*)

- pensar (*to think*)

- recomendar (*to recommend*)

✔ o/u → ue: For instance, mostrar (*to show*) changes to yo m**ue**stro (nosotros m**o**stramos), and jugar (*to play*) changes to yo j**ue**go (nosotros j**u**gamos). Here are the most frequently used Spanish verbs that fit into this category:

- acordar (*to agree*)

- acostar (*to put to bed*)

- almorzar (*to eat lunch*)

- colgar (*to hang up*)

- contar (*to tell*)

- costar (*to cost*)

- encontrar (*to meet*)

- probar (*to try [on]*)

- recordar (*to remember*)

Jugar is the only common **-ar** verb whose stem vowel changes from **u** to **ue:**

- **Yo juego al fútbol.** (*I play soccer.*)

- **Julio y yo jugamos al golf.** (*Julio and I play golf.*)

-er stem changes

Many Spanish verbs with an **-er** ending undergo stem changes in all forms except **nosotros** and **vosotros.** The following list details these changes:

✔ e → ie: For instance, querer (*to wish, want*) changes to yo qu**ie**ro (nosotros que**re**mos). Here are the most frequently used Spanish verbs that fit into this category:

- defender (*to defend*)

- encender (*to light*)

- entender (*to understand*)

- perder (*to lose*)

✔ o → ue: For instance, volver (*to return*) changes to yo v**ue**lvo (nosotros v**o**lvemos). Here are the most frequently used Spanish verbs that fit into this category:

- dev**o**lver (*to return*)

- d**o**ler (*to hurt*)

- env**o**lver (*to wrap up*)

- ll**o**ver (*to rain*)

- p**o**der (*to be able to, can*)

Some verbs with stem changes in the present tense are used impersonally in the third-person singular only:

Llueve. (*It's raining.*) (**llover;** o → ue)

Nieva. (*It's snowing.*) (**nevar;** e → ie)

Hiela. (*It's freezing.*) (**helar;** e → ie)

Truena. (*It's thundering.*) (**tronar;** o → ue)

-ir stem changes

Many Spanish verbs with an **-ir** ending undergo stem changes in all forms except **nosotros** and **vosotros.** The following list outlines these changes:

✔ e → ie: For instance, preferir (*to prefer*) changes to yo pref**ie**ro (nosotros preferimos). Here are the most frequently used Spanish verbs that fit into this category:

- adv**e**rtir (*to warn*)

- cons**e**ntir (*to allow*)

- div**e**rtir (*to amuse*)

- m**e**ntir (*to lie*)

- s**e**ntir (*to feel, regret*)

- sug**e**rir (*to suggest*)

✔ o → ue: For instance, d**o**rmir (*to sleep*) changes to yo d**ue**rmo (nosotros dormimos). Another verb conjugated like **dormir** is **morir** (*to die*).

✔ e → i: For instance, servir (*to serve*) changes to yo s**i**rvo (nosotros servimos). Here are the most frequently used Spanish verbs that fit into this category:

- desp**e**dir (*to say goodbye to*)

- exp**e**dir (*to send*)

- m**e**dir (*to measure*)

- p**e**dir (*to ask for*)

- rep**e**tir (*to repeat*)

- v**e**stir (*to clothe*)

-iar stem change (for some verbs)

Some Spanish verbs with an **-iar** ending undergo a stem change in all forms except **nosotros** and **vosotros**. This stem change is i → í. For instance, guiar (*to guide*) changes to yo guío (nosotros guiamos). Here are the most frequently used Spanish verbs that fit into this category:

- ✔ env**i**ar (*to send*)
- ✔ esqu**i**ar (*to ski*)
- ✔ fotograf**i**ar (*to photograph*)
- ✔ vac**i**ar (*to empty*)

-uar stem change (for some verbs)

Some Spanish verbs with a **-uar** ending undergo a stem change in all forms except **nosotros** and **vosotros**. This stem change is u → ú. For instance, continuar (*to continue*) changes to yo contin**ú**o (nosotros contin**u**amos). Here are the most frequently used Spanish verbs that fit into this category:

- ✔ habit**u**ar (*to accustom someone to*)
- ✔ val**u**ar (*to value*)
- ✔ eval**u**ar (*to evaluate*)

-uir (not -guir) stem change

Some Spanish verbs with a **-uir** ending (but not a **-guir** ending) undergo a stem change in all forms except **nosotros** and **vosotros**. This stem change is adding a **y** after the **u**. For instance, concluir (*to conclude*) changes to yo conclu**y**o (nosotros conclu**i**mos). Here are the most frequently used Spanish verbs that fit into this category:

- ✔ constr**u**ir (*to build*)
- ✔ contrib**u**ir (*to contribute*)
- ✔ destr**u**ir (*to destroy*)
- ✔ distrib**u**ir (*to distribute*)
- ✔ incl**u**ir (*to include*)
- ✔ sustit**u**ir (*to substitute*)

Verbs with spelling and stem changes

A few Spanish verbs have both a spelling change and a stem change in the present tense. You must conjugate these verbs to accommodate both changes. Table 4-4 provides a listing of these verbs.

Table 4-4	Verbs with Spelling and Stem Changes in the Present	
Verb	*English*	*Conjugation*
corregir	*to correct*	corr**i**jo, corr**i**ges, corr**i**ge, corr**e**gimos, corr**e**gís, corr**i**gen

(continued)

Table 4-4 (continued)

Verb	English	Conjugation
elegir	to elect	elijo, eliges, elige, elegimos, elegís, eligen
conseguir	to get, obtain	consigo, consigues, consigue, conseguimos, conseguís, consiguen
seguir	to follow	sigo, sigues, sigue, seguimos, seguís, siguen

For this exercise, write journal entries in which you express how you and your friends react to different situations. For each question, I provide a situation as well as a verbal phrase explaining the consequence of that situation in parentheses. You must conjugate the verb given in parentheses in the present tense. Here's an example to get you started:

0. Margarita quiere salir bien en su clase de español. (repetir frecuentemente las palabras del vocabulario)

A. **Repite** frecuentemente las palabras del vocabulario. (*She frequently repeats the vocabulary words.*)

19. El jefe piensa que Clarita y Rafael trabajan concienzudamente. (recomendar un aumento de salario para ellos)

_____

20. Mauricio no sale bien en su clase de ciencia. (mentir a su madre)

_____

21. Carlota no sabe como ir a la biblioteca. (pedir la ruta a un desconocido)

_____

22. Yo tengo mucho frío. (cerrar las ventanas)

_____

23. Nosotros deseamos perder peso. (empezar un régimen hoy día)

_____

24. Tu acabas de recibir un bate nuevo. (jugar al béisbol)

_____

25. Uds. tienen dos semanas de vacaciones. (querer ir a España)

_____

26. Enrique y Alfredo tienen un buen sentido de humor. (contar bromas todo el tiempo)

_____

27. Tú eres mecánico excelente. (poder ayudarme a reparar mi coche)

_____

28. Yo no estudio mucho. (escoger a menudo respuestas incorrectas)

_____

29. Yo quiero celebrar el cumpleaños de mi mejor amiga. (le ofrecer un regalo)

_____

30. Clarita está enferma. (dormir mucho)

_____

31. Ellos prefieren el invierno. (esquiar en las montañas)

_____

32. Nilda tiene mucho que hacer. (continuar trabajando)

_____

33. Tomás es ingeniero. (construir edificios)

_____

34. Yo hago muchos errores. (corregir inmediatamente mis errores)

_____

Irregular verbs

In Spanish, some present-tense verbs have irregular forms that you must memorize. There are three categories of irregular verbs in the present tense, which I cover in detail in the following sections: those that are irregular only in the **yo** form; those that are irregular in all forms except **nosotros** and **vosotros;** and those that are completely irregular.

Irregular yo forms

In the present tense, some verbs are irregular only in the first-person singular (**yo**) form. You conjugate the other verb forms in the regular fashion: by dropping the infinitive ending (**-ar, -er,** or **-ir**) and adding the ending that corresponds to the subject. The following table presents the irregular **yo** form of these verbs:

Spanish Verb	Meaning	yo Form of Present Tense
caber	to fit	quepo
caer	to fall	caigo
dar	to give	doy
hacer	to make, to do	hago
poner	to put	pongo
saber	to know a fact, to know how to	sé

Spanish Verb	Meaning	yo Form of Present Tense
salir	*to go out*	salgo
traer	*to bring*	traigo
valer	*to be worth*	valgo
ver	*to see*	veo

The following examples show these irregular forms in action:

> Yo le **doy** un reloj y él le **da** aretes. (*I give her a watch and he gives her earrings.*)

> Yo me **pongo** un abrigo y él se **pone** un suéter. (*I put on a coat and he puts on a sweater.*)

> Yo **salgo** a la una y él **sale** a las tres. (*I go out at one o'clock and he goes out at three.*)

Irregular yo, tú, él (ella, Ud.), and ellos (ellas, Uds.) forms

In the present tense, the verbs listed in Table 4-5 are irregular in all forms except **nosotros** and **vosotros.**

Table 4-5 Irregular Verbs in All Forms except nosotros and vosotros

Verb	Meaning	yo	tú	él	nosotros	vosotros	ellos
decir	*to say, to tell*	digo	dices	dice	decimos	decís	dicen
estar	*to be*	estoy	estás	está	estamos	estáis	están
oler	*to smell*	huelo	hueles	huele	olemos	oléis	huelen
tener	*to have*	tengo	tienes	tiene	tenemos	tenéis	tienen
venir	*to come*	vengo	vienes	viene	venimos	venís	vienen

Tener followed by **que** means *to have to* and shows obligation:

> **Yo tengo que trabajar ahora.** (*I have to work now.*)

> **Nosotros tenemos que partir.** (*We have to leave.*)

Completely (well, almost) irregular verbs

The verbs in Table 4-6 are irregular in all or most of their forms in the present tense; these require a bit more of your attention for memorization.

Table 4-6 Irregular Verbs in All or Most of Their Forms

Verb	Meaning	yo	tú	él	nosotros	vosotros	ellos
ir	*to go*	voy	vas	va	vamos	vais	van
oír	*to hear*	oigo	oyes	oye	oímos	oís	oyen
reír	*to laugh*	río	ríes	ríe	reímos	reís	rien
ser	*to be*	soy	eres	es	somos	sois	son

You're standing in line waiting to get into a concert. You overhear different people having conversations in Spanish. Complete their sentences with the correct form of the verb shown in bold in the question. Here's an example to get you started:

Q. **¿Es** Ud. español?

A. Sí, yo **soy** español. (*Yes, I'm Spanish.*)

A. Mis padres **son** de España. (*My parents are from Spain.*)

35. **¿Conoce** al Señor Hidalgo?

Sí, yo lo _____.

Adela y yo lo _____ también.

36. ¿A qué hora **salen** para ir a la fiesta?

Nosotros _____ a las siete y media.

Yo _____ a las ocho.

37. ¿Con quién **das** un paseo.

Yo _____ un paseo con Carlos.

Esteban y Roberto _____ con Marta.

38. **Olemos** algo.

Yo no _____ nada.

Ricardo _____ las flores.

39. ¿Adónde **van?**

Nosotros _____ al supermercado.

Yo _____ a la farmacia.

40. **¿Oyes** algo?

Sí, yo _____ un ruido.

Estos muchachos no _____ nada.

41. ¿Qué **prefiere** hacer ahora?

Nosotros _____ ir al restaurante.

Yo _____ quedarme en casa.

42. **¿Pueden** Uds. ir a la playa conmigo hoy.

    No, nosotros _____ ir a la playa mañana.

    Yo no _____ ir a la playa mañana.

43. ¿Qué **piensan** de estos zapatos?

    Nosotros _____ que son perfectos.

    Yo _____ que son demasiado estrechos.

44. **¿Ves** algo?

    Sí, yo _____ un rascacielos.

    Estos muchachos no _____ nada.

45. **¿Juega** Ud. al fútbol americano?

    Yo no _____ al fútbol americano.

    Juan y yo _____ al béisbol.

46. **¿Quieren** Uds. ir al teatro?

    No, nosotros _____ ir al cine.

    Yo _____ ir al ópera.

Expressions with irregular verbs

The irregular verbs **dar** (*to give*), **hacer** (*to make, to do*), and **tener** (*to have*), as well as a few other irregular verbs, are commonly used in everyday Spanish as part of expressions. If you want to sound like you really know the language well, and if you want readers of your prose to follow along without any hiccups, you need to devour the expressions that follow in this section and commit them to memory.

Verbs ending in **-se** are reflexive verbs; I discuss these in Chapter 11.

High-frequency expressions that use **dar** include the following:

Expression	Meaning
dar un abrazo (a)	*to hug, to embrace*
dar las gracias (a)	*to thank*
dar recuerdos (a)	*to give regards to*
dar un paseo	*to take a walk*
dar una vuelta	*to take a stroll*
darse cuenta de	*to realize*
darse prisa	*to hurry*

Here are some examples of **dar** expressions:

Yo le doy un abrazo a mi novio. (*I hug my boyfriend.*)

Ellos dan un paseo por el parque. (*They take a walk in the park.*)

High-frequency expressions that use **hacer** include the following:

Expression	*Meaning*
hacer buen (mal) tiempo	*to be nice (bad) weather*
hacer frío (calor)	*to be cold (hot) weather*
hacer una pregunta	*to ask a question*
hacer una visita	*to pay a visit*
hacer un viaje	*to take a trip*
hacer viento	*to be windy*

Here are some examples of **hacer** expressions:

Hace mal tiempo hoy. (*The weather is bad today.*)

Hacemos un viaje a Puerto Rico. (*We are taking a trip to Puerto Rico.*)

High-frequency expressions that use **tener** include the following:

Expression	*Meaning*
tener calor (frío)	*to be warm (cold)*
tener celos de	*to be jealous of* (*someone*)
tener cuidado	*to be careful*
tener dolor de . . .	*to have a . . . ache*
tener éxito	*to succeed*
tener ganas de	*to feel like*
tener hambre (sed)	*to be hungry* (*thirsty*)
tener lugar	*to take place*
tener miedo de	*to be afraid of*
tener prisa	*to be in a hurry*
tener razón	*to be right*
tener sueño	*to be sleepy*
tener suerte	*to be lucky*

Here are some examples of **tener** expressions:

Tengo un dolor de cabeza. (*I have a headache.*)

Ellos tienen razón. (*They are right.*)

What follows is a perfect example of how you can easily make a mistake in Spanish if you try to translate your English thoughts word for word. Although the verb **tener** means *to have,* Spanish speakers often use it with a noun to express a physical condition. In English, however, you use the verb *to be* followed by an adjective to express the same physical condition:

> **Tengo sed.** (*I am thirsty.* Literally: *I have thirst.*)

> **Ellos tienen miedo a los perros.** (*They are afraid of dogs.* Literally: *They have fear of dogs.*)

Common expressions that use other verbs that have a spelling change or stem change in the present tense or in another tense include the following:

Expression	Meaning
dejar caer	*to drop*
llegar a ser	*to become*
oír decir que	*to hear that*
pensar + infinitive	*to intend*
querer decir	*to mean*
volverse + adjective	*to become*

Here are some examples of these expressions in action:

> **¡Cuidado! Vas a dejar caer el vaso.** (*Be careful! You are going to drop the glass.*)

> **Pensamos hacer un viaje.** (*We intend to take a trip.*)

You're practicing your Spanish vocabulary for class. Finish your homework assignment by selecting the phrase that best completes each sentence that follows. Remember to conjugate the verb as well.

dar un paseo	pensar
dejar caer	querer decir
hacer frío	tener celos
oír decir	tener lugar

47. Paco estudia la medicina. Él _____ ser doctor algún día.

48. No comprendo esta palabra. ¿Qué _____ "palomitas?"

49. Soy muy torpe. Siempre _____ algo.

50. Siempre me informo de todo. Yo _____ que Ud. hace un viaje a México.

51. Ramón tiene un coche nuevo. Yo también quiero comprar un coche nuevo pero no tengo bastante dinero. Yo _____ de Ramón.

52. Hay una fiesta en casa de Emilio. ¿A qué hora _____?

53. Hay una temperatura de cinco grados bajo cero. _____.

54. Hace sol. Por eso yo _____ por el parque.

Answer Key

1   tomamos

2   parten

3   esperan

4   corréis

5   llega

6   asiste

7   compráis

8   debemos

9   hablas

10   miro

11   lee

12   describo

13   beben

14   compartimos

15   como

16   aprendes

17   decidís

18   applaudes

19   **Recomienda** un aumento de salario para ellos. The second **e** of **recomendar** changes to **ie** in all forms except **nosotros** and **vosotros**.

20   **Miente** a su madre. The **e** of **mentir** changes to **ie** in all forms except **nosotros** and **vosotros**.

21   **Pide** la ruta a un desconocido. The **e** of **pedir** changes to **i** in all forms except **nosotros** and **vosotros**.

22   **Cierro** las ventanas. The **e** of **cerrar** changes to **ie** in all forms except **nosotros** and **vosotros**.

23   **Empezamos** un régimen hoy día. The **e** of **empezar** doesn't change in the **nosotros** and **vosotros** forms.

24   **Juegas** al béisbol. The **u** of **jugar** changes to **ue** in all forms except **nosotros** and **vosotros**.

25   **Quieren** ir a España. The **e** of **querer** changes to **ie** in all forms except **nosotros** and **vosotros**.

26   **Cuentan** bromas todo el tiempo. The **o** of **contar** changes to **ue** in all forms except **nosotros** and **vosotros**.

27 **Puedes** ayudarme a reparar mi coche. The **o** of **poder** changes to **ue** in all forms except **nosotros** and **vosotros.**

28 **Escojo** a menudo respuestas incorrectas. For the **yo** form of this **-ger** verb, change the **g** to **j** and add **-o** as the ending.

29 **Le ofrezco** un regalo. Change the **c** to **zc,** because **-cer** is preceded by a vowel, and add **-o** as the ending for **yo.**

30 **Duerme** mucho. The **o** of **dormir** changes to **ue** in all forms except **nosotros** and **vosotros.**

31 **Esquían** en las montañas. The **i** of **esquiar** changes to **í** in all forms except **nosotros** and **vosotros.**

32 **Continúa** trabajando. The **u** of **continuar** changes to **ú** in all forms except **nosotros** and **vosotros.**

33 **Construye** edificios. You add a **y** to **construir** between the **u** and the ending in all forms except **nosotros** and **vosotros.**

34 **Corrijo** inmediatamente mis errores. For the **yo** form of the **-ger** ver, change the **e** to **i** and the **g** to **j** before addig the **-o** ending.

35 **Conozco/conocemos**

36 **Salimos/salgo**

37 **doy/dan**

38 **huelo/huele**

39 **vamos/voy**

40 **oigo/oyen**

41 **preferimos/prefiero**

42 **podemos/puedo**

43 **pensamos/pienso**

44 **veo/ven**

45 **juego/jugamos**

46 **queremos/quido**

47 **piensa**

48 **quiere decir**

49 **dejo caer**

50 **oigo decir**

51 **tengo celos**

52 **tiene lugar**

53 **hace frío**

54 **doy un paseo**

Chapter 5

Getting Answers with the Right Questions

Sometimes when you ask a question, all you want in return is a simple "yes" or "no" answer. No explanations are needed. Other times, however, you're really interested in getting information. You want all the facts. As a student, traveler, or businessperson speaking Spanish, you'll need to know names, phone numbers, addresses, how much you have to pay — any one of a thousand possible things that beg for questions and answers.

Maybe the answers you're looking for are imperative, or perhaps you just want to give in to your curiosity. It doesn't matter. You need to know how to ask questions properly in Spanish so that you receive the correct answers. And, of course, many people will have questions for you, and you'll have to provide the answers. There's no getting around that.

In this chapter, you find out how to obtain all the information you need — from easy "yes" or "no" questions to more detailed inquiries about "who?" "what?" "when?" "where?" "how?" or "why?" By the time you finish this chapter, you'll be proficient at not only asking questions, but also at giving appropriate answers to the questions others ask you.

Inquiring in Spanish

Curiosity has always been one of my most endearing personality traits. What can I say? I'm inquisitive about everything. And I'd venture to guess that many of you share my desire to learn as much as I can about everything I can. People like us ask a lot of questions. There's nothing wrong with that. Fortunately for you, asking questions in Spanish is a rather simple task.

You'll certainly need to use two main types of questions in Spanish: those that call for a "yes" or "no" answer and those that ask for more detailed facts. We cover these questions in the sections that follow.

Asking yes/no questions

It's very easy to form a question in Spanish that requires a "yes" or "no" answer. You use three simple methods:

✔ Intonation

✔ The tag **¿(No es) verdad?** (*Isn't that so?*) or **¿Está bien?** (*Is that all right?*)

✔ Inversion

The following sections break down these methods.

Unlike in English, when you want to write a question in Spanish, you put an upside-down question mark — ¿ — at the beginning of the sentence and a standard question mark — ? — at the end:

¿Tiene Ud. sed? (*Are you thirsty?*)

Also, the words *do* and *does* and sometimes *am, is,* and *are* don't translate from English into Spanish. In Spanish, these words are part of the meaning of the conjugated verb:

¿Te gusta este restaurante? (*Do you like this restaurant?*)

¿Vienen hoy? (*Are they coming today?*)

To form a negative question, you simply put **no** before the conjugated Spanish verb:

¿Ud. no quiere tomar algo? (*Don't you want to drink something?*)

Intonation

Intonation is by far the easiest way to ask a question in Spanish. If you're speaking, all you need to do is raise your voice at the end of what was a statement and add an imaginary question mark at the end of your thought. When writing, you just write down your thought and put question marks before and after it. It's that simple. Here's an example:

¿Ud. quiere tomar algo? (*Do you want to drink something?*)

The tags "¿No es verdad?" and "¿Está bien?"

¿No es verdad? and **¿Está bien?** are tags that can have a variety of meanings:

✔ Isn't that so?

✔ Right?

✔ Isn't (doesn't) he/she?

✔ Aren't (don't) they?

✔ Aren't (don't) we?

✔ Aren't (don't) you?

You generally place **¿No es verdad?** or **¿Está bien?** at the end of a statement — especially when "yes" is the expected answer:

Ud. quiere tomar algo. ¿No es verdad? (*You want to drink something, don't you?*)

Tenemos jugo. ¿Está bien? (*We have juice. Is that all right?*)

Inversion

Inversion means that you turn something around; you can invert anything from a picture to words in a sentence. When forming a "yes" or "no" question in Spanish, you may invert the word order of the pronoun or the subject noun and its accompanying verb form. The following list details some different considerations when using inversion:

✔ With inversion, pronouns tied to the conjugated verb should remain after it:

  • **¿Ud. tiene sed?** (*Are you thirsty?*) **¿Tiene Ud. sed ?** (*Are you thirsty?*)

  • **Ella va a tomar té?** (*Is she going to drink tea?*) **¿Va ella a tomar té?** (*Is she going to drink tea?*)

✔ If the subject noun or pronoun is followed by two consecutive verbs, put the subject noun or pronoun after the phrase containing the second verb (remember to keep the meaning of the phrase intact):

  • **¿Uds. quieren comer?** (*Do you want to eat?*) **¿Quieren comer Uds.?** (*Do you want to eat?*)

  • **¿Luz prefiere tomar carne?** (*Does Luz prefer to eat meat?*) **¿Prefiere tomar carne Luz?** (*Does Luz prefer to eat meat?*)

In most instances, the subject pronoun is omitted in Spanish when the subject is obvious:

¿Quieres comer algo ahora? (*Do you want to eat something now?*)

✔ To ask a negative inverted question, put **no** before the inverted verb and noun or pronoun. For verbs preceded by a direct or indirect object pronoun (see Chapter 10) or for reflexive verbs (see Chapter 11), the pronoun should remain before the conjugated verb:

  • **¿No toma frutas tu amigo?** (*Doesn't your friend eat fruit?*)

  • **¿No las toma tu amigo?** (*Doesn't your friend eat them?*)

  • **¿No se desayuna temprano Alberto?** (*Doesn't Albert eat breakfast early?*)

Asking for information

When a simple "yes" or "no" won't satisfy your curiosity, you need to know how to ask for more information in Spanish. Although the names sound a bit formidable, interrogative adjectives, interrogative adverbs, and interrogative pronouns are the tools that allow you to get all the facts you want and need. Find out how in the following sections.

Interrogative adjectives

You use the interrogative adjective **¿cuánto?** (*How much?/How many?*) before a noun when that noun may be counted or measured. **¿Cuánto?** varies and must agree in number and gender with the noun it describes (note that **cuánto, cuánta, cuántos,** and **cuántas** may also be used as interrogative pronouns):

	Masculine	*Feminine*
Singular	**¿cuánto?**	**¿cuánta?**
Plural	**¿cuántos?**	**¿cuántas?**

Here are some examples of **¿cuánto?** in use:

¿Cuánto dinero necesitas? (*How much money do you need?*)

¿Cuántos dólares ganan por hora? (*How many dollars do they earn per hour?*)

¿Cuánta moneda tiene Ud.? (*How much change [How many coins] do you have?*)

¿Cuántas horas trabajan? (*How many hours do they work?*)

The interrogative adjective **¿qué?,** on the other hand, is invariable (it doesn't change) and refers to a noun that isn't being counted. This word is equivalent to the English interrogative adjectives *what* or *which:*

¿Qué idiomas sabes hablar? (*What [Which] languages do you know how to speak?*)

You may use a preposition before an interrogative adjective where logical:

¿A qué hora sale el tren? (*At what time does the train leave?*)

Con cuánta frecuencia vas al cine? (*[With how much frequency] How often do you go to the movies?*)

¿De cuántos hombres hablan? (*How many men are you speaking about?*)

Interrogative adverbs

You use interrogative adverbs when an adverb is used to ask a question. You often use the interrogative adverbs that follow with inversion to form questions (see the earlier section "Inversion"):

English Adverb	Spanish Interrogative Adverb
How?	**¿cómo?**
When?	**¿cuándo?**
Where (to)?	**¿dónde?**
Why? (for what reason)	**¿por qué?**
Why? (for what purpose)	**¿para qué?**

Here are a couple of these adverbs at work:

¿Cómo va Ud. a la oficina? (*How do you get to work?*)

¿Dónde vive tu hermana? (*Where does your sister live?*)

You may use a preposition before an interrogative adverb where logical (note that the preposition **a** is attached to the interrogative adverb in the first example):

¿Adónde quieren ir los niños? (*Where do the children want to go?*)

¿Para que sirve esta herramienta? (*How is this tool used?*)

The interrogative adverb **¿Para qué?** asks about a purpose and, therefore, requires an answer with **para** (*for, to*):

¿Para qué usa Ud. esa brocha? (*Why [For what purpose] do you use that brush?*)

Uso esa brocha para pintar. (*I use that brush to paint.*)

¿Por qué? asks about a reason and, therefore, requires an answer with **porque** (*because*):

> **¿Por qué llora el niño?** (*Why [For what reason] is the child crying?*)
>
> **Llora porque está enfermo.** (*He's crying because he is sick.*)

Interrogative pronouns

You use an interrogative pronoun when a pronoun is used to ask a question. The following table presents the Spanish equivalents to English pronouns:

English Pronoun	Spanish Interrogative Pronoun
Who?	**¿quién(es)?**
What? (Which one[s]?)	**¿cuál(es)?**
What?	**¿qué?**
How much?	**¿cuánto?**
How many?	**¿cuántos(as)?**

The following list breaks down the characteristics of the interrogative pronouns in the previous list:

- The interrogative pronouns **¿quién(es)?** and **¿cuál(es)?** are variable pronouns and change to agree in number only with the noun they replace:
  - **¿Quién(es) llega(n)?** (*Who is arriving?*)
  - **Raquel llega.** (*Raquel is arriving.*)
  - **Raquel y Domingo llegan.** (*Raquel and Domingo are arriving.*)
  - **¿Cuál(es) de esta(s) blusa(s) prefieres?** (*Which of these blouses do you prefer?*)
  - **Prefiero la roja.** (*I prefer the red one.*)
  - **Prefiero las rojas.** (*I prefer the red ones.*)

- **¿Cuál?** means *what* or *which (one/s)* and asks about a choice or a selection:
  - **¿Cuál es tu número de teléfono?** (*What is your phone number?*)
  - **¿Cuál de los dos es el mejor?** (*Which [one] of the two is better?*)
  - **¿Cuáles son los días de la semana?** (*What are the days of the week?*)

- **¿Cuánto?,** when it means *how many,* agrees in both number and gender with the noun being replaced:
  - **¿Cuántos toman el examen?** (*How many are taking the test?*)

- **¿Cuánto?,** when it means *how much,* and **¿qué?** remain invariable:
  - **¿Cuánto vale ese coche?** (*How much is that car worth?*)
  - **¿Qué significa esto?** (*What does that mean?*)

- A preposition + **quién** refers to people. A preposition + **que** refers to things:
  - **¿De quiénes habla Ud.?** (*About whom are you speaking?*)
  - **¿De qué habla Ud.?** (*About what are you speaking?*)
  - **¿A quién se refiere él?** (*To whom is he referring?*)
  - **¿A qué se refiere él?** (*To what is he referring?*)

✔ **¿Qué?** means *what* when it precedes a verb and asks about a definition, description, or an explanation. When **¿qué?** precedes a noun, it expresses *which:*

- **¿Qué hacen durante el verano?** (*What are they doing during the summer?*)
- **¿Qué película quieres ver?** (*Which film do you want to see?*)

Hay (*there is/are* or *is/are there?*) is a present-tense form of the auxiliary verb **haber** (*to have*). You use this verb impersonally both to ask and to answer the question you ask. You can use **hay** by itself or with a preceding question word:

¿(No) Hay un buen restaurante por aquí? (*Is[n't] there a good restaurant nearby?*)

¿Dónde hay un buen restaurante por aquí? (*Where is there a good restaurant nearby?*)

You're a student. Your friend's mother wrote a note to your teacher about her grade, but your teacher had difficulty reading the letter and has come to you with questions. Write as many of those questions as you can, using interrogative adjectives, interrogative adverbs, interrogative pronouns, and **hay,** based on the underlined information contained in the note. Here's an example:

Q. Pablo vive en la ciudad.

A. **¿Quién vive en la ciudad? ¿Dónde vive Pablo?**

Estimada Señora Pueblo
Mi hija (1) Teresa no merece una nota de (2) sesenta y cinco. (3) Cada día (4) pasa dos horas estudiando (5) en la biblioteca (6) porque quiere salir bien en su clase. (7) Estudia todos los verbos y toda la gramática (8) con sus amigas. Cuando llega a casa (9) a las seis, siempre (10) está muy cansada. (11) Hay un problema. Ella (12) necesita ayuda.
Cordialmente,
Señora Colón

Your friend is a tourist writing a postcard to you. The postcard got smudged in the rain. Write down the questions you have for your friend based on the information that was written in the original postcard, which I've underlined here.

This is a handmade post-
card from the art studio of

Alma

Postcard

Place
Stamp
Here

Querida Pilar,

(13) Son <u>las dos de la tarde</u>. (14) <u>Es
jueves</u> (15) <u>el once de julio</u>. (16) Pasamos
<u>tres semanas</u> (17) <u>en España</u> (18) <u>porque</u>
(19) <u>mis hijos quieren ver</u> (20) <u>una corrida
de toros</u>. (21) <u>Mañana</u> (22) vamos a
<u>Barcelona</u> (23) porque <u>queremos hacer
una visita a la familia de mi esposo</u>. (24)
Regresamos a los Estados Unidos <u>el veinte
de julio</u>.

Alma

You've written a letter about a product your business received that doesn't work well. However, the machine in the post office crumpled and tore your letter. Write out the questions the customer relations office will write to you about the information contained in your letter, based on the underlined text that follows.

A quien corresponda,

(25) Yo devuelvo <u>inmediatamente</u> esta computadora (26) <u>porque no funciona</u>
<u>bien</u>. (27) Hay <u>muchos</u> problemas y yo no estoy satisfecha (28) <u>con ella</u>.
Además, (29) <u>el precio no es competitivo</u> y (30) <u>la computadora es de
calidad inferior</u>. (31) Yo mando la computadora <u>a su oficina en Buenos Aires</u>.
(32) <u>El número de teléfono de su oficina en Buenos Aires es (555) 23-45-67</u>.
Naturalmente, (33) <u>Ud. paga</u> los cuentos de transporte. (34) Quiero recibir
un reembolso <u>antes del fin del mes</u>.

Mariana Hidalgo

Becoming a Yes (Or No) Man: Answering Questions in Spanish

All speakers of a new language spend a lot of time asking questions, but many struggle to answer them. Where you can really shine and impress others is by providing information properly. You undoubtedly know how to answer "yes" in Spanish, because the word for "yes" is common in pop culture. Answering "no" requires a bit more work, because a simple "no" doesn't always suffice. Sometimes you need to express *nothing, nobody,* or other negative ideas. The following sections cover these topics in detail. I also explain how to answer questions that seek specific information.

Answering yes

Saying *yes* in Spanish is really quite easy. You use **sí** to answer *yes* to a question:

> **¿Quieres salir conmigo?** (*Do you want to go out with me?*)
>
> **Sí, con mucho gusto.** (*Yes, I'd be delighted.*)

Answering no

The most common negative response to a question is a plain and simple **no** (*no, not*). Other common negatives, which you may or may not use in conjunction with **no,** include the following:

Spanish	Negative English Equivalent
ni . . . ni	*neither . . . nor*
tampoco	*neither, not either*
jamás, nunca	*never, (not) ever*
nadie	*no one, nobody*
ninguno(a)	*no, none, (not) any*
nada	*nothing*

Here's a list that details some general considerations to ponder when answering negatively in Spanish:

✔ In Spanish, you generally place negative words before the conjugated verb:

> **Nunca comprendo lo que Miguel dice.** (*I never understand what Michael says.*)

Unlike in English, it's perfectly acceptable — and sometimes even necessary in common usage — for a Spanish sentence to contain a double negative. Some sentences may even contain three negatives! For example, **No le creo ni a él ni a ella./Ni él ni ella les creo.** (*I don't believe either him or her.*) If **no** is one of the negatives, it precedes the conjugated verb. When **no** is omitted, the other negative precedes the conjugated verb. Here are some examples of both:

- **No lo necesito tampoco./Tampoco lo necesito.** (*I don't need it either.*)

- **No fumo nunca./Nunca fumo.** (*I never smoke.*)

- **No viene nadie./Nadie viene.** (*No one is coming.*)
- **No tengo ninguna idea./Ninguna idea tengo.** (*I don't have any idea.*)
- **No le escucha a nadie nunca./Nunca le escucha a nadie.** (*He never listens to anyone.*)

✔ When you have two verbs in the negative answer, place **no** before the conjugated verb and put the other negative word after the second verb:

- **No puedo comer ninguna comida picante.** (*I can't eat any spicy food.*)

✔ You may also place negative words before the infinitive of the verb:

- **¿Por qué quieres no comer nada?** (*Why don't you want to eat anything?*)
- **Él prefiere no ver a nadie.** (*He doesn't want to see anyone.*)

✔ You may use negatives alone (without **no**):

- **¿Qué buscas?** (*What do you want?*)
- **Nada.** (*Nothing.*)
- **¿Dice mentiras ese muchacho?** (*Does that boy tell lies?*)
- **Nunca.** (*Never.*)

✔ A negative preceded by a preposition (see Chapter 12) retains that preposition when placed before the verb:

- **No habla de nadie./De nadie habla.** (*He doesn't speak about anyone.*)

Using no

To make a sentence negative, you can put **no** before the conjugated verb. If the conjugated verb is preceded by a pronoun, put **no** before the pronoun. **No** often is repeated for emphasis:

¿Tocas la guitarra? (*Do you play the guitar?*)

(No,) No toco la guitarra. (*[No,] I don't play the guitar.*)

¿Debe estudiar los verbos ella? (*Does she have to study the verbs?*)

(No,) Ella no los debe estudiar. (*[No,] She doesn't have to study them.*)

Using ni . . . ni

In a **ni . . . ni** construction (*neither . . . nor*), the sentence usually begins with the word **no.** Each part of the **ni . . . ni** construction precedes the word or words being stressed. Each **ni,** therefore, may be used before a noun, an adjective, or an infinitive:

No nos gusta ni el café ni el té. (*We don't like coffee or tea.*)

Su coche no es ni grande ni pequeño. (*His car is neither big nor little.*)

No puedo ni cocinar ni coser. (*I can neither cook nor sew.*)

Using nadie, nada, nunca, and jamás

You use the negatives **nadie, nada, nunca,** and **jamás** after comparisons (see Chapter 8). Note that the English translation of a Spanish negative equivalent may have an opposite meaning:

Mi madre cocina mejor que nadie. (*My mother cooks better than anyone.*)

Ella conduce más que nunca. (*She drives better than ever.*)

Quieren visitar España más que nada. (*They want to visit Spain more than anything.*)

Using ninguno

Ninguno (*no, none [not] any*), when used before a masculine singular noun, drops the final **-o** and adds an accent to the **u** (**ningún**). The feminine singular form is **ninguna.** No plural forms exist. Here's an example of its usage:

> **¿Tiene algunos problemas?** (*Do you have any problems?*)
>
> **No tengo problema ninguno.** (*I don't have a problem.*)
>
> **No tengo ningún problema.** (*I don't have a problem.*)

When used as an adjective, **ninguno/a** may be replaced by **alguno/a,** which is a more emphatic negative. This construction then follows the noun:

> **No tiene ninguna mascota./No tiene mascota alguna.** (*He doesn't have a pet.*)

Question words requiring their opposite in the negative answers

When used in questions, some words require that you use negative words of opposite meaning in the responses. The following table presents these words:

If the question contains	The negtive answer should contain
alguien (*someone, anyone*)	**nadie** (*no one, nobody*)
siempre (*always*)	**jamás/nunca** (*never*)
algo (*something*)	**nada** (*nothing*)
también (*also*)	**tampoco** (*neither, either*)
alguno(a) (*some, any*)	**ninguno(a)** (*none, [not] any*)

Here's an example sentence:

> **¿Ves algo?** (*Do you see something?*)
>
> **No veo nada.** (*I don't see anything.*)

Write a note to your parents explaining what you and your siblings didn't do around the house (in other words, you skipped out on your chores!). Use the clues I provide to fill in the appropriate negative responses. Here's an example:

Q. (not) Clarita _____ limpió la casa.

A. Clarita **no** limpió la casa.

Queridos Padres,

35. (not) Yo _____ cociné porque tenía dolor de estómago.

36. (nobody) _____ no regó el jardín.

37. (not any) Diana no lavó _____ plato.

38. (neither . . . nor) Enrique no dio de comer _____ al perro _____ al gato.

39. (nothing) Ernesto no hizo _____.

40. (either) _____ Esteban no arregló su cuarto.

41. (never) Rosa _____ planchó la ropa.

42. (never, nobody) Virginia _____ ayudó a _____.

Answering information questions

This section is chock full of tips on how to answer questions that ask you for information in Spanish. Carefully consider what's being asked so you answer each question in an appropriate manner.

- When you see a question with **¿Cómo?** (*how, what*), give the information or the explanation that's requested:

  - **¿Cómo te llamas?** (*What's your name?*)
  - **Susana.** (*Susan.*)
  - **¿Cómo estás?** (*How are you?*)
  - **Muy bien, gracias.** (*Very well, thank you.*)
  - **¿Cómo prepara Ud. este plato?** (*How do you prepare that dish?*)
  - **Con mantequilla y crema.** (*With butter and cream.*)

- When you see a question with **¿Cuánto(a)(s)** (*how much, many*), you answer with a number, an amount, or a quantity (see Chapter 1):

  - **¿Cuánto cuesta este coche?** (*How much does this car cost?*)
  - **Diez mil dólares.** (*10,000 dollars.*)
  - **¿Hace cuántas horas que está esperando Ud.?** (*How long have you been waiting?*)
  - **Dos horas.** (*Two hours.*)
  - **¿Cuántos huevos necesitas?** (*How many eggs do you need?*)
  - **Una docena.** (*A dozen.*)

- When you see a question with **¿Cuándo?** (*when*), you answer with a specific time or an expression of time:

  - **¿Cuándo empieza la película?** (*When does the film begin?*)
  - **En diez minutos.** (*In 10 minutes.*)
  - **A las tres y media.** (*At 3:30.*)
  - **En seguida.** (*Immediately.*)

- When you see a question with **¿Dónde?** (*where*), you answer with the name of a place. You use the preposition **en** to express *in:*

  - **¿Dónde vive Ud.?** (*Where do you live?*)
  - **En Nueva York.** (*In New York.*)

You must use the preposition **a** (**al, a los, a las**) + the name of a place in your answer to the question **¿adónde?** (**¿a dónde?**) (which translates literally as *to where*):

  - **¿Adónde van?** (*Where are they going?*)
  - **Van al estadio.** (*They are going to the stadium.*)

You must use the preposition **de** (**del, de la, de los**) + the name of a place in your answer to the question **¿de dónde?** (which translates literally as *from where*):

  - **¿De dónde es Ud.?** (*Where are you from?*)
  - **Soy de San Juan.** (*I'm from San Juan.*)

For more on prepositions, head to Chapter 12.

✔ When you see a question with **¿Por qué?** (*why*), answer with **porque** (*because*) + a reason:

- **¿Por qué no trabaja ella?** (*Why isn't she working?*)
- **Porque está enferma.** (*Because she's sick.*)

✔ When you see a question with **¿Quién?** (*who, whom*), answer with the name of a person.

If the question contains a preposition — **a, de, con, para,** and so on — you must use that same preposition in the answer:

- **¿Quién te acompaña al espectáculo?** (*Who is going with you to the show?*)
- **Isabel.** (*Isabel.*)
- **¿A quién espera Ud.?** (*Whom are you waiting for?*)
- **A mi novio.** (*For my boyfriend.*)
- **¿Con quién vives?** (*With whom do you live?*)
- **Con mis abuelos.** (*With my grandparents.*)

✔ When you see a question with **¿Qué?** (*what*), answer according to the situation. As with the previous bullet, if the question contains a preposition, you must use that same preposition in the answer:

- **¿Qué haces?** (*What are you doing?*)
- **Escribo algo.** (*I'm writing something.*)
- **¿Qué escribes?** (*What are you writing?*)
- **Una carta.** (*A letter.*)
- **¿Con qué escribes?** (*With what are you writing?*)
- **Con un bolígrafo.** (*With a ballpoint pen.*)

Your friend has sent you an e-mail to ask questions about your plans to go to a restaurant. Respond to his e-mail by choosing the best answer to each of his questions.

Salvador,

43. ¿Cómo quieres ir al restaurante? _____

44. ¿Cuándo quieres salir? _____

45. ¿Quién recomienda este restaurante? _____

46. ¿Por qué escojes este restaurante? _____

47. ¿Dónde está el restaurante? _____

48. ¿Cuáles platos te interesan? _____

49. ¿Cuántos amigos vas a invitar a acompañarnos? _____

50. ¿Qué prefieres hacer después de comer? _____

a. **cinco**
b. **ir al cine**
c. **porque sirve comida mexicana**
d. **los tamales y los tacos**
e. **en taxi**
f. **mi tío**
g. **en la Avenida Sexta**
h. **a eso de las siete**

Answer Key

1 ¿Cómo se llama su hija? (What is her daughter's name?)

2 ¿Qué nota no merece su hija? (What grade doesn't her daughter deserve?)

3 ¿Qué hace cada día su hija? (What does her daughter do every day?)

4 ¿Cuántas horas pasa a estudiar? (How many hours does she spend studying?)

5 ¿Dónde estudia? (Where does she study?)

6 ¿Por qué estudia? (Why does she study?)

7 ¿Qué estudia? (What does she study?)

8 ¿Con quién estudia? (WIth whom does she study?)

9 ¿A qué hora llega a casa? (At what time does she arrive home?)

10 ¿Cómo está cuando llega a casa? (How is she when she arrives home?)

11 ¿Hay un problema? (Is there a problem?)

12 ¿Qué necesita ella? (What does she need?)

13 ¿Qué hora es? (What time is it?)

14 ¿Qué día es? (What day is it?)

15 ¿Cuál es la fecha? (What is the date?)

16 ¿Cúantas semanas pasan en España? (How many weeks are you spending in Spain?)

17 ¿Dónde pasan tres semanas? (Where are you spending three weeks?)

18 ¿Por qué pasan tres semanas en España? (Why are you spending three weeks in Spain?)

19 ¿Quiénes quieren ver una corrida de toros? (Who wants to see a bullfight?)

20 ¿Qué quieren ver sus hijos? (What do your children want to see?)

21 ¿Cuándo van a Barcelona? (When are you going to Barcelona?)

22 ¿Adónde van mañana? (Where are you going tomorrow?)

23 ¿Por qué van a Barcelona? (Why are you going to Barcelona?)

24 ¿Cuándo regresan a los Estados Unidos? (When are you returning to the United States?)

25 ¿Cuándo devuelve Ud. la computadora? (When are you returning the computer?)

26 ¿Por qué devuelve Ud. la computadora? (Why are you returning the computer?)

27 ¿Cuántos problemas hay? (How many problems are there?)

28 ¿Con qué no está Ud. satisfecha? (What aren't you satisfied with?)

29 ¿Cómo es el precio? (How is the price?)

30 ¿Cómo es la calidad? (How is the quality?)

31 ¿Adónde manda Ud. la computadora? (Where are you sending the computer?)

32 ¿Cuál es el número de teléfono en Buenos Aires? (What is the telephone number in Buenos Aires?)

33 ¿Quién paga los cuentos de transporte? (Who is paying the transportation fees?)

34 ¿Cuándo quiere Ud. recibir un reembolso? (When do you want to receive a refund?)

35 no

36 nadie

37 ningún

38 ni . . . ni

39 nada

40 tampoco

41 nunca

42 nunca . . . nadie

43 e

44 h

45 f

46 c

47 g

48 d

49 a

50 b

Chapter 6

Doing It Right Now: Gerunds and the Present Progressive

● ●

In This Chapter

▶ Reviewing the different uses of gerunds in English and Spanish

▶ Forming the gerunds of regular, stem-changing, and irregular verbs

▶ Discussing the present in a progressive manner

● ●

*I*f you didn't go to school way back when, like I did, you've probably never had the distinct pleasure of diagramming a sentence and labeling all its parts on a blackboard in front of the class. Heck, I bet that the word "gerund" is probably as foreign to you as the word **gerundio.** Here, I'll give you a clue. A *gerund* is a verb form ending in -ing that you sometimes use in the present progressive tense in Spanish. Although you've undoubtedly heard of the present tense, the present progressive is a tense that may be quite unfamiliar to you, even though you use it on a daily basis.

In this chapter, you discover how to form the gerunds of Spanish verbs, as well as when to use a gerund or another verb form when you want to use the -ing ending. By the end of this chapter, you'll also be a pro at forming the present progressive — primarily by using the verb **estar** (*to be*) in conjunction with gerunds.

Gerunds: Putting the -ing in Everything

Gerunds are verb forms that end in -ing. A Spanish gerund is called a **gerundio,** and it's also derived from a verb. A Spanish gerund has two English equivalents:

✔ It may represent the English for *while* or *by* + a present participle (an English verb form ending in -ing):

Se puede aprender mucho viajando. (*One can learn a lot while traveling.*)

Estudiando, él salió bien en su examen. (*By studying, he passed his test.*)

✔ It may represent an English past participle used as an adjective that ends in -ing:

Esa niña, quien está tocando el piano, es mi hermana. (*That girl playing the piano is my sister.*)

A Spanish gerund, unlike an English gerund, may not be used as a noun subject. Spanish uses the infinitive form (the **-ar, -er,** or **-ir** form of the verb before it's conjugated) instead. In the example that follows, the English verb *swimming* is the noun subject of the verb *is*. Note the Spanish use of the infinitive:

Nadar es mi pasatiempo favorito. (*Swimming is my favorite pastime.*)

Forming the Gerunds of Regular Verbs

Forming gerunds of regular verbs — verbs that end in **-ar**, **-er**, or **-ir** without spelling or stem changes or other irregularities — is quite easy, because gerunds have only one form. Here's all you have to do:

- ✔ Drop the **-ar** from **-ar** verb infinitives and add **-ando** (the equivalent of the English -ing).
- ✔ Drop the **-er** or **-ir** from **-er** or **-ir** verb infinitives, respectively, and add **-iendo** (the equivalent of the English -ing).

The following table shows these changes for some example verbs:

Ending	Verb	Meaning	Gerund	Meaning
-ar	hablar	*to speak*	hablando	*speaking*
-er	aprender	*to learn*	aprendiendo	*learning*
-ir	escribir	*to write*	escribiendo	*writing*

Be careful! If an **-er** or **-ir** verb stem ends in a vowel, you must drop the ending and add **-yendo** (the Spanish equivalent of -ing) to form the gerund:

caer (*to fall*): ca**yendo**

construir (*to build*): constru**yendo**

creer (*to believe*): cre**yendo**

leer (*to read*): le**yendo**

oír (*to hear*): o**yendo**

traer (*to bring*): tra**yendo**

Forming the Gerunds of Stem-Changing and Irregular Verbs

Generally, but not always, the stem change of a verb is indicated in parentheses after the verb. For example, **mentir (i)** means that the internal **e** changes to **i** in certain forms and in certain tenses. However, you'll come to recognize these verbs after you work with them often enough.

You form the gerund of a stem-changing **-ir** (**-e** to **-i** or **-o** to **-u**) verb (see Chapter 4) by changing the vowel in the stem from **-e** to **-i** or from **-o** to **-u**, dropping the **-ir** infinitive ending, and adding the proper ending for a gerund (see the previous section).

From **e → i**:

decir (*to say, to tell*) → diciendo (*saying, telling*)

mentir (*to lie*) → mintiendo (*lying*)

pedir (*to ask*) → pidiendo (*asking*)

repetir (*to repeat*) → repitiendo (*repeating*)

sentir (*to feel*) → sintiendo (*feeling*)

servir (*to serve*) → sirviendo (*serving*)

venir (*to come*) → viniendo (*coming*)

From **o** → **u:**

dormir (*to sleep*) → durmiendo (*sleeping*)

morir (*to die*) → muriendo (*dying*)

Only three Spanish verbs have irregular gerunds. You don't use them very frequently, but you should still be aware of their forms. Yes, you have to memorize them in case you need to use them; at least you only have to worry about three! Here they are:

✔ **ir** (*to go*): **yendo**

✔ **poder** (*to be able*): **pudiendo**

✔ **reír** (*to laugh*): **riendo**

You work for a large international company. Your CEO just announced that the company will give a 5 percent raise to all employees. Write a note to your boss in Venezuela describing how all the workers (including yourself) reacted to the good news. Use gerunds in your answers, based on the verbs I provide. Here's an example:

O. (gritar) El señor Martí salió _____.

A. El señor Martí salió **gritando**. (*Mr. Martí left shouting.*)

Estimado Señor Ruiz,

Todos los empleados están muy contentos de recibir el aumento. Note, por favor, las reacciones favorables:

1. (llorar) La señora Gómez salió _____.

2. (aplaudir) Pablo Guzmán salió _____.

3. (correr) Yo salí _____.

4. (decir) Los hermanos Santiago salieron _____ "Ay, Caramba!"

5. (saltar) Lupe Rueda y Ricardo Rivera salieron _____ de alegría.

6. (reír) Juan López y yo salimos _____.

7. (dar) Ernesto Sánchez salió _____ gracias.

8. (leer) Elena Ramírez y María Hernández salieron _____ el nuevo contrato.

Sinceramente,

Julio Castro

Your Colombian pen pal is impressed with the quality of your Spanish writing. You decide to write him/her an e-mail in which you list the many ways a person can learn to write and speak Spanish well. Read the cues that I provide and then translate them into Spanish. Here's an example:

Q. (practicing the verbs) _____

A. **practicando los verbos**

Querido(a) _____ (name),

Muchas gracias de hacerme cumplidos. Me gusta mucho estudiar el español. Te estoy escribiendo para decirte como se aprende bien el español.

Se aprende bien el español:

9. (listening to Spanish speakers) _____

10. (studying the grammar) _____

11. (speaking with Spanish speakers) _____

12. (watching Spanish television programs) _____

13. (repeating sentences) _____

14. (memorizing vocabulary words) _____

Tu amigo(a),

_____ (your name)

The Present Progressive: Expressing an Action in Progress

For people who speak English as a first language, the concept of two present tenses — the present and the present progressive — can be very confusing. How do you determine when to use the present or the present progressive in Spanish? Good news: The choice really isn't that difficult.

You use the present tense when you want to express an action or event that the subject generally does at a given time, or that's habitual. You use the *present progressive* tense to express an action or event that's in progress or that's continuing at a given time — which calls for the use of gerunds. Here are some examples:

Él va a la oficina a las siete de la mañana. (*He goes* [does go] *to the office at seven in the morning* [every day].)

Él está trabajando. (*He is working* [at the present time].)

In the following sections, I show you the most common way to form the present progressive — by using the present tense of the verb **estar** (*to be*) and a gerund. I also explain how to use the present tense of the verbs **seguir** (*to follow, continue*) and **continuar** (*to continue*) and the present tense of verbs of motion, along with a gerund, to form the present progressive.

Using estar

You often form the present progressive tense with the present tense form of verbs to show that an action is in progress. (***Note:*** You can form the other progressive tenses by using the proper tense of the verb [preterit, imperfect, future, conditional], but they go beyond the scope of this intermediate book.)

Estar (*to be*) is the verb you most often use to form the present progressive because the present tense of **estar** expresses that something is taking place. The following table presents the present tense conjugation of this irregular verb, which you must commit to memory:

estar (*to be*)	
yo **estoy**	nosotros **estamos**
tú **estás**	vosotros **estáis**
él, ella, Ud. **está**	ellos, ellas, Uds. **están**

To form the present progressive with this verb, you simply include a gerund after the proper form of **estar.** Here are some examples:

El niño está durmiendo. (*The child is sleeping.*)

Estamos escuchando. (*We are listening.*)

Using other verbs

You use the present tense of several other verbs (not just **estar**) to form the present progressive tense as well. For instance, you can form the present progressive with the present tense of the verbs **seguir** or **continuar,** or with the present tense of verbs of motion — such as **salir, ir, andar, entrar,** and **llegar** — to show that the action or event is in progress.

The following tables list the conjugations of these verbs in the present tense so that you may use them in the present progressive:

seguir (*to continue, keep*)	
yo **sigo**	nosotros **seguimos**
tú **sigues**	vosotros **seguís**
él, ella, Ud. **sigue**	ellos, ellas, Uds. **siguen**

continuar (*to continue*)	
yo **continúo**	nosotros **continuamos**
tú **continúas**	vosotros **continuáis**
él, ella, Ud. **continúa**	ellos, ellas, Uds. **continúan**

salir (*to leave, go out*)	
yo **salgo**	nosotros **salimos**
tú **sales**	vosotros **salís**
él, ella, Ud. **sale**	ellos, ellas, Uds. **salen**

ir (*to go*)	
yo **voy**	nosotros **vamos**
tú **vas**	vosotros **vais**
él, ella, Ud. **va**	ellos, ellas, Uds. **van**

andar (*to walk*)	
yo **ando**	nosotros **andas**
tú **andas**	vosotros **andáis**
él, ella, Ud. **anda**	ellos, ellas, Uds. **andan**

Just as you do with the verb **estar,** you include a gerund with the proper present tense verb form to express the present progressive tense. Here are some examples:

> **¿Por qué sigues interrumpiendo a los demas?** (*Why do you continue interrupting others?*)

> **La muchacha continúa leyendo.** (*The girl continues reading.*)

> **Yo salgo sonriendo.** (*I leave smiling.*)

> **Su humor va cambiando.** (*Your mood is changing.*)

> **Ellos andan hablando.** (*They walk while speaking.*)

You're at a wedding that your friend, Ana, couldn't attend. Write her a short postcard to express what you and the other guests are doing. Use the correct present-tense form of the verb **estar** (*to be*) and the appropriate gerund. I provide the subject of the sentence, along with the verb you must turn into a gerund. Here's an example:

Q. los jóvenes/hablar _____

A. Los jóvenes **están hablando.** (*The young people are talking.*)

Postcard

Place
Stamp
Here

Querida Ana,
Como no puedes asistir a las bodas, te cuento lo que
pasa. Esto es lo que pasa en este momento:

15. Julia y Tomás/beber champán

   _____

16. los padres de los novios/bailar

   _____

17. la abuela de Marta/sonreír

   _____

18. los maridos/abrir regalos

   _____

19. yo/pedirle consejos a mi amigo

   _____

20. La orquesta/tocar música

   _____

21. Los niños/hacer mucho ruido

   _____

22. Silvia y yo/comer la cena

   _____

   Tu amigo(a),
   _____(your name)

You're sitting on a blanket at the beach, observing all that's going on around you. The following sentences list some of the things you see. Use the verb **estar, seguir,** or **continuar** + the appropriate gerund to write your friend a letter describing the scene. Here's an example:

Q. Two children keep arguing.

A. Dos niños **siguen discutiendo.**

23. A girl is reading a magazine.

_____

24. A few people keep playing volleyball.

_____

25. A boy continues listening to a radio.

_____

26. Two people are eating a sandwich.

_____

27. A few people are swimming.

_____

28. Three people are surfing.

_____

29. Two people continue sailing a boat.

_____

30. A woman is sunbathing.

_____

As a homework assignment for class, you have to describe a typical scene in your home. Combine the elements I provide to explain what happens in the present progressive tense. Keep the subject I provide, conjugate the first verb in the present tense, and then give the gerund of the second verb. Here's an example:

Q. mi madre/estar/hablar por teléfono

A. Mi madre **está hablando** por teléfono. (*My mother is talking on the phone.*)

31. mi perro/andar/ladrar

_____

32. mi padre lo ignora y/continuar/leer la revista

_____

33. mi madre/ir/servir la cena

_____

34. yo/estar/escuchar la radio

_____

35. mi hermano menor/seguir/pedir ayuda con su tarea

_____

36. mi hermana/llegar/traer regalos para todos

_____

37. mis abuelos/entrar/discutir

_____

38. mis amigos/salir/repetir chistes

_____

Answer Key

1 llorando

2 aplaudiendo

3 corriendo

4 diciendo

5 saltando

6 riendo

7 dando

8 leyendo

9 escuchando a hispanohablantes

10 estudiando la gramática

11 hablando con hispanohablantes

Note that you use **con** to express *with*.

12 mirando programas españoles en la televisión

The word for program is **programa,** which is masculine. To form the plural of an adjective that ends in a consonant, add **-es.**

13 repitiendo oraciones

14 aprendiendo de memoria el vocabulario

15 Julia y Tomás **están bebiendo** champán. (*Julia and Tomás are drinking champagne.*)

16 Los padres de los novios **están bailando.** (*The parents of the bride and groom are dancing.*)

17 La abuela de Marta **está sonriendo.** (*Marta's grandmother is smiling.*)

The gerund for **sonreír** is irregular and must be memorized.

18 Los novios **estan abriendo** regalos. (*The bride and groom are opening presents.*)

19 Yo le **estoy pidiendo** consejos a mi amigo. (*I am asking advice from my friends.*)

20 La orquesta **está tocando** música. (*The orchestra is playing music.*)

21 Los niños **están haciendo** mucho ruido. (*The children are making a lot of noise.*)

22 Silvia y yo **estamos comiendo** la cena. (*Silvia and I are eating dinner.*)

23 Una muchacha **está leyendo** una revista.

24 Algunas personas **siguen jugando** al voleibol.

25 Un muchacho **continúa escuchando** la radio.

26 Dos personas **están comiendo** un sándwich.

27 Algunas personas **están nadando.**

28 Tres personas **están haciendo** surf.

29 Dos personas **continúan navegando** una barca.

30 Una muchacha **está tomando** sol.

31 Mi perro **anda ladrando.** (*My dog is barking.*)

32 Mi padre lo ignora y **continúa leyendo** la revista. (*My father ignores him and continues reading the magazine.*)

33 Mi madre **va sirviendo** la cena. (*My mother is serving dinner.*)

34 Yo **estoy escuchando** la radio. (*I am listening to the radio.*)

35 Mi hermano menor **sigue pidiendo** ayuda con su tarea. (*My younger brother keeps asking for help with his homework.*)

36 Mi hermana **llega trayendo** regalos para todos. (*My sister arrives bringing presents for everyone.*)

37 Mis abuelos **entran discutiendo.** (*My grandparents are arguing.*)

38 Mis amigos **salen repitiendo** chistes. (*My friends leave repeating jokes.*)

Chapter 7

Expressing Yourself with Subjunctive Feeling

In This Chapter
▶ Creating the present subjunctive with all types of Spanish verbs
▶ Digesting the many uses of the present subjunctive

So, you're unfamiliar with the subjunctive — probably as unfamiliar as I was when I first started learning a foreign language. I'm not at all surprised. Although my teachers always seemed to concentrate on grammar, I don't remember hearing about the subjunctive until my second year of language study in high school. What exactly is the subjunctive? It isn't a tense, which tells at what time an action took place: present, past, or future. The subjunctive is a mood, meaning it indicates how the speaker feels about or perceives a situation rather than when an action occurred. The subjunctive mood exists in several tenses: the present, the past, the imperfect, and the pluperfect.

How is the present tense different from the present subjunctive? The present tense functions in the indicative mood — a mood that states a fact. The subjunctive (in any of its tenses), on the other hand, expresses unreal, hypothetical, theoretical, imaginary, uncorroborated, or unconfirmed conditions or situations. These expressions are the result of the speaker's doubts, emotions, wishes, wants, needs, desires, feelings, speculations, or suppositions. Don't be intimidated by those long lists. The subjunctive really isn't as difficult as it appears; with some practice, you'll quickly become comfortable using it.

That's where this chapter comes in. In this chapter, you discover how to form the present subjunctive of regular verbs, verbs with spelling changes, verbs with stem changes, and completely irregular verbs. After you master the technique of properly conjugating these verbs, you find many of the important uses of the subjunctive. I also give you plenty of practice on determining when to use the present tense and when to use the subjunctive mood.

Forming the Present Subjunctive

If you can form the present tense, you can form the present subjunctive — with any of the types of verbs I present in this chapter. This is because many of the subjunctive stems use the **yo** form (first-person singular) of the present tense. So, if you've mastered Chapter 4, this chapter will be less of a challenge. You discover how to form the subjunctive with many types of verbs in the following sections.

Regular verbs

You form the present subjunctive of regular verbs by dropping the **-o** from the **yo** form of the present tense and adding the subjunctive endings shown in bold in Table 7-1. These endings are relatively easy to remember, because **-ar** verbs use the present-tense endings of **-er** verbs, and **-er** and **-ir** verbs use the present-tense endings of **-ar** verbs. This is why people say that you form the present subjunctive by using the opposite verb endings on the stem.

Table 7-1	The Present Subjunctive Endings of Regular Verbs		
yo Form of Present	*-ar verbs*	*-er verbs*	*-ir verbs*
	hable (*I speak*)	comprendo (*I understand*)	escribo (*I write*)
yo	hable	comprenda	escriba
tú	hables	comprendas	escribas
él, ella, Ud.	hable	comprenda	escriba
nosotros	hablemos	comprendamos	escribamos
vosotros	habléis	comprendáis	escribáis
ellos, ellas, Uds.	hablen	comprendan	escriban

Here are some examples of these verbs in the subjunctive:

> **Es importante que yo hable con sus padres.** (*It is important that I speak to your parents.*)

> **Es esencial que Ud. comprenda las reglas.** (*It is essential that you understand the rules.*)

> **Es necesario que nosotros escribamos las notas.** (*It is necessary that we write the notes.*)

You and your business colleagues are going to a meeting. Complete the memo that your boss sent with instructions for everyone in the company, including himself and his family members, by inserting the proper form of the verbs I provide in parentheses. Here's an example:

Q. (escuchar) Es importante que Uds. _____ atentamente.

A. Es importante que Uds. **escuchen** atentamente. (*It's important that you listen attentively.*)

A Todos,

Es importante que . . .

1. (observar) tú _____ como actúan los demás.

2. (escribir) nosotros _____ notas.

3. (leer) vosotros _____ los contratos antes de firmarlos.

4. (presentar) Uds. _____ sus ideas y sus opinones con calma.

5. (negociar) yo _____ de buena fe.

6. (exprimir) tú _____ lo importante.

7. (participar) Enrique _____ en todas las discusiones.

8. (proceder) yo _____ lentamente.

9. (hablar) nosotros _____ lenta y claramente.

10. (responder) Rosa _____ cuidadosamente.

11. (reflexionar) vosotros _____ antes de hablar.

12. (describir) Felipe y Raúl _____ bien nuestra posición.

Verbs irregular in the yo form

Some verbs are irregular in the **yo** form of the present tense. These verbs use the stem of the **yo** to form the present subjunctive. You drop the final **-o** from the **yo** form and add the opposite endings. In other words, you add an ending that starts with **-a** for the **-er** and **-ir** verbs listed in Table 7-2.

Table 7-2   Subjunctive Stems Derived from the Present-Tense yo Form

Verb	Meaning	yo Form	Subjunctive Forms
caber	to fit	quepo	quepa, quepas, quepa, quepamos, quepáis, quepan
caer	to fall	caigo	caiga, caigas, caiga, caigamos, caigáis, caigan
decir	to say, to tell	digo	diga, digas, diga, digamos, digáis, digan
hacer	to make, to do	hago	haga, hagas, haga, hagamos, hagáis, hagan
oír	to hear	oigo	oiga, oigas, oiga, oigamos, oigáis, oigan
poner	to put	pongo	ponga, pongas, ponga, pongamos, pongáis, pongan
salir	to go out	salgo	salga, salgas, salga, salgamos, salgáis, salgan
tener	to have	tengo	tenga, tengas, tenga, tengamos, tengáis, tengan
traer	to bring	traigo	traiga, traigas, traiga, traigamos, traigáis, traigan
valer	to be worth	valgo	valga, valgas, valga, valgamos, valgáis, valgan
venir	to come	vengo	venga, vengas, venga, vengamos, vengáis, vengan
ver	to see	veo	vea, veas, vea, veamos, veáis, vean

Here are some examples of these types of verbs:

Es imposible que todo quepa en mi maleta. (*It's impossible that everything will fit in my suitcase.*)

Es urgente que Uds. hagan todo este trabajo ahora. (*It is urgent that you do all this work now.*)

Verbs with spelling changes

Some Spanish verbs have the same spelling change in the present subjunctive as they have in the present tense. Namely, verbs ending in **-cer/-cir, -ger/-gir,** and **-guir** (not **-uir**) undergo the same changes that occur in the **yo** form of the present. These changes are as follows:

- vowel + **-cer/-cir** verbs: c → zc
- consonant + **-cer /-cir** verbs: c → z
- **-ger/-gir** verbs: g → j
- **-guir** verbs: gu → g

Table 7-3 shows these changes in the subjunctive.

Table 7-3	Present Subjunctive of Verbs with Spelling Changes		
Infinitive	*Present yo Form*	*Stem*	*Subjunctive + Endings*
ofrecer (*to offer*)	**ofrezco**	ofrezc-	-a, -as, -a, -amos, -áis, -an
traducir (*to translate*)	**traduzco**	traduzc-	-a, -as, -a, -amos, -áis, -an
convencer (*to convince*)	**convenzo**	convenz-	-a, -as, -a, -amos, -áis, -an
esparcir (*to spread*)	**esparzo**	esparz-	-a, -as, -a, -amos, -áis, -an
escoger (*to choose*)	**escojo**	escoj-	-a, -as, -a, -amos, -áis, -an
exigir (*to demand*)	**exijo**	exij-	-a, -as, -a, -amos, -áis, -an
distinguir (*to distinguish*)	**distingo**	disting-	-a, -as, -a, -amos, -áis, -an

The following examples illustrate these spelling changes:

> **Es una lástima que el director no le ofrezca un aumento de salario.** (*It is a pity that the director isn't offering him a raise.*)

> **Es natural que el jefe exija mucho de sus empleados.** (*It is natural that the boss demands a lot from his employees.*)

You see some different spelling changes for verbs in the present subjunctive than you see for verbs with spelling changes in the present tense. In the present subjunctive, verbs ending in **-car, -gar,** and **-zar** undergo changes. They have the same changes as in the preterit (or the past tense; see Chapter 13). These changes are as follows:

- **-car** verbs: c → qu
- **-gar** verbs: g → gu
- **-zar** verbs: z → c

The following table (and examples) shows the full conjugation:

Infinitive	Stem	Subjunctive Endings
tocar (*to touch*)	to**qu**-	**-e, -es, -e, -emos, -éis, -en**
pagar (*to pay*)	pa**gu**-	**-e, -es, -e, -emos, -éis, -en**
organizar (*to organize*)	organi**c**-	**-e, -es, -e, -emos, éis, -en**

Here are some examples:

> **Es importante que no toques nada.** (*It is important that you not touch anything.*)
>
> **Es imperativo que nosotros paguemos esta factura.** (*It is imperative that we pay this bill.*)
>
> **Es necesario que él organice los datos.** (*It is necessary for him to organize the data.*)

Verbs with stem changes

Just like in the present tense, stem-changing -**ar** and -**er** verbs in the present subjunctive undergo changes in all forms except **nosotros** and **vosotros**. Table 7-4 outlines these changes.

Table 7-4		Verbs with Stem Changes in the Present Subjunctive		
Infinitive Ending	**Stem Change in the Present**	**Example Verb**	**yo, tú, él, ellos Subjunctive Stem**	**nosotros/vosotros Subjunctive Stem**
-ar	e → ie	**cerrar** (*to close*)	c**ie**rr-	cerr-
-ar	o → ue	**mostrar** (*to show*)	m**ue**str-	mostr-
-er	e → ie	**querer** (*to wish, to want*)	qu**ie**r-	quer-
-er	o → ue	**volver** (*to return*)	v**ue**lv-	volv-

Here are two example sentences with these verbs:

> **Quiero que Ud. cierre la ventana.** (*I want you to close the window.*)
>
> **Es dudoso que ellos vuelvan temprano.** (*It is doubtful that they will return early.*)

And what about -**ir** verbs? Well, -**ir** verbs with an e → ie (o → ue) stem change -**e** to -**ie** (-**o** to -**ue**) in all forms except **nosotros** and **vosotros**. Those with an e → i stem change alter -**e** to -**i** in all forms including **nosotros** and **vosotros,** as shown in Table 7-5.

Table 7-5		Certain -ir Verbs with Stem Changes	
Infinitive	**Stem Change**	**Stem**	**nosotros and vosotros Stems**
preferir (*to prefer*)	e → ie	pref**ie**r-	prefir-
dormir (*to sleep*)	o → ue	d**ue**rm-	durm-
servir (*to serve*)	e → i	s**i**rv-	sirv-

Here are some examples of **-ir** verbs in the subjunctive:

> **La profesora está contenta que nosotros prefiramos ver una película española.** (*The teacher is happy that we prefer to see a Spanish film.*)

> **Su padre está enojado que él duerma hasta las diez.** (*His father is angry that he sleeps until ten o'clock.*)

> **Es dudoso que sirvan vino en la conferencia.** (*It is doubtful that they will serve wine at the conference.*)

The changes don't end with simple **-ar, -er,** and **-ir** verbs, however. Note the stem changes for the following categories of verbs that end with an additional vowel:

✔ Verbs that end in **-iar** have accent marks in all present subjunctive forms except **nosotros:**

> **enviar** (*to send*): envíe, envíes, envíe, enviemos, enviéis, envíen

✔ Verbs that end in **-uar** have accent marks in all present subjunctive forms except **nosotros:**

> **continuar** (*to continue*): continúe, continúes, continúe, continuemos, continuéis, continúen

✔ Verbs that end in **-uir** (but not **-guir**) add a **y** after the **u** in all present subjunctive forms:

> **concluir** (*to conclude*): concluya, concluyas, concluya, concluyamos, concluyáis, concluyan

The following examples show these rules in action:

> **Es importante que Ud. envíe este paquete inmediatamente.** (*It is important that you send this package immediately.*)

> **Me enfada que Ud. no continúe estudiando español.** (*I'm annoyed that you don't continue to study Spanish.*)

> **El profesor desea que los estudiantes concluyan su trabajo.** (*The teacher wants the students to complete their work.*)

Verbs with spelling and stem changes

Some very common Spanish verbs have both spelling and stem changes in the present subjunctive form, as shown in Table 7-6.

Table 7-6	Spelling and Stem Changes in the Present Subjunctive		
Verb	*Spelling Change*	*Stem Change*	*Present Subjunctive Forms*
colgar (*to hang*)	g → gu	o → ue	**cuelgue, cuelgues, cuelgue, colguemos, colguéis, cuelguen**
jugar (*to play*)	g → gu	u → ue	**juegue, juegues, juegue, juguemos, juguéis, jueguen**

Verb	Spelling Change	Stem Change	Present Subjunctive Forms
comenzar (*to begin*)	z → c	e → ie	**comience, comiences, comience, comencemos, comencéis, comiencen**
empezar (*to begin*)	z → c	e → ie	**empiece, empieces, empiece, empecemos, empecéis, empiecen**
almorzar (*to eat lunch*)	z → c	o → ue	**almuerce, almuerces, almuerce, almorcemos, almorcéis, almuercen**

The following examples show these changes in action:

> **María está contenta de que sus perros jueguen en el jardín.** (*Maria is happy that her dogs play in the backyard.*)

> **Estoy encantada que el espectáculo empiece ahora.** (*I am delighted that the show will begin now.*)

> **La madre no permite que sus hijos almuercen en la sala.** (*The mother doesn't permit her children to eat lunch in the living room.*)

Irregular verbs

Some verbs are completely irregular in the subjunctive mood, which means you can't follow any rules or patterns to form them. You can do nothing else but memorize them. Table 7-7 presents these verbs.

Table 7-7		Irregular Verbs in the Subjunctive
Spanish Verb	*Meaning*	*Subjunctive Forms*
dar	*to give*	**dé, des, dé, demos, deis, den**
estar	*to be*	**esté, estés, esté, estemos, estéis, estén**
ir	*to go*	**vaya, vayas, vaya, vayamos, vayáis, vayan**
saber	*to know*	**sepa, sepas, sepa, sepamos, sepáis, sepan**
ser	*to be*	**sea, seas, sea, seamos, seáis, sean**

Here are some examples of irregular verbs in the subjunctive:

> **Estamos triste que tu abuela esté enferma.** (*We are sad that your grandmother is sick.*)

> **Yo dudo que él sepa reparar la computadora.** (*I doubt that he knows how to repair the computer.*)

You and your classmates know exactly what your Spanish teacher expects from you. Write an e-mail to your friend explaining your class rules. In the space provided, insert the correct form of the verb in parentheses. Here's an example:

Q. (saber) Es importante que nosotros _____ conjugar todos los verbos.

A. Es importante que nosotros **sepamos** conjugar todos los verbos. (*It is important that we know how to conjugate all the verbs.*)

Querido Federico,

Es importante que

13. (llegar) tú no _____ tarde a la clase y que Isabel y yo no _____ tarde a la clase tampoco.

14. (perder) tú no _____ y que Isabel y yo no lo _____ tampoco.

15. (tener) tú no _____ miedo y que Isabel y yo no lo _____ tampoco.

16. (continuar) tú no _____ hablando todo el tiempo y que Isabel y yo no _____ hablando tampoco.

17. (mostrar) tú no _____ la tarea a su compañero de clase y que Isabel y yo no la _____ a nuestra compañera de clase tampoco.

18. (estar) tú no _____ nervioso en clase y que Isabel yo no _____ nerviosas tampoco.

19. (masticar) tú no _____ chicle y que Isabel y yo no lo _____ tampoco.

20. (ir) tú no _____ al baño y que Isabel y yo no _____ al baño tampoco.

21. (mentir) tú no _____ y que Isabel y yo no _____ tampoco.

22. (empezar) tú no _____ la tarea en clase y que Isabel y yo no la _____ tampoco.

23. (enviar) tú no _____ notas a los demás y que Isabel y yo no las _____ tampoco.

24. (dormir) tú no _____ en clase y que Isabel y yo no _____ en clase tampoco.

25. (hacer) tú no _____ la tarea en clase y que Isabel y yo no la _____ en clase tampoco.

26. (salir) tú no _____ de la clase sin permiso y que Isabel y yo no _____ de la tampoco.

27. (cerrar) tú no _____ el libro y que Isabel y yo no _____ el libro tampoco.

28. (traducir) tú no _____ las frases en inglés y que Isabel y yo no las _____ tampoco.

29. (pedir) tú no _____ el permiso y que Isabel y yo no lo _____ tampoco.

30. (escoger) tú no _____ respuestas incorrectas y que Isabel y yo no las _____ tampoco.

31. (jugar) tú no _____ en la clase y que Isabel y yo no _____ en la tampoco.

32. (almorzar) tú no _____ en clase y que Isabel y yo no _____ en la tampoco.

33. (ser) tú no _____ irresponsable y que Isabel y yo no _____ irresponsables tampoco.

34. (dar) tú no _____ tu tarea a tus amigos y que Isabel y yo no la _____ a nuestros amigos tampoco.

Tu amiga,

Pilar

Spanning the Uses of the Present Subjunctive

The present subjunctive has many applications, which makes it a very useful tool for you to have. The subjunctive allows you to express your innermost hopes, desires, and dreams; your most pressing needs; your wildest doubts; and your most humble opinions. Furthermore, it allows you to give advice, to insist on receiving what you want, to offer suggestions, and to demand the necessities of life. And you can execute these expressions in a very low-key, gentle way.

How do you know when to use the present subjunctive? Allow me to make it clear cut. You must use the present subjunctive in Spanish (whether or not you'd use it in English) when all the following conditions exist within a sentence:

✔ The sentence contains a main (or independent) clause — a group of words containing a subject and a verb that can stand alone as a sentence — and a subordinate (or dependent) clause — a group of words containing a subject and a verb that can't stand alone. Generally, each clause must contain a different subject.

✔ The main clause shows, among other things, wishing, wanting, emotion, doubt, need, necessity, feelings, emotions, commands or orders, supposition, speculation, or opinion.

✔ **Que** (*that*) joins the main clause to the dependent clause, which contains a verb in the subjunctive.

When you use the subjunctive in English (and most people do so without even realizing it), you often omit the word *that*. In Spanish, however, you must always use **que** to join the two clauses:

> • **Es improbable que yo salga esta noche.** (*It is improbable [that] I'll go out tonight.*)
>
> • **(No) Es extraño que él haga eso.** (*It is [not] strange [that] he's doing that.*)
>
> ✔ The verb in the main clause is in the present, the future (see Chapter 15), or a command (see Chapter 9).

Here are two examples to get you into the swing of things before the following sections dig deeper into the inner workings of the present subjunctive.

> **La profesora de español quiere que los estudiantes no hablen inglés en clase.** (*The Spanish teacher doesn't want the students to speak English in class.*)
>
> **El gerente insiste en que los empleados trabajen el sábado.** (*The manager insists that the workers work on Saturday.*)

After impersonal expressions

Just because you use an impersonal expression doesn't mean you're being impersonal. On the contrary, you can use this construction to convey some very personal information and ideas. An impersonal expression acts as the main clause of the sentence and is joined to the thoughts you want to relate by **que** (*that*). When this expression shows wishing, uncertainty, need, emotion, and so on, it requires the subjunctive in the dependent clause that follows.

Because it isn't a tense but a mood, the present subjunctive may refer to present or future actions:

> **Conviene que Ud. estudie mucho.** (*It is advisable that you study a lot.*)
>
> **Es dudoso que yo termine todo mi trabajo esta noche.** (*It is doubtful that I will finish all my work tonight.*)

Many (although not all) impersonal expressions begin with **es** (*it is*) and are followed by adjectives showing wishing, emotion, doubt, need, and so on. They require the subjunctive even if they're negated:

> **No es urgente que me telefonee.** (*It isn't urgent that you call me.*)

The following table lists some of the most common Spanish impersonal expressions that require the subjunctive:

English	Spanish
it is absurd that	**es absurdo que**
it is advisable that	**conviene que**
it is amazing that	**es asombroso que**
it is amusing that	**es divertido que**
it is bad that	**es malo que**
it is better that	**es mejor que, más vale que**
it is curious that	**es curioso que**

English	Spanish
it is difficult that	**es difícil que**
it is doubtful that	**es dudoso que**
it is easy that	**es fácil que**
it is enough that	**es suficiente que, basta que**
it is essential that	**es esencial que**
it is fair that	**es justo que**
it is fitting that	**es conveniente que**
it is good that	**es bueno que**
it is imperative that	**es imperativo que**
it is important that	**es importante que, importa que**
it is impossible that	**es imposible que**
it is improbable that	**es improbable que**
it is incredible that	**es increíble que**
it is indispensable that	**es indispensable que**
it is interesting that	**es interesante que**
it is ironic that	**es irónico que**
it is natural that	**es natural que**
it is necessary that	**es necesario que, es preciso que, es menester que**
it is nice that	**es bueno que**
it is a pity that	**es una lástima que**
it is possible that	**es posible que**
it is preferable that	**es preferible que**
it is probable that	**es probable que**
it is rare that	**es raro que**
it is regrettable that	**es lamentable que**
it seems untrue that	**parece mentira que**
it is strange that	**es extraño que**
it is surprising that	**es sorprendente que**
it is unfair that	**es injusto que**
it is urgent that	**es urgente que**
it is useful that	**es útil que**

Here are some examples that show how an impersonal expression can communicate a very personal thought, feeling, or opinion:

Es sorprendente que esa mujer sea tan irresponsable. (*It is surprising that that woman is so irresponsible.*)

Es injusto que estas personas no puedan votar. (*It is unfair that these people can't vote.*)

Be careful! When impersonal expressions show certainty, you must use the indicative (present, past, or future):

English	Spanish
it is certain, it is sure	**es cierto**
it is clear	**es claro**
it is evident	**es evidente**
it is exact	**es exacto**
it is obvious	**es obvio**
it is sure	**es seguro**
it is true	**es verdad**
it seems	**parece**

> **Es obvio que nuestros precios son competitivos.** (*It is obvious that our prices are competitive.*)
>
> **Es claro que Ud. tiene razón.** (*It is clear that you are right.*)

However, impersonal expressions that show certainty when used in the affirmative express doubt or denial when they're negated and, therefore, require the subjunctive:

> **Es cierto que el avión despega pronto.** (*It is certain that the plane will take off soon.*)
>
> **No es cierto que el avión despegue pronto.** (*It is uncertain that the plane will take off soon.*)

Your friend is having a party, and you want to offer suggestions on what people have to do to prepare for the party and what the party will be like. Do so by writing her a note, in which you combine the fragments I provide to form your sentences. Here's an example to get you started:

O. importante/Yolanda/hablar con los invitados.

A. **Es** importante **que** Yolanda **hable** con los invitados. (*It is important that Yolanda speak with the guests.*)

Querida Linda,

35. preciso/todos/buscar una orquesta

_____

36. urgente/Daniel/le decir el menú al cocinero

_____

37. seguro/todo el mundo/estar nervioso

_____

38. indispensable/yo/enviar las invitaciones

_____

39. importante/vosotros/escoger un buen restaurante

_____

40. no/evidente/todos los invitados/venir

_____

41. imperativo/tú/saber a quienes quieres invitar

_____

42. cierto/vosotros/tener muchos amigos

_____

43. esencial/tu esposo/pagar con antelación

_____

44. necesario/Estela/le dar una lista de los invitados al propietario

_____

45. conviene que/yo/organizar actividades

_____

46. claro/esta fiesta/ir a ser maravillosa

_____

Susana

To express wishing, emotion, need, and doubt

When used in a main clause, certain verbs require the use of the subjunctive in the dependent clause. This is because these verbs show not only wishing, emotion, need, or doubt, but also other related thoughts such as advice, command, demand, desire, hope, permission, preference, prohibition, request, suggestion, or wanting. The following table lists some of these verbs:

Spanish	*English*
aconsejar	*to advise*
alegrarse (de)	*to be glad, to be happy*
avergonzarse de	*to be ashamed of*
(no) creer	*to believe (disbelieve)*
desear	*to desire, to wish, to want*
dudar	*to doubt*
enfadarse	*to become angry*
enojarse	*to become angry*
esperar	*to hope*

Spanish	*English*
exigir	*to require, to demand*
insistir	*to insist*
lamentar	*to regret*
mandar	*to command, to order*
necesitar	*to need*
negar	*to deny*
ojalá (que) . . .	*if only . . .*
ordenar	*to order*
pedir	*to ask for, to request*
permitir	*to permit*
preferir	*to prefer*
prohibir	*to forbid*
querer	*to wish, to want*
reclamar	*to demand*
recomendar	*to recommend*
requerir	*to require*
rogar	*to beg, to request*
sentir	*to be sorry, to regret*
solicitar	*to request*
sorprenderse de	*to be surprised*
sugerir	*to suggest*
suplicar	*to beg, to plead*
temer	*to fear*
tener miedo de	*to fear*

Here's how you use many of these verbs:

> **Siento que Uds. no vengan a mi fiesta.** (*I am sorry that you aren't coming to my party.*)

> **El patrón manda que Ud. llegue a tiempo.** (*The boss demands that you arrive on time.*)

> **Ojalá que yo gane la loteria.** (*If only I win the lottery.*)

If no doubt exists in the thought you want to express, you use the indicative (past, present, or future):

> **Él no duda que yo merezco el premio.** (*He doesn't doubt that I deserve the award.*)

> **Yo creo que ella es muy inteligente.** (*I believe she is very intelligent.*)

If the certainty is negated or questioned, however, you use the subjunctive:

> **¿No piensas que ese libro sea interesante?** (*Don't you think that book is interesting?*)

You and your classmates are practicing for a school play. The teacher has written out some suggestions for the cast. Complete his sentences by filling in the missing words, using the correct forms of the verbs I provide in parentheses. Here's an example:

Q. (prestar) Quiero que todos _____ atención.

A. Quiero que todos **presten** atención. (*I want everyone to pay attention.*)

47. (hacer) Deseo que Blanca _____ lo que yo le digo.

48. (seguir) Aconsejo que todos _____ las instrucciones.

49. (cantar) No niego que Guillermo _____ bien.

50. (aprender) Exijo que Rosa _____ su papel de memoria.

51. (saber) Ojalá que Gregorio y Salvador _____ las palabras de la canción.

52. (ir) Prefiero que Ricardo _____ a la derecha en esta escena.

53. (hablar) Creo que los muchachos siempre _____ con voz firme.

54. (poder) Dudo que el público _____ oír a Esteban.

After adjectives that express feelings or emotions

When the main clause of a Spanish sentence contains the word **estar** (*to be*) followed by an adjective that expresses feelings or emotions, you use the subjunctive in the dependent clause. To complete the sentence, you insert the words **de que** (*that*) after the adjective:

> **Estoy alegre de que Uds. me acompañen al cine.** (*I'm happy that you are accompanying me to the movies.*)

> **No estamos contentos de que tú pierdas el tiempo.** (*We are not happy that you are wasting time.*)

The following table lists many Spanish adjectives that express feelings or emotions (for more on adjectives, head to Chapter 8):

Spanish Adjective	English Meaning
alegre	happy
asustado (-a)	afraid
avergonzado (-a)	embarrassed, ashamed
contento (-a)	happy
encantado (-a)	delighted
enfadado (-a)	displeased
enojado (-a)	angry
fastidiado (-a)	bothered
feliz	happy
furioso (-a)	furious

Spanish Adjective	English Meaning
infeliz	_unhappy_
irritado (-a)	_irritated_
lisonjeado (-a)	_flattered_
orgulloso (-a)	_proud_
triste	_sad_

You use the subjunctive after the adverbs **tal vez** (_perhaps_) and **quizás** (_perhaps_) to imply doubt or uncertainty. When you want to express certainty, you use the indicative:

> **Tal vez (Quizás) vayan a la América del Sur.** (_Perhaps they will go to South America._)

> **Si Ud. no llega a tiempo a la oficina, tal vez tiene que despertarse más temprano.** (_If you don't arrive at the office on time, perhaps you need to wake up earlier._)

Josefina is very happy today. Complete the e-mail she plans to send to a friend, in which she wants to explain why she's happy, by joining the phrases I supply. Provide any missing parts and conjugate the verbs as necessary. Here's an example:

Q. contenta/mi hija/recibir buenas notas

A. **Estoy** contenta **de que** mi hija **reciba** buenas notas. (_I am glad that my daughter receives good grades._)

Verónica

55. alegre/mi casa/valer mucho _____

56. contenta/mi jefe/me ofrecer un aumento de salario _____

57. feliz/mi hijo/demostrar una aptitud para las ciencias _____

58. orgullosa/mis hijos/salir bien en la escuela _____

59. encantada/mi familia/venir a visitarnos _____

60. lisonjeada/tú/querer acompañarnos a Costa Rica _____

Josefina

In relative clauses

You use the subjunctive in relative clauses, where the person or thing mentioned in the main clause

- ✔ Is indefinite
- ✔ Is nonexistent
- ✔ Is sought after but not yet attained
- ✔ May or may not exist

In other words, the subject of the sentence just isn't sure or is in doubt about the availability of the person or thing. Here are two examples:

> **Busco a un mecánico que <u>sepa</u> reparar mi coche.** (*I am looking for a mechanic who knows how to repare my car.*)

> **Conozco a un mecánico que <u>sabe</u> reparar mi coche.** (*I know a mechanic who knows how to repair my car.*)

Note that in the first sentence, the subject is unsure if such a person can be found. In the second sentence, however, the subject has no doubt that the person exists, so the present tense, rather than the present subjunctive, is required.

You're on a tour in a Spanish-speaking country. Write an e-mail to practice your Spanish in which you explain what's happening on your trip. For each exercise, I provide two sentences. You must join them with **que** and use either the present tense or the present subjunctive in the second part of the new sentence. Here's an example:

0. No es evidente. El guía conoce bien la región

A. No es evidente **que** el guía **conozca** bien la región. (*It is not evident that the guide knows the region well.*)

Diego

61. Yo busco una tienda. Vende recuerdos. _____

62. Yo estoy sorprendido. El tren no va al centro. _____

63. Es natural. El guía sabe las rutas más bellas. _____

64. ¿Conoces a un chófer aquí? Conduce bien. _____

65. Yo no dudo. La visita turística es interesante. _____

66. Yo no creo. El museo está cerrado. _____

67. Es una lástima. Estos hombres cuelgan un cartel que indica: "No hay billetes."

_____

68. Es claro. El guía es bueno. _____

Felipe

Answer Key

1	observes
2	escribamos
3	leáis
4	presenten
5	negocie
6	exprimas
7	participes
8	proceda
9	hablemos
10	responda
11	reflexionéis
12	describa

13 **llegues, lleguemos.** In -**gar** verbs, **g** changes to **gu** in the subjunctive.

14 **pierdas, perdamos.** The stem vowel changes from **e** to **ie** in all forms except **nosotros** and **vosotros.**

15 **tengas, tengamos.** To form the subjunctive, take the **yo** form of the present tense and drop -**o.**

16 **continúes, continuemos.** The stem vowel changes from **u** to **ú** in all forms except **nosotros** and **vosotros.**

17 **muestres, mostremos.** The stem vowel changes from **o** to **ue** in all forms except **nosotros** and **vosotros.**

18 **estés, estemos. Estar** has irregular subjunctive forms that must be memorized.

19 **mastiques, mastiquemos.** In -**car** verbs, **c** changes to **qu** in the subjunctive.

20 **vayas, vayamos. Ir** has irregular subjunctive forms that must be memorized.

21 **mientas, mintamos.** The **nosotros** form is irregular.

22 **empieces, empecemos.** In -**zar** verbs, **z** changes to **c** in the subjunctive. The stem vowel changes from **e** to **ie** in all forms except **nosotros** and **vosotros.**

23 **envíes, enviemos.** The stem vowel changes from **i** to **í** in all forms except **nosotros** and **vosotros.**

24 **duermas, durmamos.** The stem vowel changes from **o** to **u** in all forms except **nosotros** and **vosotros.** The **nosotros** form is irregular.

25 **hagas, hagamos**

26 **salgas, salgamos**

27 **cierres, cerremos**

28 **traduzcas, traduzcamos**

29 **pidas, pidamos.** The stem vowel changes from **e** to **i** in all forms including **nosotros** and **vosotros.**

30 **escojas, escojamos.** In **-ger** verbs, **g** changes to **j** in the subjunctive.

31 **juegues, juguemos**

32 **almuerces, almorcemos.** In **-zar** verbs, **z** changes to **c** in the subjunctive. The stem vowel changes from **o** to **ue** in all forms except **nosotros** and **vosotros.**

33 **seas, seamos. Ser** has irregular subjunctive forms that must be memorized.

34 **dés, demos. Dar** has irregular subjunctive forms that must be memorized.

35 **Es** preciso **que** todos **busquen** una orquesta. (*It is necessary that everyone look for an orchestra.*)

36 **Es** urgente **que** Daniel **le diga** el menú al cocinero. (*It is urgent that Daniel tells the menu to the cook.*)

37 **Es** seguro **que** todo el mundo **está** nervioso. (*It is certain that everyone is nervous.*) The indicative is used because there is no doubt.

38 **Es** indispensable **que** yo **envíe** las invitaciones. (*It is indispensible that I send the invitations.*)

39 **Es** importante **que** vosotros **escojáis** un buen restaurante. (*It is important that you choose a good restaurant.*)

40 **No es** evidente **que** todos los invitados **vengan.** (*It is not evident that all the guests will come.*)

41 **Es** imperativo **que** tú **sepas** a quienes quieres invitar. (*It is imperative that you know whom you want to invite.*)

42 **Es** cierto **que** vosotros **tenéis** muchos amigos. (*It is certain that you have a lot of friends.*)

43 **Es** esencial **que** tu esposo **pague** con antelación. (*It is essential that your husband pays in advance.*)

44 **Es** necesario **que** Estela **le dé** una lista de los invitados al propietario. (*It is necessary that Estela gives a list of the guests to the owner.*)

45 Conviene **que** yo **organice** actividades. (*It is advisable that I organize activities.*)

46 **Es** claro **que** esta fiesta **va** a ser maravillosa. (*It is clear that this party is going to be marvelous.*)

47 **haga**

48 **siguen**

49 **canta.** The indicative is used because there is no doubt.

50 **aprenda**

51 **sepan**

52 **vaya**

53 **hablan.** The indicative is used because there is no doubt.

54 **pueda**

55 **Estoy** alegre **de que** mi casa **valga** mucho. (*I am happy that my house is worth so much.*)

56 **Estoy** contenta **de que** mi jefe me **ofrezca** un aumento de salario. (*I am content that my boss is offering me a raise.*)

57 **Estoy** feliz **de que** mi hijo **demuestre** una aptitud para las ciencias. (*I am happy that my son shows an aptitude for the sciences.*)

58 **Estoy** orgullosa **de que** mis hijos **salgan** bien en la escuela. (*I am proud that my children do well in school.*)

59 **Estoy** encantada **de que** mi familia **venga** a visitarnos. (*I am delighted that my family is coming to visit us.*)

60 **Estoy** lisonjeda **de que** tú **quieras** acompañarnos a Costa Rica. (*I am flattered that you want to accompany me to Costa Rica.*)

61 Yo busco una tienda **que venda** recuerdos. (*I am looking for a store that sells souvenirs.*) **Vender** is a regular verb in the subjunctive.

62 Yo estoy sorprendido **de que** el tren no **vaya** al centro. (*I am surprised that the train doesn't go downtown.*)

63 Es natural **que** el guía **sepa** las rutas más bellas. (*It is natural that the guide knows the most beautiful routes.*)

64 ¿Conoces a un chófer aquí **que conduzca** bien? (*Do you know a driver here who drives well?*)

65 Yo no dudo **que** la visita turística **es** interesante. (*I don't doubt that the tour is interesting.*)

66 Yo no creo **que** el museo **esté** cerrado. (*I don't believe that the museum is closed.*)

67 Es una lástima **que** estos hombres **cuelguen** un cartel que indica: "No hay billetes." (*It's a pity that these men are hanging a sign that says: "There are no tickets."*)

68 Es claro **que** el **guía es** bueno. (*It is clear that the guide is good.*)

Part III
Writing for Specific Clarity

The 5th Wave   By Rich Tennant

©RICHTENNANT

Obviously you're pronouncing the phrase "Throw us a...," correctly in Spanish, but the word for "lifesaver" just isn't coming out right.

Pollo Del Mar

In this part . . .

1f you want to fine tune your writing skills after perfecting the basics, this is the part you want to concentrate on. The chapters here take you through the nitty gritty elements essential to putting together good, coherent sentences.

I include a chapter on adjectives that points out significant differences between English and Spanish and shows you how to use and place them in Spanish sentences. I show you how to form, use, and place adverbs. If you insist on comparing things, you're in luck, because I explain how to make comparisons of equality, comparisons of inequality, and how to express that something is absolutely superlative.

Giving commands in Spanish can prove to be a challenge, but the explanations presented here will help you fly through the material. I also introduce when to use direct and indirect object pronouns, as well as how to express your likes and dislikes. Reflexive verbs are for those who are a bit egocentric at times, and I give these people their day in the sun here, too. Finally, prepositions in another language can be extremely challenging because they aren't translated literally from one language to the next; the last chapter in this part teaches you to think about the purpose of the preposition in order to avoid mistakes in your writing.

Chapter 8

Coloring Your Sentences with Adjectives and Adverbs

In This Chapter

▶ Spicing up your descriptions with adjectives

▶ Using adverbs to describe actions

▶ Comparing nouns and actions

To be a good writer, you need to be descriptive. And to be descriptive, you must have a good command of adjectives and adverbs. Your writing will be far more interesting if you can zero in on the physical qualities or personality traits of the person you're portraying or the characteristics of the place or thing you want to discuss. Your writing will also be much more informative if you can vividly describe how the objects in your environment work or how the people who surround you act. Another useful writing tool is making comparisons. Comparisons will enrich your e-mails, notes, letters, prose, and compositions. The bottom line is that writing well means being able to go beyond a simple, declarative sentence by adding color and excitement to your thoughts. And yes, you can certainly do this in Spanish with only a small amount of effort.

This chapter illustrates how adjectives in Spanish are different from adjectives in English and presents all that you need to know to use them properly. You also discover how to form and place adverbs within Spanish sentences. Finally, I include an explanation on how to compare and contrast people, places, things, ideas, and activities. By the end of this chapter, you'll be able to write all your descriptive thoughts in Spanish.

Describing People and Things with Adjectives

The function of an adjective is to describe a noun or pronoun so that your audience gains a better understanding of what that noun or pronoun is like. Is the house *big?* Are the trees *green?* You should use adjectives frequently when you write so that your readers will have the most information about, and the best possible understanding of, what you want to describe. The following sections show you how to use adjectives by discussing their agreement and positioning in sentences.

Unlike in English, where adjectives have only one form, Spanish adjectives agree in gender (masculine or feminine) and number (singular or plural) and with the nouns they describe. When the noun or pronoun is feminine, the adjective describing it must also be feminine. When the noun or pronoun is singular/plural, its verb and any adjectives describing it must also be singular/plural.

Agreement of adjectives

In the following sections, you discover how to make adjectives agree in gender (masculine or feminine) and number (singular or plural) with the nouns they modify. I also present some high-frequency Spanish adjectives that will come in handy in most everyday learning, traveling, and business situations.

The gender of adjectives

Most Spanish adjectives end in **-o** in their masculine form or **-a** in their feminine form. Adjectives that end in **-o**, like most nouns, are masculine. (In some instances, however, masculine adjectives end in another vowel and maybe even in a consonant; see the following section.) As you may expect, a masculine, singular adjective ending in **-o** forms its feminine counterpart by changing **-o** to **-a.**

Table 8-1 lists many common adjectives that you may find especially useful in Spanish.

Table 8-1	Common Spanish Adjectives	
Masculine	*Feminine*	*Meaning*
aburrido	aburrida	*boring*
afortunado	afortunada	*fortunate*
alto	alta	*tall*
atractivo	atractiva	*attractive*
bajo	baja	*short*
bonito	bonita	*pretty*
bueno	buena	*good*
delgado	delgada	*thin*
delicioso	deliciosa	*delicious*
divertido	divertida	*fun*
enfermo	enferma	*sick*
enojado	enojada	*angry*
famoso	famosa	*famous*
feo	fea	*ugly*
flaco	flaca	*thin*
generoso	generosa	*generous*
gordo	gorda	*fat*
guapo	guapa	*pretty, good-looking*
listo	lista	*ready*
magnífico	magnífica	*magnificent*
malo	mala	*bad*

Masculine	Feminine	Meaning
moderno	moderna	modern
moreno	morena	dark-haired
necesario	necesaria	necessary
negro	negra	black
nuevo	nueva	new
ordinario	ordinaria	ordinary
orgulloso	orgullosa	proud
pardo	parda	brown, drab
peligroso	peligrosa	dangerous
pequeño	pequeña	small
perezoso	perezosa	lazy
perfecto	perfecta	perfect
rico	rica	rich
romántico	romántica	romantic
rubio	rubia	blond
serio	seria	serious
simpatico	simpática	nice
sincero	sincera	sincere
tímido	tímida	shy
todo	toda	all
viejo	vieja	old

Here's an example of an adjective in action:

> **Mi primo, Jaime, es tímido, y mi prima, Francisca, es tímida también.** (*My cousin, James, is shy, and my cousin, Francisca, is shy, too.*)

Exceptions to the rules

You want a rule in life? There are some exceptions to every rule. In Spanish, masculine, singular adjectives may end in **-a, -e,** or a consonant (other than **-or**). The adjectives in Table 8-2 don't change in their feminine form.

Table 8-2	Adjectives that End in -a or -e	
Masculine	Feminine	Meaning
egoísta	egoísta	selfish
materialista	materialista	materialistic

(continued)

Table 8-2 (continued)

Masculine	Feminine	Meaning
optimista	optimista	optimistic
pesimista	pesimista	pessimistic
realista	realista	realistic
alegre	alegre	happy
amable	amable	nice
eficiente	eficiente	efficient
elegante	elegante	elegant
excelente	excelente	excellent
grande	grande	big
horrible	horrible	horrible
importante	importante	important
inteligente	inteligente	intelligent
interesante	interesante	interesting
pobre	pobre	poor
responsable	responsable	responsible
sociable	sociable	sociable
triste	triste	sad
valiente	valiente	brave

And the adjectives in Table 8-3 end in consonants and undergo no change for gender.

Table 8-3 Adjectives that End in Consonants

Masculine	Feminine	Meaning
cortés	cortés	courteous
azul	azul	blue
débil	débil	weak
fácil	fácil	easy
fiel	fiel	loyal
genial	genial	pleasant
leal	leal	loyal
puntual	puntual	punctual
tropical	tropical	tropical

Masculine	Feminine	Meaning
joven	joven	*young*
popular	popular	*popular*
feroz	feroz	*ferocious*
sagaz	sagaz	*astute*
suspicaz	suspicaz	*suspicious*

Here's an example of one of these adjectives at work:

Mi padre es joven, y mi madre es joven también. (*My father is young, and my mother is young, too.*)

In Spanish, some adjectives of nationality with a masculine form ending in a consonant add **-a** to form the feminine. The adjectives **inglés** (and other adjectives of nationality that end in **-és**) and **alemán** also drop the accent on their final vowel to maintain their original stresses:

Masculine	Feminine	Meaning
español	española	*Spanish*
inglés	inglesa	*English*
alemán	alemana	*German*

And some adjectives with a masculine form ending in **-or** add **-a** to form the feminine:

Masculine	Feminine	Meaning
encantador	encantadora	*enchanting*
hablador	habladora	*talkative*
trabjador	trabajadora	*hard-working*

Here are some examples:

Fritz es alemán, y Heidi es alemana también. (*Fritz is German, and Heidi is German, too.*)

Carlota es trabajadora, pero su hermano no es trabajador. (*Carlota is hard-working, but her brother isn't hard-working.*)

The plural of adjectives

There are two basic rules to follow to form the plural of adjectives in Spanish. First, you add **-s** to singular adjectives ending in a vowel:

Singular	Plural	Meaning
alto	altos	*tall*
rubia	rubias	*blond*
interesante	interesantes	*interesting*

Second, you add **-es** to singular adjectives ending in a consonant:

Singular	Plural	Meaning
fácil	*fáciles*	*easy*
trabajador	*trabajadores*	*hard-working*

Just like with some nouns and pronouns, when speaking about mixed company (males and females, with no mind to number) make sure to use the masculine form of the adjective:

> **Mi hermana y mis hermanos son rubios.** (*My sister and my brothers are blond.*)

Some singular Spanish adjectives don't follow the basic rules for making plurals. They follow the same or similar rules for plural formation as Spanish nouns (see Chapter 3):

- Singular adjectives ending in **-z** change **-z** to **-c** in the plural:

  feliz → felices (*happy*)

- Some adjectives add or drop an accent mark to maintain original stress:

  joven → jóvenes (*young*)

  inglés → ingleses (*English*)

  alemán → alemanes (*German*)

You're writing an e-mail to a friend in which you describe certain other friends and family members. Select an adjective from the list I provide that would more clearly describe the person. Make sure the adjective agrees in number and gender with the noun. Here's an example:

O. Mis primos no son pesimistas. Son _____.

A. Mis primos no son pesimistas. Son **optimistas.** (*My cousins aren't pessimistic. They are optimistic.*)

alemán	inglés
cómico	joven
débil	perezoso
descuidado	popular
egoísta	sagaz
fiel	sincero
francés	suspicaz
generoso	valiente

1. Mis padres son astutos y prudentes. Son _____.

2. Mi hermana tiene sospecha o desconfianza en todo. Es _____.

3. Mi amiga, Linda, no es trabajadora. Es _____.

4. Eduardo no comparte nada con nadie. Es _____.

5. Antonio y Santiago no tienen miedo de nada. Son _____.

6. Juanita hace reír a otros. Es _____.

7. Enrique y Carmen siempre dicen la verdad. Son _____.

8. Margarita no traiciona (betray) a nadie. Es _____.

9. Mis abuelos son muy magnánimos. Son _____.

10. Mi tío nunca tiene cuidado. Es _____.

11. Mis hermanas tienen muchos amigos. Son _____.

12. Mi tía es de Francia. Es _____.

13. Mercedes no tiene suficiente fuerza física. Es _____.

14. Mis tías no son viejas. Son _____.

15. Mis amigos son de Inglaterra. Son _____.

16. Mi padre es de Alemania. Es _____.

Positioning of adjectives

In Spanish, adjectives may precede or follow the noun they modify. Most adjectives follow the noun. The placement depends on the type of adjective being used, the connotation the speaker wants to convey, and the emphasis being used. And sometimes, when more than one adjective describes a noun, the rules for placement vary according to the type of adjectives being used. For example, possessive adjectives, demonstrative adjectives, and adjectives of quantity precede the noun they modify, whereas descriptive adjectives generally follow the noun they modify. The following sections dig deeper into these topics.

Adjectives that follow the noun

In Spanish, most descriptive adjectives follow the noun they modify. The descriptive adjectives **feos, querido, delgado,** and **interesantes** are descriptive adjectives that follow the noun:

> **dos gatos feos** (*two ugly cats*)
>
> **mi padre querido** (*my dear father*)
>
> **ese hombre delgado** (*that thin man*)
>
> **algunas cosas interesantes** (*some interesting things*)

Adjectives that precede the noun

Adjectives that impose limits — numbers, possessive adjectives, demonstrative adjectives, and adjectives of quantity — usually precede the noun they modify. The possessive adjective **su** and the number **una** precede the noun, for instance:

> **su novia francesa** (*his French girlfriend*)
>
> **una compañía próspera** (*a successful company*)

Descriptive adjectives that emphasize qualities or inherent characteristics appear before the noun:

Tenemos buenos recuerdos de su fiesta. (*We have good memories of her party.*)

In this example, the speaker is emphasizing the quality of the memories.

Shortened forms of adjectives

Some Spanish adjectives get shortened in certain situations. The following list details when this occurs:

- ✔ The following adjectives drop their final **-o** before a masculine, singular noun. **Alguno** and **ninguno** add an accent to the **-u** when the **-o** is dropped:
    - **uno** (*one*) → **un coche** (*one car*)
    - **bueno** (*good*) → **un buen viaje** (*a good trip*)
    - **malo** (*bad*) → **un mal muchacho** (*a bad boy*)
    - **primero** (*first*) → **el primer acto** (*the first act*)
    - **tercero** (*third*) → **el tercer presidente** (*the third president*)
    - **alguno** (*some*) → **algún día** (*some day*)
    - **ninguno** (*no*) → **ningún hombre** (*no man*)

When a preposition separates the adjective from its noun, you use the original form of the adjective (don't drop the **-o**):

uno de tus primos (*one of your cousins*)

- ✔ **Grande** becomes **gran** (*great, important, famous*) before a singular masculine or feminine noun:
    - **un gran profesor** (*a great teacher* [male])
    - **una gran profesora** (*a great teacher* [female])

But it remains **grande** after the noun:

- **un escritorio grande** (*a large desk*)
- **una mesa grande** (*a large table*)

- ✔ **Ciento** (*one hundred*) becomes **cien** before nouns and before the numbers **mil** and **millones**:
    - **cien hombres y cien mujeres** (*one hundred men and one hundred women*)
    - **cien mil habitantes** (*one hundred thousand inhabitants*)
    - **cien millones de euros** (*one hundred million euros*)

You're a tourist who has seen many things while traveling. Create a journal entry in which you organize your notes by making all the adjectives agree and by putting them in the proper position. I provide an adjective before the slash and another adjective after it. You must determine the correct form of the adjectives (masculine or feminine; singular or plural) and place each adjective in its correct place. Here's an example:

Q. playa: un/espléndido

A. Nosotros vimos **una playa espléndida.** (*We saw a splendid beach.*)

17. flores: rojo/cien _____

18. lago: ninguno/largo _____

19. nubes: blanco/mucho _____

20. selva: un/magnífico _____

21. montañas: alto/poco _____

22. río: grande/un _____

23. cascadas: estupéndo/alguno _____

24. animales: mucho/feroz _____

25. cielo: un/azul _____

26. plantas: peligroso/ninguno _____

Describing Verbs with Adverbs

The function of an adverb is to describe a verb, another adverb, or an adjective so that your audience has a better understanding of how or to what degree or intensity an action is performed. Does a person run (very) quickly? Is his or her house very big? You use adverbs frequently when you write to express the manner in which things are done. The following sections work on helping you form adverbs and position them correctly in sentences.

Forming adverbs

Many English adverbs end in **-ly,** and the equivalent Spanish ending is **-mente.** To form an adverb in Spanish, you add **-mente** to the feminine singular form of an adjective. Table 8-4 illustrates how it's done.

Unlike adjectives, which require agreement in gender and number with the noun they describe, adverbs require no agreement because they modify a verb and not a noun or pronoun.

Table 8-4		Forming Various Types of Adverbs	
Masc. Adj.	*Fem. Adj.*	*Adverb*	*Meaning*
completo	completa	completamente	completely
lento	lenta	lentamente	slowly
rápido	rápida	rápidamente	quickly
alegre	alegre	alegremente	happily
breve	breve	brevemente	briefly

(continued)

Table 8-4 *(continued)*			
Masc. Adj.	*Fem. Adj.*	*Adverb*	*Meaning*
frecuente	frecuente	frecuentemente	*frequently*
especial	especial	especialmente	*especially*
final	final	finalmente	*finally*
feroz	feroz	ferozmente	*ferociously*

The following example shows an adverb in action:

Él entra rápidamente, y ella sale rápidamente. (*He enters quickly, and she leaves quickly.*)

Adverbial phrases

Sometimes, it's quite awkward to form an adverb in Spanish by using the feminine singular form of the adjective. When writing, you may find the spelling tricky. And at other times, you may not recall the feminine form of the adjective. Luckily, you have an easy way out. You can use the preposition **con** (*with*) + the noun to form an adverbial phrase, which functions in the same way as an adverb.

For instance, if you have trouble remembering or writing **cuidadosamente** (*carefully*), you can substitute **con cuidado** (*with care*) and your Spanish will be perfect. Here are some examples of how this works:

con + noun	*Adverb*	*Meaning*
con alegría	**alegremente**	*happily*
con claridad	**claramente**	*clearly*
con cortesía	**cortésmente**	*courteously*
con energía	**enérgicamente**	*energetically*
con habilidad	**hábilmente**	*skillfully*
con paciencia	**pacientemente**	*patiently*
con rapidez	**rápidamente**	*quickly*
con respeto	**respetuosamente**	*respectfully*

Here's an example of this construction:

Ella habla con respeto (respetuosamente). (*She speaks with respect [respectfully].*)

Simple adverbs

Some adverbs and adverbial expressions aren't formed from adjectives; they're words or phrases in and of themselves. Table 8-5 lists some of the most frequently used expressions that fit this description.

Table 8-5	Frequently Used Unique Phrases		
Adverb	*Meaning*	*Adverb*	*Meaning*
a menudo	*often*	menos	*less*
a veces	*sometimes*	mientras	*meanwhile*

Adverb	Meaning	Adverb	Meaning
ahora	now	más tarde	later
ahora mismo	right now	mejor	better
al fin	finally	muy	very
allá	there	peor	worse
aquí	here	poco	little
bastante	quite, rather, enough	por consiguiente	consequently
casi	almost	por supuesto	of course
cerca	near	pronto	soon
de buena gana	willingly	pues	then
de nuevo	again	siempre	always
de repente	suddenly	sin embargo	however, nevertheless
de vez en cuando	from time to time	también	also, too
demasiado	too	tan	as, so
despacio	slowly	tarde	late
después	afterward	temprano	soon, early
en seguida	immediately	todavía	still, yet
hoy día	nowadays	todos los días	everyday
lejos	far	ya	already
más	more	ya no	no longer

Here's an example of one of these phrases in use:

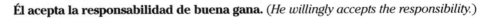

Él acepta la responsabilidad de buena gana. (*He willingly accepts the responsibility.*)

Express how different people in your office work by replacing the phrase **con** + noun and using an adverb in the following sentences. This example shows you the way:

0. Jaime responde con respeto.

A. Jaime responde **respetuosamente.** (*Jaime answers respectfully.*)

27. Estas mujeres hablan con franqueza.

_____

28. Ese hombre trabaja con cuidado.

_____

29. El jefe reacciona con rapidez.

_____

30. Yo escucho con atención.

_____

31. Clara se explica con claridad.

_____

32. Pilar contesta con cortesía.

_____

33. Miguel hace preguntas con frecuencia.

_____

34. Ana participa con felicidad.

_____

Adjectives versus adverbs

The use of certain adjectives and adverbs can require some thought and an understanding of the function of the parts of speech in English. Alas, their use in Spanish can be just as tricky. The following list presents some adjective/adverb situations that can trip you up when learning how to use these tools in Spanish:

✔ **Buen(o/a)(s)** and **mal(o/a)(s)** are adjectives (and must agree in number and gender with the nouns they modify) that mean _good_ and _bad_, respectively, and **bien** and **mal** are adverbs (requiring no agreement) that mean _well_ and _badly/poorly,_ respectively.

  • **Ellas tienen muchas buenas (malas) ideas.** (_They have many good [bad] ideas._)

  • **Elena juega bien (mal).** (_Elena plays well [poorly]._)

✔ The Spanish words **más** (_more_), **menos** (_less, fewer_), **mejor** (_better_), **peor** (_worse_), **mucho** (_much, many_), **poco** (_little, few_), and **demasiado** (_too much, too many_) may be used as adjectives or adverbs.

As adjectives, **más** and **menos** remain invariable; **mejor** and **peor** add **-es** to agree only with noun plurals that they modify; and **mucho, poco,** and **demasiado** agree in number and gender with the nouns they modify. As adverbs, all these words remain invariable. Look at the following sentences where adjectives appear in the first examples and adverbs are used in the second examples:

  • **Samuel tiene más (menos) energía.** (_Samuel has more [less] energy._)

  Samuel trabaja más (menos) enérgicamente. (_Samuel works more [less] energetically._)

  • **Teodoro tiene mejores (peores) notas.** (_Theodore has better [worse] grades._)

  Teodoro se aplica mejor (peor). (_Theodore applies himself better [worse]._)

  • **Da muchas (pocas, demasiadas) excusas.** (_He gives many [few, too many] excuses._)

  Piensa mucho (poco, demasiado). (_He thinks a lot [a little, too much]._)

Positioning of adverbs

You generally place adverbs directly after the verb they modify. Sometimes, however, the position of the adverb is variable and is placed where you'd logically put an English adverb:

  ¿Hablas español elocuentemente? (_Do you speak Spanish eloquently?_)

  Afortunadamente, yo recibí el paquete. (_Fortunately, I received the package._)

Describe the following workers by completing each sentence with the correct form of the adjective or adverb indicated. Here's an example:

O. (mucho) Alonso gana _____ porque hace _____ trabajo.

A. Alonso gana **mucho** porque hace **mucho** trabajo. (*Alonso earns a lot because he does a lot of work.*)

35. (malo) Antonio reacciona _____ porque recibe _____ noticias.

36. (mejor) Carolina tiene _____ resultados porque trabaja _____.

37. (bien) El señor López es un _____ profesor porque enseña _____.

38. (más) Vicente tiene _____ dinero porque ahorra _____.

39. (demasiado) Felipe tiene _____ problemas porque se preocupa _____ de todo.

40. (poco) Clara tiene _____ energía porque come _____.

Making Comparisons

You generally make comparisons by using adjectives or adverbs. You can make comparisons of equality or inequality, and you can use superlatives. Making comparisons in Spanish isn't easy, but the previous sections of this chapter, along with the following sections, present you with all the tools you need.

English, comparatives usually end in **-er:**

> She is tall**er** than I.

> He runs fast**er** than they.

Comparisons of equality

Comparisons of equality show that two things or people are the same. In Spanish, whether you're using an adjective or an adverb, you make the comparison the same way. You use **tan** (*as*) + adjective or adverb + **como** (*as*), as shown here:

> **Dolores es tan conscienzuda como Jorge.** (*Dolores is as conscientious as George.*)

> **Ella estudia tan diligentemente como él.** (*She studies as diligently as he does.*)

Remember that when you use an adjective, it must agree in number and gender with the subject.

You can make negative comparisons by putting **no** before the verb:

> **Tú no eres tan trabajadora como él.** (*You are not as hard-working as he is.*)

> **Tú no escuchas tan atentamente como Juan.** (*You don't listen as attentively as Juan.*)

Comparisons of inequality

Comparisons of inequality show that two things or people are not the same. As with comparisons of equality, whether you're using an adjective or an adverb, you make the comparison the same way. You create the comparison of inequality with **más** (*more*) or **menos** (*less*):

> **más** (**menos**) + adjective or adverb + **que** (*than*)

Here are two examples:

> **Diego es más (menos) hablador que yo.** (*Diego is more [less] talkative than I.*)
>
> **Diego habla más (menos) que yo.** (*Diego talks more [less] than I.*)

The superlative

The *superlative* shows that something (or someone) is the best or worst of its (or his or her) kind. You form the superlatives of adjectives as follows:

> Subject + verb + **el** (**la, los, las**) + **más** (**menos**) (*more [less]*) + adjective + **de** (*in*)

Here's an example:

> **Ella es la más alta de su clase.** (*She is the tallest in her class.*)

If the sentence contains a direct object, you form the superlative by inserting the noun after **el** (**la, los, las**):

> **Ella prepara la paella más deliciosa del mundo.** (*She prepares the best paella in the world.*)

English superlatives usually end in **-est:**

> She is the tall**est** in her class.
>
> He runs the fast**est** of them all.

Now we come to adverbs. Superlatives of adverbs aren't distinguished from their comparative forms (see the previous sections):

> **Él acepta críticas más (menos) pacientemente que los otros.** (*He accepts criticism more [less] patiently than others.*)

Irregular comparatives

As adjectives, **bueno** (*good*), **malo** (*bad*), **grande** (*big*), and **pequeño** (*small*) have irregular forms in the comparative and superlative. Note that **grande** and **pequeño** each have two different meanings in their comparative and superlative forms.

Table 8-6 displays all the changes that these adjectives undergo.

Table 8-6	Irregular Adjectives in the Comparative and Superlative	
Adjective	*Comparative*	*Superlative*
bueno (buena) (*good*) **buenos (buenas)**	**mejor** (*better*) **mejores**	**el (la) mejor** (*the best*) **los (las) mejores**
malo (mala) (*bad*) **malos (malas)**	**peor** (*worse*) **peores**	**el (la) peor** (*the worst*) **los (las) peores**
grande (*great, big*)	**mayor** (*older, greater in age or status*) **más (menos) grande** (*larger [less large in size]*)	**el (la) mayor** (*the oldest, greatest*) **el más (menos) grande** (*the largest [the least large]*)
pequeño (pequeña) (*small*) **pequeños (pequeñas)**	**menor** (*minor, lesser, younger in age or status*) **más (menos) pequeño (pequeña)** (*smaller [less small in size]*) **más (menos) pequeños (pequeñas)** (*smaller [less small in size]*)	**el (la) menor** (*the least, the youngest*) **el (la) más pequeño (pequeña)** (*the smallest*) **los (las) más (menos) pequeños (pequeñas)** (*the smallest [least small]*)

The adverbs **bien** (*well*) and **mal** (*poorly*) become **mejor** (*better*) and **peor** (*worse*), respectively, in their comparative forms and follow the verb or verb phrase they modify:

> **Tomás juega al fútbol mejor que Javier.** (*Thomas plays soccer better than Javier.*)

> **Ella cocina peor que yo.** (*She cooks worse than I do.*)

For this exercise, write a journal entry in which you describe the things and people in town by forming comparisons with adjectives and adverbs. For each question, I provide the noun and the verb. You use the +, –, and = signs to determine the type of comparison in play and whether you should use an adjective or an adverb. Make sure that all your adjectives agree with the nouns they modify. These examples get you started:

Q. la iglesia es = magnífico/la catedral

A. La iglesia es **tan mágnifica como** la catedral. (*The church is as magnificent as the cathedral.*)

Q. el metro llega + frecuente/el autobús

A. El metro llega **más frecuentemente que** el autobús. (*The subway arrives more frequently than the bus.*)

41. este rascacielos es + alto/ese edificio

_____

42. estas calles son – estrecho/esas avenidas

_____

43. esta boutique es = elegante/esos almacenes

_____

44. este juez escucha – atento/ese abogado

_____

45. estos choferes de autobús conducen + bien/esos choferes de taxi

_____

46. este doctor reflexiona = profundo/ese cirujano

_____

The absolute superlative

The *absolute superlative* expresses the ultimate; you use it when no comparison is made. To form this basic construction, you add **-ísimo** (masc.); **-ísima** (fem.); **-ísimos** (masc. plural); **-ísimas** (fem. plural) to the adjective according to the gender (masculine or feminine) and number (singular or plural) of the noun being described. The meaning is the same as **muy** (*very*) + adjective:

> **La catedral es muy bella. La catedral es bellísima.** (*The cathedral is very beautiful.*)
>
> **Los edificios son muy altos. Los edificios son altísimos.** (*The buildings are very tall.*)

Here are some more things you need to know to form the absolute superlative:

- You drop the final vowel of an adjective before adding **-ísimo** (**-a, -os, -as**):

  La casa es grande. La casa es grandísima. (*The house is very large.*)

- You use **muchísimo** to express *very much:*

  Te adoro muchísimo. (*I adore you very much.*)

- Adjectives ending in **-co** (**-ca**), **-go** (**-ga**), or **-z** change **c** to **qu**, **g** to **gu**, and **z** to **c**, respectively, before adding **-ísimo:**

  - **La torta es muy rica. La torta es riquísima.** (*The pie is very tasty.*)

  - **El suéter es muy largo. El suéter es larguísimo.** (*The sweater is very long.*)

  - **El juez es muy sagaz. El juez es sagacísimo.** (*The judge is very shrewd.*)

Your friend is having a very bad day and is complaining about *everything*. Write down what he says so you can show it to him at a later date for a laugh. I provide the adjective in parentheses, and you create the absolute superlative form. Here's an example:

O. (grande) Mis problemas son _____.

A. Mis problemas son **grandísimos.** (*My problems are very big.*)

47. (rico) Este pastel es _____.

48. (atroz) Estos crímenes son _____.

49. (largo) Este día es _____.

50. (mal) Estos hombres son _____.

51. (difícil) Esta situación es _____.

52. (aburrido) Estas películas son _____.

Answer Key

1 sagaces

2 suspicaz

3 perezosa

4 egoísta

5 valientes

6 cómica

7 sinceros

8 fiel

9 generosos

10 descuidado

11 populares

12 francesa

13 débil

14 jóvenes

15 ingleses

16 alemán

17 Nosotros vimos **cien flores rojas.** (*We saw 100 red flowers.*)

18 Nosotros vimos **ningún lago largo.** (*We didn't see any wide lake.*)

19 Nosotros vimos **muchas nubes blancas.** (*We saw many white clouds.*)

20 Nosotros vimos **una selva magnífica.** (*We saw a magnificent jungle.*)

21 Nosotros vimos **pocas montañas altas.** (*We saw few high mountains.*)

22 Nosotros vimos **un río grande.** (*We saw a large river.*)

23 Nosotros vimos **algunas cascadas estupéndas.** (*We saw some fantastic waterfalls.*)

24 Nosotros vimos **muchos animales feroces.** (*We saw many ferocious animals.*)

25 Nosotros vimos **un cielo azul.** (*We saw a blue sky.*)

26 Nosotros vimos **ningunas plantas peligrosas.** (*We didn't see any dangerous plants.*)

27 Estas mujeras hablan **francamente.** (*These women speak frankly.*)

28 Ese hombre trabaja **cuidadosamente.** (*That man works carefully.*)

29 El jefe reacciona **rápidamente.** (*The boss reacts quickly.*)

30   Yo escucho **atentamente.** (*I listen attentively.*)

31   Clara se explica **claramente.** (*Clara explains herself clearly.*)

32   Pilar contesta **cortésmente.** (*Pilar answers courteously.*)

33   Miguel hace preguntas **frecuentemente.** (*Miguel frequently asks questions.*)

34   Ana participa **felizmente.** (*Ana participates happily.*)

35   **mal/malas**

36   **mejores/mejor**

37   **buen/bien**

38   **más/más**

39   **demasiados/demasiado**

40   **poca/poco**

41   Este rascacielos es **más alto que** ese edificio. (*This skyscraper is taller than that building.*)

42   Estas calles son **menos estrechas que** esas avenidas. (*These streets are less narrow than those avenues.*)

43   Esta boutique es **tan elegante como** esos almacenes. (*This boutique is as elegant as those department stores.*)

44   Este juez escucha **menos atentamente que** ese abogado. (*This judge listens less attentively than that lawyer.*)

45   Estos choferes de autobus conducen **mejor que** esos choferes de taxi. (*These bus drivers drive better than those taxi drivers.*)

46   Este doctor reflexiona **tan profoundamente como** ese cirujano. (*This doctor thinks as profoundly as that surgeon.*)

47   **riquísimo**

48   **atrocísimos**

49   **larguísimo**

50   **malísimos**

51   **dificilísima**

52   **aburridísimas**

Chapter 9

Getting Attention with Commands

· ·

In This Chapter

▶ Reviewing the basics of the imperative mood

▶ Making requests and commands politely

▶ Giving commands to those you know

· ·

Can you guess how many times you've had to give people directions to your home or to a restaurant? Perhaps you often give instructions on how to do something, like how to fix a broken object, how to lose weight, or how to succeed at a job interview. Maybe, if you're a cook and baker like me, you've had to explain recipes and procedures. And at different points in life, we all have to ask others for help or for favors.

In all these situations, you've had to use the *imperative,* which is a fancy way of saying that you've given commands. Just like in English, the imperative isn't a tense in Spanish because it doesn't show time. It's called a *mood* because it indicates the manner in which the action occurs.

In this chapter, you discover much more about the imperative mood. You review the different ways to give a command in Spanish so that whatever needs to get done gets done.

You will, in all probability, have to refer to Chapter 7 when reading this chapter because some of the imperative forms are based on or are identical to subjunctive forms. If you've successfully mastered the subjunctive, the imperative will be a piece of cake.

The Imperative Mood

When something is imperative, it just *has* to be done — and right away at that. In such an instance, it's only logical to command someone to do something to ensure that the job gets done. When you're talking about the "imperative" in Spanish, you're talking about giving a command. And just like in English, the subject of most commands in Spanish is *you.*

Unlike English, where you have only one way to say *you,* in Spanish you have four ways. The approach you use depends on whether you're being formal (polite) or informal (familiar), and whether you're addressing one person or multiple people.

Here's a short guide on the ways to say *you,* along with two examples:

	Singular	Plural
Informal (familiar)	tú	vosotros
Formal (polite)	Ud.	Uds.

¡Escucha (tú)/Escuchad (vosotros)! (*Listen!*)

¡Escuche (Ud.)/Escuchen (Uds.)! (*Listen!*)

In English, you may put an exclamation mark at the end of a command. In Spanish, you must place an inverted exclamation mark (¡) at the beginning of an emphasized command and a regular exclamation mark (!) at the end:

¡**Abra la ventana!** (*Open the window!*)

¡**No discuten!** (*Don't argue!*)

Forming Formal Commands

You give formal (or polite) commands to people who are older and wiser or to people who are unfamiliar to you. Of course, in a formal situation you don't want to be rude, so you'll use the Spanish words for please: **por favor.** Giving a formal command can also mean that you're asking a person to help you or to do a favor for you.

The subjects of formal commands are **Ud.** (if you're addressing only one person) and **Uds.** (if you're addressing more than one person):

Abra (Ud.) la puerta, por favor. (*Open the window, please.*)

Por favor, hablen (Uds.) más despacio. (*Please speak more slowly.*)

In English, you never actually say the word *you* when you give a command or make a request. In Spanish, the use of a subject pronoun (**Ud., Uds., tú,** or **vosotros**) in a command is optional and not used all that frequently. You can identify the subject by a quick look at the verb form being used:

Pase (Ud.) la sal, por favor. (*Pass the salt, please.*)

Presten (Uds.) atención. (*Pay attention.*)

Commanding with regular verbs

The subjunctive comes in handy when you want to give a formal command. You use the present subjunctive of the **Ud.** or **Uds.** form of a verb to form either an affirmative or negative formal command. Here's a quick refresher course on forming the present subjunctive:

1. Drop the final **-o** from the **yo** form of the present tense.

2. For infinitives ending in **-ar,** add **-e** for **Ud.** and **-en** for **Uds.** For infinitives ending in **-er** or **-ir,** add **-a** for **Ud.** and **-an** for **Uds.**

3. To form the negative, simply put **no** before the verb.

Here's a chart to help you see these changes in action:

-ar verbs	*-er verbs*	*-ir verbs*
firmar (*to sign*)	**comer** (*to eat*)	**subir** (*to go up*)
yo firmo (*I sign*)	**yo como** (*I eat*)	**yo subo** (*I go up*)
[No] Firme (Ud.) ([*Don't*] *Sign.*)	**[No] Coma (Ud.)** ([*Don't*] *Eat.*)	**[No] Suba (Ud.)** ([*Don't*] *Go up.*)
[No] Firmen (Uds.) ([*Don't*] *Sign.*)	**[No] Coman (Uds.)** ([*Don't*] *Eat.*)	**[No] Suban (Uds.)** ([*Don't*] *Go up.*)

The following list shows some regular verbs in action in commands:

> **Trabajen cuidadosamente.** (*Work carefully.*)
>
> **No trabajen tan despacio.** (*Don't work so slowly.*)
>
> **Lea en voz alta.** (*Read aloud.*)
>
> **No lea esa carta.** (*Don't read that letter.*)
>
> **Escriba cómo se llega a su casa.** (*Write how to get to your house.*)
>
> **No escriba nada.** (*Don't write anything.*)

You don't feel well and decide to go to the doctor for a checkup. Complete her written instructions to you by giving the formal singular command form of the verbs I provide in parentheses. Here's an example:

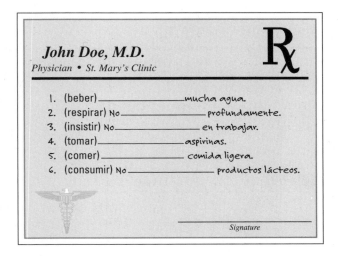

John Doe, M.D.
Physician • St. Mary's Clinic

Rx

1. (beber) _____ mucha agua.
2. (respirar) No _____ profundamente.
3. (insistir) No _____ en trabajar.
4. (tomar) _____ aspirinas.
5. (comer) _____ comida ligera.
6. (consumir) No _____ productos lácteos.

_____
Signature

Commanding with other verbs

To create both affirmative and negative commands in Spanish, you have to use the present subjunctive forms (see Chapter 7) for all verbs with irregular **yo** forms, with spelling changes, with stem changes, and with a combination. And some verbs have irregular command forms that have to be memorized. Fortunately for you, there are very few of these verbs. Table 9-1 starts you off by helping you navigate verbs with irregular **yo** forms.

Table 9-1	Verbs with Irregular yo Forms	
Spanish Verbs	*Commands*	*Meaning*
decir	**(no) diga(n)**	(*don't*) *tell*
hacer	**(no) haga(n)**	(*don't*) *do*
oír	**(no) oiga(n)**	(*don't*) *hear*
poner	**(no) ponga(n)**	(*don't*) *put*
salir	**(no) salga(n)**	(*don't*) *leave*
tener	**(no) tenga(n)**	(*don't*) *have* (*be*)
traer	**(no) traiga(n)**	(*don't*) *bring*
valer	**(no) valga(n)**	(*don't*) *be worth* (*cost*)
venir	**(no) venga(n)**	(*don't*) *come*

The examples that follow show you how to use these verbs in the imperative:

Siempre digan la verdad. (*Always tell the truth.*)

No tenga miedo. (*Don't be afraid.*)

Table 9-2 highlights Spanish verbs with spelling changes in the imperative.

Table 9-2	Verbs with Spelling Changes	
Spanish Verbs	*Commands*	*Meaning*
-ar verbs		
sa**car**	(no) sa**que**(n)	(*don't*) *take out*
pa**gar**	(no) pa**gue**(n)	(*don't*) *pay*
organi**zar**	(no) organi**ce**(n)	(*don't*) *organize*
-er and **-ir** verbs		
obede**cer**	(no) obede**zca**(n)	(*don't*) *obey*
condu**cir**	(no) condu**zca**(n)	(*don't*) *drive*
esco**ger**	(no) esco**ja**(n)	(*don't*) *choose*
exi**gir**	(no) exi**ja**(n)	(*don't*) *demand*
distin**guir**	(no) distin**ga**(n)	(*don't*) *distinguish*

These examples show how to use verbs with spelling changes in commands:

Saque su tarjeta de crédito. (*Take out your credit card.*)

No conduzca tan rápidamente. (*Don't drive so fast.*)

Table 9-3 covers verbs that require stem changes in the imperative mood.

Table 9-3	Verbs with Stem Changes	
Spanish Verbs	*Commands*	*Meaning*
-ar verbs		
cerrar (e to ie)	**(no) cierre(n)**	(*don't*) *close*
mostrar (o to ue)	**(no) muestre(n)**	(*don't*) *show*
enviar (i to í)	**(no) envíe(n)**	(*don't*) *send*
continuar (u to ú)	**(no) continúe(n)**	(*don't*) *continue*
-er and **-ir** verbs		
perder (e to ie)	**(no) pierda(n)**	(*don't*) *lose*
volver (o to ue)	**(no) vuelva(n)**	(*don't*) *return*
mentir (e to ie)	**(no) mienta(n)**	(*don't*) *lie*
dormir (o to ue)	**(no) duerma(n)**	(*don't*) *sleep*
pedir (e to i)	**(no) pida(n)**	(*don't*) *ask* (*for*)
destruir (add y)	**(no) destruya(n)**	(*don't*) *destroy*

Here are some examples that show how to use these verbs in commands:

> **Envíe este paquete inmediatamente.** (*Send this package immediately.*)

> **No destruya ese documento.** (*Don't destroy that document.*)

Some Spanish verbs undergo both spelling and stem changes when used in commands. Table 9-4 presents these verbs.

Table 9-4	Verbs with Spelling and Stem Changes	
Spanish Verbs	*Commands*	*Meaning*
colgar (o to ue/g to gu)	**(no) cuelgue(n)**	(*don't*) *hang*
jugar (u to ue/g to gu)	**(no) juegue(n)**	(*don't*) *play*
comenzar (e to ie/z to c)	**(no) comience(n)**	(*don't*) *begin*
empezar (e to ie/z to c)	**(no) empiece(n)**	(*don't*) *begin*
almorzar (o to ue/z to c)	**(no) almuerce(n)**	(*don't*) *eat lunch*
corregir (e to i/g to j)	**(no) corrija(n)**	(*don't*) *correct*
seguir (e to i/gu to g)	**(no) siga(n)**	(*don't*) *follow*

Here are some sample commands containing verbs with both spelling and stem changes:

> **No jueguen allá.** (*Don't play there.*)

> **Empiecen inmediatamente.** (*Begin immediately.*)

Finally, Table 9-5 presents irregular verbs that you have to memorize in order to use them in commands.

Table 9-5	Irregular Verbs	
Spanish Verbs	*Commands*	*Meaning*
estar	(no) esté(n)	*(don't) be*
ir	(no) vaya(n)	*(don't) go*
saber	(no) sepa(n)	*(don't) know*

Here's how you include these irregular verbs in commands:

> **Estén listos a las siete.** (*Be ready at 7 o'clock.*)

> **Vaya a la tienda ahora.** (*Go to the store now.*)

You have some family members from out of town who are staying at your house for an extended time. How about you put them to work? Leave them a list explaining what they should and shouldn't do. Use the plural, formal command form of the verbs I provide in parentheses. Here's an example:

Q. (almorzar) No _____ en la sala.

A. No **almuercen** en la sala. (*Don't eat in the living room.*)

7. (destruir) No _____ nada.

8. (cerrar) No _____ las ventanas.

9. (mentir) Si hay un problema, no _____.

10. (decir) Siempre _____ la verdad.

11. (perder) No _____ nada.

12. (pedir) _____ ayuda si sea necesario.

13. (hacer) _____ las camas.

14. (poner) _____ la mesa.

15. (estar) No _____ de retraso al trabajo.

16. (organizar) _____ los gabinetes.

17. (tener) _____ cuidado.

18. (ir) _____ al supermercado.

19. (colgar) No _____ nada afuera.

20. (empezar) _____ su trabajo inmediatamente.

21. (apagar) _____ todas las luces.

22. (sacar) _____ la basura.

23. (recoger) _____ la ropa del suelo.

24. (seguir) _____ todas las instrucciones.

Issuing Informal Commands

You give informal (or familiar) commands to people you know: friends, peers, family members, or pets. The subject of an informal Spanish command is **tú** (if you're addressing one person) or **vosotros** (if you're addressing more than one person).

The **vosotros** (second person plural) command is used primarily in Spain. In Spanish American countries, people use the **Uds.** form for plural informal commands.

The sections that follow explain how to create singular and plural informal commands with both regular and irregular verbs.

Giving singular commands with tú

Singular, affirmative, familiar commands are very easy to form. You just take the present tense **tú** form of the verb and drop the final **-s**. This rule holds true for regular verbs, verbs with irregular **yo** forms, verbs with spelling changes, verbs with stem changes, and verbs with both spelling and stem changes. Also, a few verbs have irregular singular, familiar, affirmative command forms and must be memorized.

In a negative command, these irregular verbs follow the same rules as all the other verbs. To form a singular, negative, familiar command with any verb when **tú** is the subject, you use the present subjunctive **tú** form. Here's a refresher on how to form the present subjunctive (see Chapter 7):

1. Drop the final **-o** from the **yo** form of the present tense.

2. For infinitives ending in **-ar,** add **-es** for the **tú** form. For infinitives ending in **-er** or **-ir,** add **-as** for the **tú** form.

3. To form the negative, put **no** before the verb.

Using regular verbs

The following table illustrates the difference between singular familiar commands in their affirmative and negative forms for regular verbs:

Regular Verbs	Affirmative Commands	Negative Commands	English
firm**ar**	firm**a**	no firm**es**	*(don't) sign*
com**er**	com**e**	no com**as**	*(don't) eat*
sub**ir**	sub**e**	no sub**as**	*(don't) go up*

Here are some examples that show how singular familiar commands should look with regular verbs:

> **Usa (No uses) este libro.** (*[Don't] Use this book.*)
>
> **Corre (¡No corras!)** (*¡[Don't] Run!*)
>
> **Cubre (No cubras) los ojos.** (*[Don't] Cover your eyes.*)

Your friend wants to help you cook. Write down instructions for her, using the singular familiar command form. I provide the regular verbs in parentheses and you insert the proper command form. Here's an example:

Q. (abrir) _____ el saco de legumbres.

A. **Abre** el saco de legumbres. (*Open the bag of vegetables.*)

25. (proceder) _____ lentamente.

26. (leer) _____ la receta.

27. (limpiar) _____ las verduras.

28. (pelar) _____ las zanahorias.

29. (mezclar) _____ los guisantes con las zanahorias.

30. (cortar) _____ cebollas.

31. (combinar) _____ todos los ingredientes en una caserola.

32. (añadir) _____ mantequilla y aqua.

33. (cubrir) _____ la caserola.

34. (dejar) _____ cocinar por treinta minutos.

Using other types of verbs

Verbs with irregular **yo** forms, verbs with spelling changes, verbs with stem changes, and verbs with both spelling and stem changes follow the same rules for forming familiar commands as regular verbs. You must, however, take into account the changes, so the verb forms may look a little strange at first. There also are a handful of verbs that have irregular singular, familiar command forms that you must memorize. Consult the tables in this section to see how these types of verbs look in the imperative.

Table 9-6 presents verbs that have irregular **yo** forms when used in singular, familiar commands.

Table 9-6	Verbs with Irregular yo Forms		
Spanish Verbs	**Affirmative**	**Negative**	**Meaning**
oír	oye	no oigas	(*don't*) hear
traer	trae	no traigas	(*don't*) bring

Two examples show how to use these verbs in their imperative forms:

¡Oye lo que digo! (*Hear what I am saying!*)

Trae (No traiga) el periódico. (*[Don't] Bring the newspaper.*)

Table 9-7 presents verbs that have spelling changes in their singular, familiar commands. As you'll see, these verbs only have changes in the negative form.

Table 9-7	Verbs with Spelling Changes		
Spanish Verbs	*Affirmative*	*Negative*	*Meaning*
-ar verbs			
sacar	saca	no saques	(*don't*) *take out*
pagar	paga	no pagues	(*don't*) *pay*
organizar	organiza	no organices	(*don't*) *organize*
-er and **-ir** verbs			
obedecer	obedece	no obedezcas	(*don't*) *obey*
conducir	conduce	no conduzcas	(*don't*) *drive*
escoger	escoge	no escojas	(*don't*) *choose*
exigir	exige	no exijas	(*don't*) *demand*
distinguir	distingue	no distingas	(*don't*) *distinguish*

The following examples show how to use these verbs:

Paga (No pagues) la cuenta. (*[Don't]Pay the bill.*)

Obedece (No obedezcas) a esa mujer. (*[Don't] Obey that woman.*)

Table 9-8 lists verbs with stem changes in singular, familiar commands. These verbs experience changes in both their affirmative and negative forms.

Table 9-8	Verbs with Stem Changes		
Spanish Verbs	*Affirmative*	*Negative*	*Meaning*
-ar verbs			
cerrar (e to ie)	cierra	**no cierres**	(*don't*) *close*
mostrar (o to ue)	muestra	**no muestres**	(*don't*) *show*
enviar (i to í)	envía	**no envíes**	(*don't*) *send*
continuar (u to ú)	continúa	**no continúes**	(*don't*) *continue*
-er and **-ir** verbs			
perder (e to ie)	pierde	**no pierdas**	(*don't*) *lose*
volver (o to ue)	vuelve	**no vuelvas**	(*don't*) *return*
mentir (e to ie)	miente	**no mientas**	(*don't*) *lie*
dormir (o to ue)	duerme	**no duermas**	(*don't*) *sleep*
pedir (e to i)	pide	**no pidas**	(*don't*) *ask (for)*
destruir (add y)	destruye	**no destruyas**	(*don't*) *destroy*

Here are some examples of these verbs in action:

> **Continúa (No continúes) hablando.** (*[Don't] Continue speaking.*)
>
> **Pide (No pidas) la verdad.** (*[Don't] Ask for the truth.*)

Table 9-9 presents verbs with both spelling and stem changes. You'll see just a vowel change in the affirmative, singular, familiar command; the singular, negative, familiar command will feature that change and another spelling change.

Table 9-9	Verbs with Spelling and Stem Changes		
Spanish Verbs	*Affirmative*	*Negative*	*Meaning*
colgar (o to ue/g to gu)	cuelga	no cuelgues	(*don't*) hang
jugar (u to ue/g to gu)	juega	no juegues	(*don't*) play
comenzar (e to ie/z to c)	comienza	no comiences	(*don't*) begin
empezar (e to ie/z to c)	empieza	no empieces	(*don't*) begin
almorzar (o to ue/z to c)	almuerza	no almuerces	(*don't*) eat lunch
corregir (e to i/g to j)	corrige	no corrijas	(*don't*) correct
seguir (e to i/gu to g)	sigue	no sigas	(*don't*) follow

The examples here show these verbs in the singular, familiar command form:

> **Cuelga. (No cuelgues.)** (*Hang up. [Don't hang up.]*)
>
> **Almuerza (No almuerces) conmigo.** (*[Don't] Eat lunch with me.*)

Table 9-10 displays irregular verbs in their singular, familiar, affirmative or negative command forms. You must memorize these verbs and the changes they undergo.

Table 9-10		Irregular Verbs	
Spanish Verbs	*Affirmative*	*Negative*	*Meaning*
decir	di	no digas	(*don't*) say, tell
hacer	haz	no hagas	(*don't*) do, make
ir	ve	no vayas	(*don't*) go
poner	pon	no pongas	(*don't*) put
salir	sal	no salgas	(*don't*) leave
ser	sé	no seas	(*don't*) be
tener	ten	no tengas	(*don't*) have
valer	val or vale	no valgas	(*don't*) be worth
venir	ven	no vengas	(*don't*) come

Here are a couple of examples of these irregular verbs in commanding action:

> **Pon (No pongas) tu abrigo.** *([Don't] Put on your coat.)*
>
> **Ven (No vengas) aquí.** *([Don't] Come here.)*

Your friend Verónica wants to lose weight. Write out your suggestions for her by using the singular, familiar, affirmative, and negative command form of the verb I provide in parentheses. I'll start you off with an example:

Q. (exigir) No _____ helado, _____ ensalada.

A. No **exijas** helado, **exige** ensalada. *(Don't demand ice cream, demand salad.)*

35. (tener) No _____ dudas, _____ confianza.

36. (salir) _____ del gimnasio contenta, no _____ triste.

37. (pedir) No _____ una porción grande, _____ una porción pequeña.

38. (poner) No _____ mayonesa en tu sándwich, _____ mostaza.

39. (hacer) _____ ejercicios físicos frecuentemente, no _____ ejercicios raramente.

40. (jugar) No _____ a las damas, _____ a un deporte.

41. (almorzar) _____ cuando tienes hambre, no _____ después de comer algo.

42. (seguir) _____ tu régimen conscienzudamente, no _____ tu régimen solamente de vez en cuando.

43. (perder) No _____ diez libras, _____ veinte libras.

44. (continuar) _____ el régimen cuando estás bien, no _____ el régimen cuando estás enferma.

45. (ser) _____ optimista, no _____ pesimista.

46. (mostrar) No _____ tu menú a tus amigas, _____ tu menú a tu entrenadora.

47. (escoger) Siempre _____ verduras, no _____ nunca postres.

48. (ir) No _____ al cine, _____ al gimnasio.

49. (gozar) _____ de la comida saludable, no _____ de la comida poco saludable.

Giving plural commands with vosotros

Forming plural, affirmative, familiar commands is a cinch. You just drop the final **-r** of the infinitive and add **-d.** This rule holds true for regular verbs, verbs with irregular **yo** forms, verbs with spelling changes, verbs with stem changes, verbs with both spelling and stem changes, and all irregular verbs. You form all plural, negative, familiar commands by using the present subjunctive **vosotros** form of the verb (see Chapter 7).

To form a negative command with any verb when **vosotros** is the subject, use the present subjunctive **vosotros** form:

1. Drop the final **-o** from the **yo** form of the present tense.

2. For infinitives ending in **-ar,** add **-éis** for the **vosotros** form. For infinitives ending in **-er** or **-ir,** add **-áis** for the **vosotros** form.

3. To form the negative, put **no** before the verb.

Using regular verbs

The following table illustrates the difference between plural, familiar commands in their affirmative and negative forms for regular verbs:

Regular Verbs	Affirmative	Negative	Meaning
firmar	firmad	no firméis	(don't) sign
comer	comed	no comáis	(don't) eat
subir	subid	no subáis	(don't) go up

Here's how your **vosotros** commands should look when using regular verbs:

> **Tirad (No tiréis) la cuerda.** *([Don't] Pull the cord.)*

> **Bebed (No bebáis) café.** *([Don't] Drink coffee.)*

> **Resistid (No restistáis).** *(Resist. [Don't resist.])*

Your two nieces are coming over to babysit for your children. Write them a note to tell them what to do. Use the affirmative, plural, familiar form of the verb I provide for each question to form a full sentence. Here's an example:

Q. hablar/con ellos.

A. **Hablad** con ellos. *(Speak with them.)*

50. mirar/la televisión con ellos _____

51. insistir en/ comer temprano _____

52. ayudar/a los niños con sus tareas _____

53. leer/historias a los niños _____

54. prometer/de acostar a los niños a las ocho _____

55. escribir/una nota si hay problemas _____

Using other types of verbs

Verbs with irregular **yo** forms, verbs with spelling changes, verbs with stem changes, and verbs with both spelling and stem changes follow the same rules for forming plural commands as regular verbs. You must remember to make any necessary changes, though. You also must memorize a few verbs that have irregular plural, familiar command forms. Consult the tables in this section to see how these types of verbs look in the imperative.

Table 9-11 presents the verbs with irregular **yo** forms when used in the plural, familiar command form.

Table 9-11	Verbs with Irregular yo Forms		
Spanish Verbs	*Affirmative*	*Negative*	*Meaning*
oír	**oíd**	**no oigáis**	(*don't*) *hear*
traer	**traed**	**no traigáis**	(*don't*) *bring*

Here are these verbs shown in examples:

> **Oíd esto.** (*Hear this.*)
>
> **Traed (No tragáis) el libro.** (*[Don't] Bring the book.*)

Table 9-12 lists verbs that require spelling changes in the plural command form. However, you only see the change in the negative plural, familiar command form.

Table 9-12	Verbs with Spelling Changes		
Spanish Verbs	*Affirmative*	*Negative*	*Meaning*
-ar verbs			
sacar	saca**d**	no sa**quéis**	(*don't*) *take out*
pagar	paga**d**	no pa**guéis**	(*don't*) *pay*
organizar	organiza**d**	no organi**céis**	(*don't*) *organize*
-er and **-ir** verbs			
obedecer	obedece**d**	no obede**zcáis**	(*don't*) *obey*
conducir	conduci**d**	no condu**zcáis**	(*don't*) *drive*
escoger	escoge**d**	no esco**jáis**	(*don't*) *choose*
exigir	exigi**d**	no exi**jáis**	(*don't*) *demand*
distinguir	distingui**d**	no distin**gáis**	(*don't*) *distinguish*

The following examples show these verbs with spelling changes:

> **Organizad (No organicéis) una reunión.** (*[Don't] Organize a meeting.*)
>
> **Exigid (No exijáis) esto.** (*[Don't] Demand that.*)

Table 9-13 outines verbs that require stem changes in the plural, familiar command form. As you'll see, stem changes occur only in verbs that end in **-ir** in their original infinitive form.

Table 9-13	Verbs with Stem Changes		
Spanish Verbs	*Affirmative*	*Negative*	*Meaning*
-ar verbs			
cerrar (e to ie)	cerra**d**	no cerr**éis**	(*don't*) *close*
mostrar (o to ue)	mostra**d**	no mostr**éis**	(*don't*) *show*
enviar (i to í)	envia**d**	no envi**éis**	(*don't*) *send*
continuar (u to ú)	continua**d**	no continu**éis**	(*don't*) *continue*
-er and **-ir** verbs			
perder (e to ie)	perde**d**	no perd**áis**	(*don't*) *lose*
volver (o to ue)	volve**d**	no volv**áis**	(*don't*) *return*
mentir (e to ie)	menti**d**	no mint**áis**	(*don't*) *lie*
dormir (o to ue)	dormi**d**	no **durmáis**	(*don't*) *sleep*
pedir (e to i)	pedi**d**	no **pidáis**	(*don't*) *ask (for)*
destruir (add y)	destrui**d**	no **destruyáis**	(*don't*) *destroy*

The verbs **mentir** (e to ie) and **dormir** (o to ue) change the **e** to **i** and the **o** to **u**, respectively, in the present subjunctive **vosotros** form (see Chapter 7).

Here are two examples of these stem-changing verbs in the affirmative and negative plural familiar:

> **Mostrad (No mostréis) la foto a Ana.** (*[Don't] Show the photo to Ana.*)
>
> **Dormid (No durmáis) hasta el mediodía.** (*[Don't] Sleep until noon.*)

For the plural, familiar command construction, when a verb has both a spelling change and a stem change, only the spelling change occurs, and it occurs only in the negative form. Table 9-14 shows you this construction.

Table 9-14	Verbs with Spelling and Stem Changes		
Spanish Verbs	*Affirmative*	*Negative*	*Meaning*
colgar (o to ue/g to gu)	colga**d**	no col**guéis**	(*don't*) *hang*
jugar (u to ue/g to gu)	juga**d**	no ju**guéis**	(*don't*) *play*
comenzar (e to ie/z to c)	comenza**d**	no comen**céis**	(*don't*) *begin*
empezar (e to ie/z to c)	empeza**d**	no empe**céis**	(*don't*) *begin*
almorzar (o to ue/z to c)	almorza**d**	no almor**céis**	(*don't*) *eat lunch*
corregir (e to i/g to j)	corregi**d**	no corri**jáis**	(*don't*) *correct*
seguir (e to i/gu to g)	segui**d**	no si**gáis**	(*don't*) *follow*

The following examples show these verbs in action:

> **Colgad (No colguéis) la noticia aquí.** (*[Don't] Hang the notice here.*)
>
> **Comenzad (No comencéis).** (*[Don't] Begin.*)

Finally, Table 9-15 lists the irregular verbs that you must simply memorize in order to give plural, familiar commands in Spanish.

Table 9-15		Irregular Verbs	
Spanish Verbs	*Affirmative*	*Negative*	*Meaning*
decir	decid	no digáis	(*don't*) say, tell
hacer	haced	no hagáis	(*don't*) do
ir	id	no vayáis	(*don't*) go
poner	poned	no pongáis	(*don't*) put
salir	salid	no salgáis	(*don't*) leave
ser	sed	no seáis	(*don't*) be
tener	tened	no tengáis	(*don't*) have, be
valer	valed	no valgáis	(*don't*) be worth
venir	venid	no vengáis	(*don't*) come

Here are two examples of these irregular verbs in commands:

> **Id (No vayáis) allá.** (*[Don't] Go there.*)
>
> **Sed (No seáis) optimista.** (*[Don't] Be optimistic.*)

Your friends will be doing some traveling and you want to give them some advice so they don't make any big mistakes. Use the plural, negative, familiar form of the verbs I provide in parentheses. Here's an example:

Q. (caminar) No _____ solos.

A. No **caminéis** solos. (*Don't walk alone.*)

56. (ir) No _____ al aeropuerto tarde.

57. (pagar) No _____ en efectivo.

58. (dar) No _____ vuestros nombres a un desconocido.

59. (hacer) No _____ vuestras maletas a última hora.

60. (llevar) No _____ ningún artículo peligroso en su equipaje.

61. (olvidar) No _____ vuestros pasaportes.

You need advice, so you seek help from a friend and a teacher. Both say the same things to you, but your friend uses the **tú** command form and your teacher uses the **Ud.** command form. I provide verb phrases in parentheses; you write each verb in the familiar and in the polite command form. Here are some examples:

Q. Yo no salgo bien en mi clase. (estudiar más)

A. Friend: **Estudia** más. (*Study more.*)

A. Teacher: **Estudie** más.

Q. Mis padres no están contentos de mis notas. (no salir tan frecuentemente)

A. Friend: **No salgas** tan frecuentemente. (*Don't go out so frequently.*)

A. Teacher: **No salga** tan frecuentemente.

62. Estoy enfermo. (no venir a la escuela)

Friend: _____

Teacher: _____

63. Tengo una cita con mi profesor. (no llegar tarde)

Friend: _____

Teacher: _____

64. Quiero comprar un abrigo muy caro. (pagar con una tarjeta de crédito)

Friend: _____

Teacher: _____

65. Quiero regresar tarde a casa. (pedir permiso)

Friend: _____

Teacher: _____

66. No sé nadar. (no ir a la playa)

Friend: _____

Teacher: _____

67. No me gustan los perros. (no tener miedo de Fido.)

Friend: _____

Teacher: _____

68. Hago muchos errores. (corregir el trabajo)

Friend: _____

Teacher: _____

69. Estoy cansado. (cerrar los ojos)

Friend: _____

Teacher: _____

Answer Key

1 **beba.** Regular -er verb.

2 **respire.** Regular -ar verb.

3 **insista.** Regular -ir verb.

4 **tome.** Regular -ar verb.

5 **coma.** Regular -er verb.

6 **consuma.** Regular -ir verb.

7 **destruyan.** Stem-changing verb that adds a y.

8 **cierren.** Stem-changing -e to ie (-ar) verb.

9 **mientan.** Stem-changing -e to ie (-ir) verb.

10 **digan.** Irregular yo form verb.

11 **pierdan.** Stem-changing -e to ie (-er) verb.

12 **pidan.** Stem-changing -e to i (-ir) verb.

13 **hagan.** Irregular yo form verb.

14 **pongan.** Irregular yo form verb.

15 **estén.** Irregular verb.

16 **organicen.** Verb with -zar spelling change.

17 **tengan.** Irregular yo form verb.

18 **vayan.** Irregular verb.

19 **cuelguen.** Stem-changing -o to ue (-ar) verb. Verb with -gar spelling change.

20 **empiecen.** Stem-changing -e to ie verb. Verb with -zar spelling change.

21 **apaguen.** Verb with -gar spelling change.

22 **saquen.** Verb with -car spelling change.

23 **recojan.** Verb with -ger spelling change.

24 **sigan.** Stem-changing -e to i verb. Verb with gu to g spelling change.

25 **procede.** Regular -er verb.

26 **lee.** Regular -er verb.

27 **limpia.** Regular -ar verb.

28 **pela.** Regular -ar verb.

29 **mezcla.** Regular -ar verb.

30 **corta.** Regular -ar verb.

31 **combina.** Regular -ar verb.

32 **añade.** Regular -ir verb.

33 **cubre.** Regular -ir verb.

34 **deja.** Regular -ar verb.

35 **tengas/ten.** Irregular verb./Irregular yo form verb.

36 **sal/salgas.** Irregular verb./Irregular yo form verb.

37 **pidas/pide.** Stem-changing -e to i (-ir) verb.

38 **pongas/pon.** Irregular verb./Irregular yo form verb.

39 **haz/hagas.** Irregular verb./Irregular yo form verb.

40 **juegues/juega.** Stem-changing -u to ue (-ar) verb. Verb with -zar spelling change.

41 **almuerza/almuerces.** Stem-changing -o to ue (-zar) verb. Verb with -zar spelling change.

42 **sigue/sigas.** Stem-changing -e to i (-guir) verb. Verb with gu to g spelling change.

43 **pierdas/pierde.** Stem-changing -e to ie (-er) verb.

44 **continúa/continúes.** Verb with u to ú stem change.

45 **sé/seas.** Irregular verb.

46 **muestres/muestra.** Stem-changing -o to ue (-ar) verb.

47 **escoge/escojas.** Verb with -ger spelling change.

48 **vayas/ve.** Irregular verb.

49 **goza/goces.** Verb with -zar spelling change.

50 **Mirad** la televisión con ellos. (*Watch television with them.*)

51 **Insistid** en comer temprano. (*Insist on eating early.*)

52 **Ayudad** a los niños con sus tareas. (*Help the children with their homework.*)

53 **Leed** historias a los niños. (*Read stories to the children.*)

54 **Prometed** de acostar a los niños a las ocho. (*Promise to put the children to bed at 8 p.m.*)

55 **Escribid** una nota si hay problemas. (*Write a note if there are any problems.*)

56 **vayáis.** Irregular verb.

57 **paguéis.** Verb with -gar spelling change.

58 **deis.** Regular -ar verb.

59 **hagáis.** Irregular yo form verb.

60 **llevéis.** Regular -ar verb.

61 **olvidéis.** Regular -ar verb.

62 Friend: **No vengas** a la escuela. (*Don't come to school.*)

Teacher: **No venga** a la escuela.

63 Friend: **No llegues** tarde. (*Don't arrive late.*)

Teacher: **No llegue** tarde.

64 Friend: **Paga** con una tarjeta de crédito. (*Pay with a credit card.*)

Teacher: **Pague** con una tarjeta de crédito.

65 Friend: **Pide** permiso. (*Ask for permission.*)

Teacher: **Pida** permiso.

66 Friend: **No vayas** a la piscina. (*Don't go to the swimming pool.*)

Teacher: **No vaya** a la piscina.

67 Friend: **No tengas** miedo de Fido. (*Don't be afraid of Fido.*)

Teacher: **No tenga** miedo de Fido.

68 Friend: **Corrige** el trabajo. (*Correct the work.*)

Teacher: **Corrija** el trabajo.

69 Friend: **Cierra** los ojos. (*Close your eyes.*)

Teacher: **Cierre** los ojos.

Chapter 10

Being Clear and Concise with Object Pronouns

*I*magine that you're sitting in the food court of your local mall, eating a fabulous looking hot-fudge sundae with mint chocolate chip ice cream. A friend stops to chat and says: "Wow! What a delicious looking sundae! Can I see your sundae? Can I taste your sundae? Give me the sundae. Where can I buy that sundae? Do they make that sundae every day? I want that sundae!" Overly fixated on what you're consuming, your friend uses the word "sundae" to the point of being boring and downright annoying. Can you help your friend expand his horizons? Sure you can.

If you want to speak freely and naturally, and if you want to sound as if Spanish comes quite naturally to you, you must step up and master the use of direct and indirect object pronouns. You'll be glad you did, because your Spanish will sound more colloquial and more fluent. In the previous example, the trick is to use the direct object pronoun *it* to avoid repetition of the direct object noun *sundae*. Can an indirect object pronoun also substitute for an indirect object noun? Of course. Here's an example: "My grandfather is old. I read to my grandfather. I send cards to my grandfather. I write e-mails to my grandfather." You can vary your wording by substituting the indirect object pronoun *him* for the indirect object noun *my grandfather*.

In this chapter, you see the difference between direct and indirect object nouns and pronouns, and you find out how to use them properly in the sentences you want to create. You must know which verbs require a direct or indirect object pronoun so that selecting the one you need isn't a guessing game. You also discover how to place these words correctly within your sentences. By the end of this chapter, you'll be writing and speaking a much clearer and more concise sentence in Spanish.

Dealing Directly with Direct Object Pronouns

A direct object pronoun is a replacement word for a direct object noun. This pronoun helps you avoid unnecessary, continuous repetition of the noun, which allows for a more colloquial, free-flowing conversational tone when you're speaking or writing. Don't be tricked by these pronouns, though; always remember that the verb in your sentence must agree with the subject pronoun. The following sections walk you through the world of direct object pronouns.

Understanding direct object pronouns

Direct object nouns or *pronouns* answer the question "Whom or what is the subject acting upon?" Direct objects may refer to people, places, things, or ideas. A direct object pronoun simply replaces a direct object noun and agrees with it in number and gender.

In both English and Spanish, a direct object noun follows the subject and its verb:

Veo la casa. (*I see the house.*)

Unlike in English, however, you usually place a Spanish direct object pronoun before the conjugated verb:

La veo. (*I see it.*)

Table 10-1 lists the direct object pronouns in Spanish.

Table 10-1	Spanish Direct Object Pronouns		
Singular Pronouns	*Meaning*	*Plural Pronouns*	*Meaning*
me	*me*	**nos**	*us*
te	*you* (familiar)	**os**	*you* (polite)
lo	*him, it, you*	**los**	*them, you*
la	*her, it, you*	**las**	*them, you*

Here are some example sentences that show how you use Spanish direct object pronouns:

Él me comprende. (*He understands me.*)

¿Nos ve Ud.? (*Do you see us?*)

¿Los periódicos? Yo los leo cada día. (*The newspapers? I read them every day.*)

People often use **le** rather than **lo** in Spain to express *you* (masculine) or *him*. **Lo** is used as a direct object pronoun in Spanish America. The plural of **lo** and **le** is **los,** which means *them* or *you*. Here are some examples:

>   **Cuido al niño.** (*I watch the child.*)
>
>   **Lo [Le] cuido.** (*I watch him.*)
>
>   **Cuido a los niños.** (*I watch the children.*)
>
>   **Los cuido.** (*I watch them.*)
>
>   **Miro el programa.** (*I watch the program.*)
>
>   **Lo miro.** (*I watch it.*)
>
>   **Miro los programas.** (*I watch the programs.*)
>
>   **Los miro.** (*I watch them.*)

Complete the following journal entries in which you explain what you bought during your travels and what you did with these items. To complete an entry, you must insert the correct direct object pronoun. Here's an example to get you started:

0. Compré un poster y _____ admiré.

A. Compré un poster y **lo** admiré. (*I bought a poster and I admired it.*)

1. Compré una chaqueta y _____ llevé.

2. Compré tarjetas postales y _____ envié a mis amigos.

3. Compré un libro y _____ leí.

4. Compré recuerdos y _____ guardé.

5. Compré camisetas y _____ mostré a mi amiga.

6. Compré una guía y _____ estudié.

7. Compré discos compactos y _____ escuché.

8. Compré un plano de la ciudad y _____ miré.

Getting personal with the personal a

In Spanish, the personal **a** conveys absolutely no meaning and is used only before a direct object noun (not before a direct object pronoun or any indirect objects) to indicate that it refers to a person or a beloved pet. The following list explains in more detail how to use the personal **a:**

✔ You use the personal **a** before a common or proper noun that refers to a person or persons. The personal **a** combines with the definite article **el** to form the contraction **al,** but it doesn't combine with the other definite articles:

   No conozco a ellas. (*I don't know them.*)

   Busco al señor Gómez. (*I'm looking for Mr. Gómez.*)

   Visitamos a la señora Perón. (*We visited Mrs. Perón.*)

✔ You use the personal **a** before the name of your pooch, tabby, hamster, turtle, or other pet:

Adiestró a Fido. (*She tamed Fido.*)

Llamé a Boots. (*I called Boots.*)

✔ You use the personal **a** before a pronoun that refers to a person:

No espero a nadie. (*I'm not waiting for anyone.*)

You don't, however, use the personal **a** with the verb **tener** (*to have*):

Tengo dos hermanos. (*I have two brothers.*)

Write a journal entry in which you express what you and your family members intend to do when you take a trip to Argentina. For each exercise, I provide the subject, the verb, and the direct object noun. You must combine the elements by conjugating the verb pensar in the present tense and by correctly adding the personal **a.** Here's an example:

Q. nosotros/ver/nuestros primos

A. Nosotros **pensamos** ver **a** nuestros primos. (*We intend to see our cousins.*)

9. yo/ver/mi familia

_____

10. mis hijos/conocer/alcalde de Buenos Aires

_____

11. nosotros/invitar/las primas de nuestros amigos

_____

12. José/visitar/Carlota Hernández

_____

13. tú/buscar/señor Rueda

_____

14. vosotros/admirar/todos los niños

_____

Using Indirect Object Pronouns

Indirect object nouns or *pronouns* refer only to people (and to beloved pets); they answer the question: "To or for whom is the subject doing something?" An indirect object pronoun can replace an indirect object noun but also is used in Spanish when the indirect object noun is mentioned. The indirect object pronoun never agrees with the noun to which it refers. And just like with direct object pronouns, indirect object pronouns generally are placed before the conjugated verb. For example:

> **Le escribo un e-mail.** (*I'm writing an e-mail to him.*)
>
> **Le escribo a Gloria un e-mail.** (*I'm writing an e-mail to Gloria.*)

Table 10-2 presents the indirect object pronouns in Spanish.

Table 10-2	Spanish Indirect Object Pronouns		
Singular Pronouns	*Meaning*	*Plural Pronouns*	*Meaning*
me	to/for me	nos	to/for us
te	to/for you (familiar)	os	to/for you (familiar)
le	to/for him, her, you (formal)	les	to/for them, you (formal)

The following sentences show how you use indirect object pronouns:

> **¿Me dices la verdad?** (*Are you telling me the truth?*)
>
> **La mujer nos ofrece un refresco.** (*The lady offers us a drink.*)
>
> **Les doy un abrazo.** (*I give them a hug.*)

A clue that may indicate that you need an indirect object pronoun is the use of the preposition **a** (**al, a la, a los,** or **a las**), which means *to* or *for* (unlike the personal **a,** which has no meaning [see the previous section]), followed by the name of or reference to a person. You may use **a él, a ella,** or **a Ud.** or the person's name to clarify to whom you're referring:

> **Yo le escribo a Rosa.** (*I write to Rosa.*)
>
> **Yo le escribo.** (*I write to her.*)
>
> **Ella le habla al muchacho.** (*She speaks to the boy.*)
>
> **Ella le habla.** (*She speaks to him.*)
>
> **Ella le habla a él.** (*She speaks to him.*)
>
> **Ella le habla a Juan.** (*She speaks to Juan.*)

Although you may use the prepositions *to* and *for* in English, you omit these prepositions in Spanish sentences before an indirect object pronoun:

> **Te compro un regalo.** (*I'm buying a present for you; I'm buying you a present.*)
>
> **Me escriben.** (*They are writing to me; They are writing me.*)

Write a text message to a friend explaining what's happening at Linda's party by combining all the elements I provide (conjugate the verb in the present tense) and by inserting the proper indirect object pronoun. Here's an example:

Q. Linda/leer una carta/a sus padres

A. Linda **les lee** una carta a sus padres. (*Linda reads a card to her parents.*)

15. Carlos/pedir un trozo de la torta/a vosotros

_____

16. yo/contar todo/a tí

_____

17. tú/telefonear/a tus amigos

_____

18. Juana y yo/dar un regalo/a Linda

_____

19. Linda/servir refrescos/a nosotros

_____

20. Gloria/ofrecer un sándwich/a mí

_____

Selecting a Direct or an Indirect Object Pronoun

Sometimes people get confused when trying to figure out whether to use a direct object pronoun or an indirect object pronoun. The good news is you'll have absolutely no problem with **me, te, nos,** and **os** because they act as both direct and indirect object pronouns. They're also reflexive pronouns (see Chapter 11):

> **Me respeta.** (*He respects me.*)
>
> **Me dice un secreto.** (*He tells me a secret.*)
>
> **Nos visita.** (*She visits us.*)
>
> **Nos trae flores.** (*She brings us flowers.*)

Here's one tip: If you can use the word *to* or *for* in an English sentence before a reference to a person — no matter how awkward the construction may seem — you must use an indirect object pronoun in your Spanish sentence:

> **Quiero mostrarte esta foto.** (*I want to show* [to] *you this photo.*)

The following sections give you some more "insider" tips that will help you decide between direct and indirect object pronouns.

Common Spanish verbs requiring a direct object

Verbs that require an indirect object in English may require a direct object in Spanish because *to* or *for* is included in the meaning of the infinitive. (Remember that any **a** you see will be the personal **a** [see the earlier section on this topic].) Some of these high-frequency verbs include the following:

- **buscar** (*to look for*)
- **escuchar** (*to listen to*)
- **esperar** (*to wait for*)
- **llamar** (*to call*)
- **mirar** (*to look at*)

The following examples illustrate how you use these verbs:

Nosotros esperamos a nuestros amigos. (*We are waiting for our friends.*)

Nosotros los esperamos. (*We are waiting for them.*)

Busco a mi perro. (*I'm looking for my dog.*)

Lo busco. (*I'm looking for it.*)

Common Spanish verbs requiring an indirect object

Verbs that require a direct object in English don't necessarily require a direct object in Spanish. The verbs that follow take indirect objects in Spanish, regardless of the object used in English. This is because *to* or *for* is implied when speaking about a person or because the verb generally is followed by the preposition **a:**

acompañar (*to accompany*)

aconsejar (*to advise*)

contar (*to relate, tell*)

contestar (*to answer*)

dar (*to give*)

decir (*to say, tell*)

enviar (*to send*)

escribir (*to write*)

explicar (*to explain*)

llamar (*to call*)

mandar (*to send*)

obedecer (*to obey*)

ofrecer (*to offer*)

pedir (*to ask*)

preguntar (*to ask*)

presentar (*to introduce*)

prestar (*to lend*)

prohibir (*to forbid*)

prometer (*to promise*)

regalar (*to give a gift*)

telefonear (*to call*)

Here are a few examples:

> **Te aconsejo practicar más.** (_I advise you to practice more._)
>
> **Ella le pide disculpa a su amiga.** (_She asks her friend for an apology._)
>
> **Me regala un reloj.** (_He is giving me a watch as a gift._)

Your friend Marta is having problems. Complete the following e-mail to another friend with the proper direct or indirect object pronoun in order to explain what you do to help. Here's an example:

_**O.**_ Yo _____ telefoneo a menudo.

_**A.**_ Yo **le** telefoneo a menudo. (_I call her often on the phone._)

21. Yo _____ llamo.

22. Yo _____ aconsejo.

23. Yo _____ busco todo el tiempo.

24. Yo _____ escucho.

25. Yo _____ doy mi opinión.

26. Yo _____ digo francamente lo que pienso.

27. Yo _____ ofrezco ayuda.

28. Yo _____ espero cuando quiere hablarme.

Placing Object Pronouns Correctly

How do you decide where to place a direct or indirect object pronoun in a Spanish sentence? Generally, you place these pronouns before the conjugated verb:

> **Nosotros los necesitamos.** (_We need them._)
>
> **Siempre les cuentas chistes.** (_You always tell them jokes._)

In sentences with two verbs that follow one subject or in sentences with a gerund (the **-ando** or **-iendo** forms; see Chapter 6), you have the choice of placing the object pronoun before the conjugated verb or after and attached to the infinitive or the gerund. The following list provides some examples of this construction.

When you attach the pronoun to the gerund, an accent is required on the stressed vowel. In general, to correctly place the accent, you count back three vowels and add the accent. Also, remember that negatives go before the pronoun when it precedes the verb.

✔ With a gerund:
- **(No) Lo estoy haciendo.** (*I'm [not] doing it.*)
- **(No) Estoy haciéndolo.** (*I'm [not] doing it.*)

✔ With an infinitive:
- **(No) Lo quiero hacer.** (*I [don't] want to do it.*)
- **(No) Quiero hacerlo.** (*I [don't] want to do it.*)

In a negative command, the object pronoun precedes the verb. In an affirmative command, however, the object pronoun must follow the verb and be attached to it (for more on commands, refer to Chapter 9). An accent mark normally is required on the stressed vowel (if there are only two vowels, no accent is needed). To properly place the accent, count back three vowels and add it.

Here's what affirmative commands look like:

Prepárela. (*Prepare it.*)

Hazlo. (*Do it.*)

Now take a look at the negatives:

No la prepare. (*Don't prepare it.*)

No lo hagas. (*Don't do it.*)

For this exercise, write out what you would like to ask or say to an acquaintance about your plans. I provide the direct or indirect object noun in parentheses; you must decide whether to use a direct or indirect object pronoun to replace the indicated noun, and then you must put the pronoun in its proper place in the sentence. Where appropriate, provide both correct responses. Here's an example to get you started:

Q. (las muchachas) Necesito telefonear.

A. Necesito **telefonearles.** (**Les** necesito telefonear.) (*I need to call them on the phone.*)

29. (programas en la televisión) ¿Por qué estás mirando?

_____

30. (a María) No digas nuestros planes.

_____

31. (los billetes) Puedo comprar.

_____

32. (a Ramón y a Jorge) Llama.

_____

33. (a Julia) ¿No estás hablando?

_____

34. (a mi padre) Quiero pedir dinero.

_____

Doing Double Duty with Double Object Pronouns

It's quite common in Spanish that a sentence requires both a direct and an indirect object pronoun. You have many rules to consider when creating these sentences, as the following list shows:

✔ When the verb has two object pronouns, the indirect object pronoun (a person) precedes the direct object pronoun (usually a thing):

- **Ella nos muestra las revistas.** (_She shows us the magazines._)

- **Ella nos las muestra.** (_She shows them to us._)

- **Nosotros te damos el boleto.** (_We give you the ticket._)

- **Nosotros te lo damos.** (_We give it to you._)

✔ When a sentence has two third-person object pronouns, the indirect object pronouns **le** and **les** change to **se** before the direct object pronouns **lo, la, los,** and **las:**

- **Él les lee las revistas a sus abuelos.** (_He reads the magazines to his grandparents._)

- **Él se las lee.** (_He reads them to you [him, her]._)

To clarify the meaning of **se** — because it can mean _to/for you, him, her,_ and _them_ — you may include the phrase **a Ud. (Uds.), a él (ellos),** or **a ella (ellas):**

Yo se los digo a él (a ella) (a Uds.). (_I tell them to him [her] [you]._)

✔ The same rules for the positioning of single object pronouns apply for double object pronouns (see the previous section). The following examples show how you use and place double object pronouns:

With an infinitive, you may place the two separate pronouns before the conjugated verb, or you may connect and attach them to the end of the infinitive:

- **(No) Te los quiero mostrar.** (_I [don't] want to show them to you._)

- **(No) Quiero mostrártelos.** (_I [don't] want to show them to you._)

With a gerund, you may place the two separate pronouns before the conjugated form of **estar,** or you may connect and attach them to the end of the gerund:

- **(No) Se la estoy leyendo a él.** (_I'm [not] reading it to him._)

- **(No) Estoy leyéndosela a él.** (_I'm [not] reading it to him._)

With commands:

- Formal:

    Affirmative: **Dígamelo.** (*Tell it to me.*)

    Negative: **No me lo diga.** (*Don't tell it to me.*)

- Informal:

    Affirmative: **Dímelo.** (*Tell it to me.*)

    Negative: **No me lo digas.** (*Don't tell it to me.*)

✔ When two pronouns appear in a sentence with an infinitive, you generally count back three vowels and add an accent:

Yo voy a escribírselo a Ud. (*I'm going to write it to you.*)

When you add two pronouns to a gerund or an affirmative command, however, you generally count back four vowels when adding an accent:

- **Estamos comprándoselas a ellos.** (*We are buying it for them.*)

- **Muéstramelo.** (*Show it to me.*)

With a diphthong (two vowels blended together that stand for only one vowel sound), you may have to count back as many as five vowels:

Tráiganoslos. (*Bring them to us.*)

You're helping your younger brother do his homework, in which he must discuss the jobs people perform. Make his sentences shorter by replacing the direct and indirect object nouns with pronouns. I provide the subject and the conjugated verb forms, along with the object nouns in parentheses. You must replace the nouns with pronouns and place them properly within the sentence. Here's an example:

Q. el peluquero corta (el pelo/a ti)

A. El peluquero **te lo** corta. (*The barber cuts it for you.*)

35. el cartero trae (el correo/a la gente)

_____

36. profesora, ¡enseña! (la gramática/a los alumnos)

_____

37. el dentista quiere extraer (los dientes/a ti)

_____

38. el cajero está dando (la moneda/a nosotros)

_____

39. comerciante, ¡no venda! (las mercancías/a sus competidores)

_____

40. el banquero no va a cambiar (dinero/a todos los turistas)

_____

41. el juez está explicando (las leyes/a los criminales)

_____

42. poeta ¡escriba! (poemas/a tu novia)

_____

43. el artista muestra (sus obras/a vosotros)

_____

44. el panadero puede vender (pasteles/a mí)

_____

45. el doctor está recetando (medicina/a los enfermos)

_____

46. la secretaria no escribe (cartas/a Uds.)

_____

Getting by with Gustar and Other Similar Verbs

During any average day, most people have occasion to express their likes and dislikes. To do so in Spanish, you have to use the verb **gustar** (_to please_) or **disgustar** (_to displease_). Verbs like **gustar** and **disgustar** require special attention because although you can say _I like_ in English, in Spanish you have to say that something is pleasing to you. This means that Spanish sentences appear somewhat backward to English speakers. This also means (because something is pleasing "to" the subject) that **gustar,** and verbs similar to **gustar,** require the use of an indirect object pronoun. Note how the English and Spanish sentences convey the same meaning but are expressed in a totally different fashion:

English: I like chocolate.

Spanish: Chocolate is pleasing to me.

As you can see, in English the subject _I_ is followed by the verb _like,_ which in turn is followed by the direct object _chocolate._ In Spanish, however, _chocolate_ becomes the subject. The verb _pleasing_ agrees with the subject _chocolate,_ and _to me_ is the indirect object. So, your sentence in Spanish reads as follows: **Me gusta el chocolate.** Using **gustar** or **disgustar** is a little confusing at first, but you'll quickly get the hang of it.

The following table presents other Spanish verbs that work like **gustar:**

Spanish Verb	Meaning
agradar	*to please, to be pleased with*
convenir (ie)	*to be suitable, convenient*
disgustar	*to upset, displease*
doler (ue)	*to be painful*
encantar	*to enchant*
entusiasmar	*to enthuse*
faltar	*to lack, need*
fascinar	*to fascinate*
importar	*to be important*
interesar	*to interest*
parecer	*to seem*
quedar	*to remain to someone, have left*
tocar	*to be one's turn*

Here are some examples that show how you use these verbs in Spanish sentences. Note that the subject is now at the end of the sentence and the verb must agree with the subject:

> **Me duele la espalda.** (*My back hurts.* Literally: *My back is hurting to me.*)
>
> **¿Te gustan los deportes?** (*Do you like sports?* Literally: *Are sports pleasing to you?*)
>
> **Nos encanta nadar.** (*We love to swim.* Literally: *Swimming enchants us.*)

You use the third-person singular form of any verb from the previous list with one or more infinitives:

> **Me gusta cantar.** (*I like to sing.*)
>
> **Me gusta cantar y bailar.** (*I like to sing and dance.*)

The following list presents some more details you should know about using these verbs:

✔ An indirect object pronoun may be preceded by the preposition **a** + the corresponding prepositional pronoun — **mí, ti, él, ella, Ud, nosotros, vosotros, ellos, ellas, Uds.** — for stress or clarification (see Chapter 12):

> • **A mí me parece claro.** (*It seems clear to me.*)
>
> • **A ellas les interesa la música.** (*Music interests them.*)

✔ An indirect object pronoun may be preceded by the preposition **a** + the indirect object noun:

> • **A Miguel no le gusta trabajar.** (*Michael doesn't like to work.*)
>
> • **A las niñas les gusta el helado.** (*The girls like ice cream.*)

For this exercise, write a letter to your pen pal in which you state what your friends like. I provide the Spanish indirect object, the Spanish infinitive of the verb that takes an indirect object, and the Spanish subject. You must give the indirect object, its related pronoun, and the proper form of the verb that agrees with the Spanish subject. This example gets you started:

Q. a nosotros/gustar/leer

A. A nosotros **nos gusta** leer. (*We like to read.*)

47. a Julio/fascinar/los deportes

_____

48. a mí/importar/el ballet y la ópera

_____

49. a Roberto y a mí/gustar/la natación

_____

50. a las muchachas/interesar/levantar pesos

_____

51. a Carmen/entusiasmar/tocar la guitarra y jugar al fútbol

_____

52. a tí/encantar/las películas

_____

Answer Key

1. **la.** The noun is feminine singular.

2. **las.** The noun is feminine plural.

3. **lo.** The noun is masculine singular.

4. **los.** The noun is masculine plural.

5. **las.** The noun is feminine plural.

6. **la.** The noun is feminine singular.

7. **los.** The noun is masculine plural.

8. **lo.** The noun is masculine singular.

9. Yo **pienso** ver **a** mi familia. (*I intend to see my family.*)

10. Mis hijos **piensan** conocer **al** alcalde de Buenos Aires. (*My children intend to meet the mayor of Buenos Aires.*)

11. Nosotros **pensamos** invitar **a** las primas de nuestros amigos. (*We intend to invite our friends' cousins.*)

12. José **piensa** visitar **a** Carlota Hernández. (*José intends to visit Carlota Hernández.*)

13. Tú **piensas** buscar **al** señor Rueda. (*You intend to look for Mr. Rueda.*)

14. Vosotros **pensáis** admirar **a** todos los niños. (*You intend to admire all the children.*)

15. Carlos **os pide** un trozo de la tarta a vosotros. (*Carlos asks you for a piece of cake.*)

16. Yo **te cuento** todo a tí. (*I tell you everything.*)

17. Tú **les telefoneas** a tus amigos. (*You call your friends on the phone.*)

18. Juana y yo **le damos** un regalo a Linda. (*Juana and I give a gift to Linda.*)

19. Linda **nos sirve** refrescos a nosotros. (*Linda serves us soft drinks.*)

20. Gloria **me ofrece** un sándwich a mí. (*Gloria offers me a sandwich.*)

21. **la**

22. **le**

23. **la**

24. **la**

25. **le**

26. **le**

27. **le**

28. **la**

29 ¿Por qué estás **mirándolos?** (¿Por qué **los** estás mirándo?) (*Why are you looking at them?*)

30 No **le digas** nuestros planes. (*Don't tell her your plans.*)

31 Puedo **comprarlos.** (**Los** puedo comprar.) (*I can buy them.*)

32 **Llámalos.** (*Call them.*)

33 ¿No estás **hablandole?** (¿No **le** estás hablando?) (*Aren't you speaking to her?*)

34 Quiero **pedirle** dinero. (**Le** quiero pedir dinero.) (*I want to ask him/her for money.*)

35 El cartero **se lo** trae. (*The mailman brings it to them.*)

36 Profesora, **¡enséñasela!** (*Teacher, teach it to them!*)

37 El dentista **te los** quiere extraer. (El dentista quiere **extraértelos.**) (*The dentist wants to extract them from you.*)

38 El cajero **nos la** está dando. (El cajero está **dándonosla.**) (*The cashier is giving it to us.*)

39 Comerciante, ¡no **se las** venda! (*Merchant, don't sell them to them!*)

40 El banquero no **se lo** va a cambiar. (El banquero no va a **cambiárselo.**) (*The banker isn't going to change it for them.*)

41 El juez **se las** está explicando. (El juez está **explicándoselas.**) (*The judge is explaining them to them.*)

42 Poeta **¡escríbaselos!** (*Poet, write them to her!*)

43 El artista **os las** muestra. (*The artist shows them to you.*)

44 El panadero **me los** puede vender. (El panadero puede **vendérmelos.**) (*The baker can sell them to me.*)

45 El doctor **se la** está recetando. (El doctor está **recetándosela.**) (*The doctor is prescribing it to them.*)

46 La secretaria no **se las** escribe. (*The secretary doesn't write them to you.*)

47 A Julio **le fascinan** los deportes. (*Sports fascinate Julio.*)

48 A mí **me importan** el ballet y la ópera. (*The ballet and the opera are important to me.*)

49 A Roberto y a mí **nos gusta** la natación. (*Robert and I like swimming.*)

50 A las muchachas **les interesa** levantar pesos. (*Lifting weights interests the girls.*)

51 A Carmen **le entusiasma** tocar la guitarra y jugar al fútbol. (*Playing the guitar and playing soccer enthuse Carmen.*)

52 A tí **te encantan** las películas. (*Movies enchant you.*)

Chapter 11

Reflecting on Reflexive Pronouns and Verbs

I'm willing to wager that if you've ever heard of reflexive verbs, it's because your foreign language teacher explained them to you. Most assuredly, your English teachers haven't covered them at all. *A reflexive verb* shows that the subject is acting upon itself and, therefore, requires a reflexive pronoun that expresses *myself, yourself, himself, herself, ourselves, yourselves,* or *themselves.*

Are you thinking, "Oh no, not more pronouns"? Don't worry, reflexive pronouns act as either direct or indirect object pronouns and are almost exactly the same as the pronouns in Chapter 10. In fact, you have to remember only two small, simple differences. So, if you've mastered object pronouns, reflexive pronouns will be a snap.

In this chapter, I explain how you recognize and use reflexive verbs in Spanish, as well as which pronouns are used for different subjects. The placement of reflexive pronouns in different types of sentences (regular present tense [Chapter 4], sentences with two verbs, present progressive tense [Chapter 6], and commands [Chapter 9]) should come as no surprise if you've practiced the materials in the preceding chapters. I also cover the special meaning of some reflexive verbs so that you can use them properly when speaking and writing Spanish. Finally, you discover how you can use reflexive verbs to indicate a passive action.

Recognizing and Using Reflexive Verbs

Reflexive verbs have several applications. Not only are they used to express that an action is performed by a subject on itself, but also to show how subjects act toward one another. Plus, they have limited use in passive constructions, where instead of doing the acting, the subject is acted upon (see the following section for more).

Are you wondering how to recognize a reflexive verb? It's really quite easy. If an **-ar, -er,** or **-ir** infinitive has **-se** attached to its end, you know you have a reflexive verb (**lavarse** [*to wash oneself*], **bañarse** [*to bathe oneself*]). That **-se** ending shows that the reflexive verb has a reflexive pronoun as its direct or indirect object. The subject of a reflexive verb, like subjects with other verbs, may be omitted. Whether you use or imply the subject, however, in the sentence the subject and its reflexive pronoun must refer to the same person or thing:

> **(Yo) Me llamo Gloria.** (*My name is Gloria.* [Literally: *I call myself Gloria.*])

> **(Nosotros) Nos levantamos.** (*We get up.*)

Compare the sentences that follow:

> **Ella se lava.** (*She washes herself.*)

> **Ella se lava la cara.** (*She washes her face.*)

In the first example, the reflexive pronoun (**se**) acts as a direct object. To determine this, ask yourself this question: Whom is she washing? The answer is: "herself." (Remember, a direct object indicates "whom" or "what" the subject is acting upon — in this case, herself.)

In the second example, the reflexive pronoun acts as an indirect object. To determine this, ask yourself this question: "What is she washing?" The answer is: "her face." "Her face" is now the direct object. Now ask this question: "For whom is she washing this face?" The answer is: "for herself." (Remember, an indirect object indicates "to" or "for" whom the subject is acting — in this case, "for herself.")

Note: In the conjugation, you drop the **-se** and always add (**se**) as a reflexive pronoun.

Some verbs may throw you off a bit. Depending on what you want to say, a verb may have both a reflexive and a non-reflexive form. How's that possible? Well, a reflexive verb requires that the subject act upon itself. What if, however, that subject acts upon someone or something else? In that case, the sentence doesn't need a reflexive pronoun.

Look carefully at the examples that follow:

> **Ella se lava.** (*She washes herself.*)

> **Ella lava a su perro.** (*She washes her dog.*)

In the first example, the verb requires a reflexive pronoun (**se**) because the subject, "she," is washing "herself." In the second example, however, the subject, "she," is washing "her dog." Because the subject isn't acting upon herself in this case, you don't use the reflexive pronoun. You simply use the possessive adjective **su** before the noun **perro** (see Chapter 3).

Conversely, some verbs that generally aren't used reflexively can be made reflexive (if the subject is acting upon itself) by adding a reflexive pronoun:

> **Él prepara la comida.** (*He prepares the meal.*)

> **Él se prepara.** (*He prepares himself.*)

In the first example, the verb doesn't require a reflexive pronoun because the subject, "he," is preparing someone or something else ("the meal"). In the second example, however, the subject, "he," is preparing "himself," which requires a reflexive pronoun.

The rest of the sections in this chapter dig deeper into many issues I present here. For now, Table 11-1 presents many common reflexive verbs (letters in parentheses indicate a spelling change).

Table 11-1	Common Reflexive Verbs		
Verb	*Meaning*	*Verb*	*Meaning*
abrazarse	*to hug each other*	**fijarse (en)**	*to notice*
abrocharse	*to fasten*	**hacerse**	*to become*
aburrirse	*to become bored*	**irse**	*to go away*
acostarse (ue)	*to go to bed*	**lavarse**	*to wash oneself*
afeitarse	*to shave*	**levantarse**	*to get up*
alegrarse (de)	*to be glad*	**llamarse**	*to be called, named*
aplicarse	*to apply oneself*	**maquillarse**	*to put on makeup*
apresurarse	*to hurry*	**marcharse**	*to go away*
asegurarse de	*to make sure*	**olvidarse (de)**	*to forget*
bañarse	*to bathe oneself*	**pasearse**	*to go for a walk*
burlarse (de)	*to make fun of*	**peinarse**	*to comb one's hair*
callarse	*to be silent*	**ponerse**	*to put on, become, place oneself*
cansarse	*to become tired*	**preocuparse (de)**	*to worry*
casarse	*to get married*	**quedarse**	*to remain*
cepillarse	*to brush (hair, teeth)*	**quejarse (de)**	*to complain*
despedirse (i)	*to say goodbye*	**quitarse**	*to remove*
despertarse (ie)	*to wake up*	**refriarse**	*to catch a cold*
desvestirse (i)	*to get undressed*	**reírse (de)**	*to laugh at*
divertirse (ie)	*to have fun*	**relajarse**	*to relax*
dormirse (ue)	*to fall asleep*	**romperse**	*to break (a part of the body)*
ducharse	*to take a shower*	**secarse**	*to dry oneself*
encontrarse (ue)	*to be located, meet*	**sentarse (ie)**	*to sit down*
enfadarse (con)	*to get angry*	**sentirse (ie)**	*to feel*
engañarse	*to be mistaken*	**vestirse (i)**	*to get dressed*
enojarse	*to become angry*	**volverse (ue)**	*to become*
equivocarse	*to be mistaken*		

Manuela is getting into some mischief today. Read what she's doing in the following exercise sentences and insert the reflexive pronoun **se** only if it's necessary because Manuela is performing an action upon herself. Here's an example to get you started:

Q. Lava _____ el coche con agua sucia y después _____ lava.

A. Lava el coche con agua sucia y después **se** lava.

1. _____ afeita y después _____ al perro.

2. _____ pone un impermeable y después _____ su gato en la bañera.

3. _____ maquilla a su hermana menor y después _____ maquilla.

4. _____ despierta a las tres de la mañana y después _____ despierta a su familia.

5. _____ viste a su prima en ropa de niña y después _____ viste.

6. Ella rompe _____ el juguete de su hermana y después _____ rompe la pierna.

Using Reflexive Verbs in Special Cases

Some situations in Spanish call for special reflexive constructions. For instance, you may use a plural reflexive construction if you want to convey an English reciprocal action that expresses "one another" or "each other." Here's the simple way to construct this:

> **Nos respetamos.** (*We respect one another [each other].*)

> **Se abrazan.** (*They hug one another [each other].*)

To clarify or reinforce the meaning of the reflexive pronoun in a reciprocal construction, you can add these singular forms: **uno a otro** (**una a otra**) or **el uno al otro** (**la una a la otra**) (*one another [each other]*). Or you can add these plural forms: **unos a otros** (**unas a otras**) or **los unos a los otros** (**las unas a las otras**) (*each other*).

> **Las muchachas se miran.** (*The girls look at each other [at themselves].*)

> **Ellas se miran (una a otra) la una a la otra.** (*They look at each other.*)

For more on adding reflexive pronouns, see the later section "Implementing Reflexive Pronouns."

Estela and Luis will be married soon. Express how they're acting by creating reciprocal constructions based on the information I provide. Here's an example:

Q. repestarse

A. **Ellos se respetan.**

7. amarse _____

8. hablarse todo el tiempo _____

9. abrazarse a menudo _____

10. mirarse con cariño _____

11. besarse mucho _____

12. casarse dentro de poco _____

You use the *passive voice* when the subject, instead of performing an action, is acted upon by another person or thing. Normally, you avoid the passive voice in Spanish just as you do in English. In certain cases, however, the passive can really come in handy.

You may use reflexive verbs in Spanish to express the passive voice when the English subject is a thing (not a person) and when the person performing the action isn't indicated. To form the passive with a reflexive verb, use the third person reflexive pronoun **se** and the third-person singular (**él, ella, Ud.**) or third person plural (**ellos, ellas, Uds.**) form of the present tense. You'll undoubtedly recognize the reflexive construction in this first example:

Aquí se habla español. (*Spanish is spoken here.*)

Se venden periódicos allá. (*They sell newspapers over there.*)

Write down what happens in a restaurant in Spanish by using the passive reflexive construction. Complete the parts I give you with the proper pronoun and verb conjugation. Here's an example:

Q. prohibir salir sin pagar

A. **Se prohibe** salir sin pagar. (*You can't leave without paying.* [Literally: *It is prohibited to leave without paying.*])

13. comer queso al fin de la comida

_____

14. beber vino blanco con el pescado

_____

15. poner la mesa con un mantel

_____

16. sacar su foto

_____

17. preparar la comida en la cocina

_____

18. abrir el restaurante todos los días

_____

Considering Verbs with Special Reflexive Meanings

As I say earlier in this chapter, some Spanish verbs can be reflexive or not, depending upon whom the subject is acting. Well, now you must become familiar with other Spanish verbs that have special meanings, depending on whether or not they're used reflexively. Be careful when you use the verbs in Table 11-2 (letters in parentheses indicate a spelling change).

Table 11-2	Spanish Verbs with Different Reflexive Meanings		
General Form	*General Meaning*	*Reflexive Form*	*Reflexive Meaning*
aburrir	*to bore*	**aburrirse**	*to become bored*
acordar (ue)	*to agree*	**acordarse de (ue)**	*to remember*
acostar (ue)	*to put to bed*	**acostarse (ue)**	*to go to bed*
bañar	*to bathe (someone)*	**bañarse**	*to bathe oneself*
cansar	*to tire*	**cansarse**	*to become tired*
colocar	*to place (something)*	**colocarse**	*to place oneself; to get a job*
dormir (ue)	*to sleep*	**dormirse (u)**	*to fall asleep*
enfadar	*to anger, irritate*	**enfadarse (con)**	*to get angry, annoyed*
engañar	*to deceive*	**engañarse**	*to be mistaken*
esconder	*to hide (something)*	**esconderse**	*to hide oneself*
ir	*to go*	**irse**	*to go away*
levantar	*to raise (something)*	**levantarse**	*to get up*
llamar	*to call*	**llamarse**	*to be called, to call oneself*

General Form	General Meaning	Reflexive Form	Reflexive Meaning
parar	*to stop (something)*	pararse	*to stop oneself*
poner	*to put (something)*	ponerse	*to put (something on), to become, to place oneself*
quitar	*to remove*	quitarse	*to take off*
sentar (ie)	*to seat*	sentarse (ie)	*to sit down*

Here are two examples that show you how the meanings of these verbs differ when you use them reflexively and non-reflexively:

> **La profesora se sienta después de sentar los alumnos por orden alfabético.** (*The teacher sits after seating the students in alphabetical order.*)

> **Ella llama a su amiga que se llama Emilia.** (*She calls her friend whose name is Emilia.*)

You're spending the day at the movies with your friend, Juan. Complete the following sentences with the correct form of the verb I provide (reflexive or non-reflexive) and a reflexive pronoun, if necessary. Here's an example:

Q. (levantar/levantarse) Yo _____ tarde.

A. Yo **me levanto** tarde. (*I get up late.*)

19. (llamar/llamarse) Yo _____ a Juan.

20. (ir/irse) Él quiere _____ al cine.

21. (duchar/ducharse) Antes, yo tengo que _____.

22. (parar/pararse) El autobús _____ delante del cine.

23. (sentar/sentarse) Nosotros _____ enfrente de la pantalla.

24. (dormir/dormirse) Cuando empieza la película Juan _____.

You're writing an e-mail to a pen pal about what you do on a typical school day. Translate the following English sentences into Spanish. Be careful! Not all the verbs are reflexive. Remember to write your answers in first person.

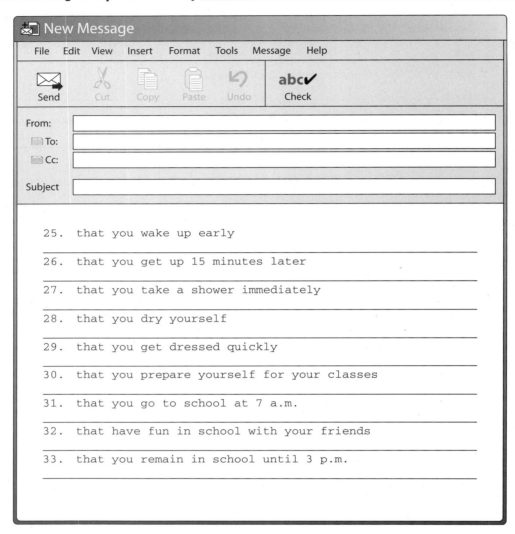

25. that you wake up early

26. that you get up 15 minutes later

27. that you take a shower immediately

28. that you dry yourself

29. that you get dressed quickly

30. that you prepare yourself for your classes

31. that you go to school at 7 a.m.

32. that have fun in school with your friends

33. that you remain in school until 3 p.m.

Using Reflexive Pronouns

You always conjugate a reflexive verb with the reflexive pronoun that agrees with the subject. Generally, these pronouns, like the direct and indirect object pronouns you study in Chapter 10, precede the conjugated verbs. The verb conjugation isn't affected by the use of the pronoun. Table 11-3 shows example verbs and the reflexive pronoun for each subject.

Reflexive pronouns are exactly the same as direct and indirect object pronouns except for the third-person singular and plural (**se**) forms. Because you use **se** when double object pronouns appear in a sentence (see Chapter 10), it should be relatively easy to remember to use it as the reflexive pronoun:

Ella se llama Mariana. (*Her name is Mariana.*)

Table 11-3	Properly Using Reflexive Pronouns		
Infinitive	*Subject*	*Reflexive Pronoun*	*Verb*
dormirse (ue) (*to fall asleep*)	yo	**me**	**duermo**
despertarse (ie) (*to wake up*)	tú	**te**	**despiertas**
desvestirse (i) (*to undress*)	él, ella, Ud.	**se**	**desviste**
relajarse (*to relax*)	nosostros	**nos**	**relajamos**
callarse (*to be silent*)	vosotros	**os**	**calláis**
marcharse (*to go away*)	ellos, ellas, Uds.	**se**	**marchan**

Here are some examples that show you how to use these reflexive pronouns:

¿De qué se queja Ud? (*What are you complaining about?*)

Me quejo de los precios. (*I'm complaining about the prices.*)

¿A qué hora se acuestan los niños? (*At what time do the children go to bed?*)

Los niños se acuestan a las nueve. (*The children go to bed at nine o'clock.*)

To negate a reflexive verb, you put **no** or the proper negative word (see Chapter 5) before the reflexive pronoun:

¿Se enoja Ud. a menudo? (*Do you often get angry?*)

No, no me enojo a menudo. (*No, I don't get angry often.*)

Nunca me enojo. (*I never get angry.*)

No me enojo nunca. (*I never get angry.*)

You're writing a journal entry in which you talk about your bad habits and those of your acquaintances. I provide the subject and the reflexive verb and you provide the reflexive pronoun and conjugate the verb. Here's an example:

Q. yo/acostarse tarde

A. Yo **me acuesto** tarde. (*I go to bed late.*)

34. Isabel y yo/preocuparse de todo

_____

35. Gloria/enfadarse fácilmente

_____

36. mis hermanos/equivocarse a menudo

_____

37. yo/reírse de mis amigos

_____

38. tú/quejarse de vez en cuando

_____

39. vosotros/dormirse en clase

_____

Properly Placing Reflexive Pronouns

Just like with direct and indirect object pronouns (see Chapter 10), you generally place reflexive pronouns before the conjugated verbs:

> **Me aplico en la clase de español.** (*I apply myself in Spanish class.*)
>
> **¿Por qué te pones enojado?** (*Why are you becoming angry?*)
>
> **Ella no se siente bien.** (*She doesn't feel well.*)

In sentences with two verbs that follow one subject (as in the first two examples that follow [see Chapter 4]) or in sentences with a gerund (as in the second two examples that follow [see Chapter 6]), you have the choice of placing the reflexive pronoun before the conjugated verb or after and attached to the infinitive or the gerund. When you attach the pronoun to a gerund, an accent is required on the stressed vowel:

> **(No) Voy a maquillarme.** (*I'm [not] going to put on my make-up.*)
>
> **(No) Me voy a maquillar.** (*I'm [not] going to put on my make-up.*)
>
> **(No) Estoy maquillándome.** (*I am [not] putting on my make-up.*)
>
> **(No) Me estoy maquillando.** (*I am [not] putting on my make-up.*)

Did you notice the accent I added in the third sentence from the previous list, when the pronoun was attached to the gerund? In general, to correctly place this accent, count back three vowels and add the accent:

> **Ella (no) está peinándose.** (*She [isn't] combing her hair.*)
>
> **Ella (no) se está peinando.** (*She [isn't] combing her hair.*)

A negative (see Chapter 5) goes before the pronoun when it precedes the verb:

> **(No) Voy a maquillarme.** (*I'm [not] going to put on my make-up.*)
>
> **(No) Me voy a maquillar.** (*I'm [not] going to put on my make-up.*)

Write a journal entry in which you state what each person wants to do under the given circumstances. Conjugate the first verb I provide in the present tense, and leave the second verb in its infinitive form. In your first sentence, place the correct reflexive pronoun before the conjugated present-tense verb form. In your second sentence, place the correct reflexive pronoun after the infinitive and attached to it. Here's an example that illustrates these instructions:

Q. Ella tiene miedo. (querer/esconderse)

A. **Se quiere esconder. Quiere esconderse.** (*She wants to hide [herself].*)

40. Yo tengo sueño. (querer/acostarse)

_____

41. Nosotros tenemos hombre. (deber/prepararse el desayuno*)*

_____

42. Tú estás sucio. (ir a/bañarse)

_____

43. Alberto está mojado. (pensar/secarse)

_____

44. Las muchachas están cansadas. (poder/sentarse)

_____

45. Uds. están enfermos. (preferir/quedarse en casa)

_____

Did you see what just happened? Write down in your journal what the people around you are doing. For this exercise, you conjugate the verb **estar** (*to be*) in the present tense and put the verb I provide in its gerund form. In your first sentence, place the correct reflexive pronoun before the conjugated present tense form of **estar**. In your second sentence, place the correct reflexive pronoun after the gerund and attached to it. Here's an example:

Q. Ellos acaban de disputar con su amigo. (pelearse)

A. **Se están peleando. Están peleándose.**

46. Yo acabo de oír truenos y de ver relámpagos. (esconderse)

_____

47. Susana acaba de recibir una invitación al cine. (vestirse)

_____

48. Los muchachos acaban de jugar al fútbol en el lodo. (ducharse)

_____

49. Tú acabas de derramar jugo de uva en tus panatalones. (cambiarse de ropa)

_____

50. Nosotros acabamos de oír sonar el timbre de la puerta. (levantarse)

_____

51. Uds. acaban de terminar su tarea. (relajarse)

_____

When used with a command, a reflexive pronoun (just like a direct or indirect object pronoun) precedes a negative command and follows (and is attached to) an affirmative command (formal or informal):

Láve<u>se</u>. (Láva<u>te</u>.) (_Wash yourself._)

No <u>se</u> lave. (No <u>te</u> laves.) (_Don't wash yourself._)

General rules about placement are: When one pronoun is attached, count back three vowels and add an accent:

Acuésta<u>te</u> temprano. (_Go to bed early._)

When two pronouns are attached, count back four vowels and add an accent:

Póngaselo. (_Put it on._)

You're on a class trip. Write down the instructions your teacher gives to you and your classmates. I give you a yes or no clue to show you whether the command is affirmative or negative. Change the reflexive verb to an affirmative or negative command, and add accent marks as necessary. Here's an example:

_0._ (no) pasearse por el parque

_A._ No **se paseen** Uds. por el parque.

_0._ (sí) sentarse

_A._ **Siéntense** Uds.

52. (sí) quedarse en grupos de dos _____

53. (no) irse sin permiso_____

54. (no) tardarse en el baño _____

55. (sí) fiarse en mí _____

56. (no) ponerse nerviosos _____

57. (sí) divertirse mucho _____

Answer Key

1 **se/—**. In the first action, she's shaving herself, and in the second action, she's shaving the dog.

2 **se/—**. In the first action, she's putting on a raincoat, and in the second action, she's putting her cat in the bathtub.

3 **—/se**. In the first action, she's putting make-up on her younger sister, and in the second action, she's putting make-up on herself.

4 **se/—**. In the first action, she's waking up at 3 a.m., and in the second action, she's waking her family.

5 **—/se**. In the first action, she's dressing her cousin in girls' clothing, and in the second action, she's dressing herself.

6 **—/se**. In the first action, she's breaking her sister's toy, and in the second action, she's breaking her own leg.

7 Ellos **se aman.** (*They love each other.*)

8 Ellos **se hablan** todo el tiempo. (*They speak to each other all the time.*)

9 Ellos **se abrazan** a menudo. (*They hug each other often.*)

10 Ellos **se miran** con cariño. (*They look at each other affectionately.*)

11 Ellos **se besan** mucho. (*They kiss each other a lot.*)

12 Ellos **se casan** dentro de poco. (*They get married to each other within a short time.*)

13 **Se come** queso al fin de la comida. (*Cheese is eaten at the end of the meal.*)

14 **Se bebe** vino blanco con el pescado. (*White wine is drunk with fish.*)

15 **Se pone** la mesa con un mantel. (*The table is set with a tablecloth.*)

16 **Se saca** su foto. (*They take your photograph.*)

17 **Se prepara** la comida en la cocina. (*The food is prepared in the kitchen.*)

18 **Se abre** el restaurante todos los días. (*The restaurant is open every day.*)

19 **llamo.** The subject isn't acting upon itself.

20 **ir.** The subject isn't acting upon itself.

21 **ducharme.** The subject is acting upon itself.

22 **se para.** The subject is acting upon itself.

23 **nos sentamos.** The subject is acting upon itself.

24 **se duerme.** The subject is acting upon itself. (***Note:* Dormir** is a verb with an **o** to **ue** stem change.)

25 **Me despierto temprano. Despertarse** is a verb with an **e** to **ie** stem change.

26 **Me levanto quince minutos después.**

27 **Me ducho inmediatamente.**

28 **Me seco.**

29 **Me visto rápidamente. Vestirse** is a verb with an **e** to **i** stem change.

30 **Me preparo para mis (las) clases.**

31 **Voy a la escuela a las siete de la mañana.** A reflexive isn't needed because the meaning is *to go* and not *to go away.*

32 **Me divierto en la escuela con mis amigos. Divertirse** is a verb with an **e** to **ie** stem change.

33 **Me quedo en la escuela hasta las tres de la tarde.**

34 Isabel y yo **nos preocupamos** de todo. (*Isabel and I worry about everything.*)

35 Gloria **se enfada** fácilmente. (*Gloria gets angry easily.*)

36 Mis hermanos **se equivocan** a menudo. (*My brothers are often wrong.*)

37 Yo **me río** de mis amigos. (*I laugh at my friends.*) **Reír** is an irregular verb.

38 Tú **te quejas** de vez en cuando. (*You complain from time to time.*)

39 Vosotros **os durmís** en clase. (*You fall asleep in class.*)

40 **Me quiero acostar. Quiero acostarme.** (*I want to go to bed.*) **Querer** is a verb with an **e** to **ie** stem change.

41 **Nos debemos preparar el desayuno. Debemos prepararnos el desayuno.** (*We have to prepare breakfast for ourselves.*)

42 **Te vas a bañar. Vas a bañarte.** (*You are going to bathe yourself.*) **Ir** is an irregular verb.

43 **Se piensa secar. Piensa secarse.** (*He thinks about drying himself.*) **Pensar** is a verb with an **e** to **ie** stem change.

44 **Se pueden sentar. Pueden sentarse.** (*They can sit down.*) **Poder** is a verb with an **o** to **ue** stem change.

45 **Se prefieren quedar** en casa. **Prefieren quedarse** en casa. (*You prefer to remain at home.*) **Preferir** is a verb with an **e** to **ie** stem change.

46 **Me estoy escondiendo. Estoy escondiéndome.** (*I am hiding [myself].*)

47 **Se está vistiendo. Está vistiéndose.** (*She is getting dressed.*) **Vestir** is a verb with an **e** to **i** stem change.

48 **Se están duchando. Están duchándose.** (*They are taking a shower.*)

49 **Te estás cambiando** de ropa. **Estás cambiándote** de ropa. (*You are changing your clothing.*)

50 **Nos estamos levantando. Estamos levantándonos.** (*We are getting up.*)

51 **Se están relajando. Están relajándose.** (*You are relaxing.*)

52 **Quédense Uds.** en grupos de dos. (*Remain in groups of two.*)

53 **No se vayan Uds.** sin permiso. (*Don't go away without permission.*)

54 **No se tarden Uds.** en el baño. (*Don't take too long in the bathroom.*)

55 **Fíense** en mí. (*Trust me.*)

56 **No se pongan** nerviosos. (*Don't get nervous.*) **Poner** is an irregular **-go** verb.

57 **Diviértanse** mucho. (*Have a lot of fun.*) **Divertir** is a verb with an **e** to **ie** stem change.

Chapter 12

Preparing to Connect with Prepositions

*P*repositions are words used before nouns or pronouns to relate them to other words in the sentence. Think of prepositions as words that join different words, clauses, or phrases. Have you ever heard of a dangling preposition? Writing a sentence with one is a big no-no among grammarians. Here's an example: "That's the car I'm dreaming *about.*" Why is this sentence grammatically incorrect? Because prepositions should always be followed by objects to create prepositional phrases. How should the sentence read? "That's the car *about* which I'm dreaming." Yes, it definitely sounds awkward, but that's the proper way to express that thought.

In this chapter I introduce you to common Spanish prepositions and I explain how to select the most appropriate preposition for your sentence. Certain Spanish verbs require a preposition before an infinitive, so being familiar with them will enhance your speaking and writing skills. Also, you find out about the pronouns that follow prepositions. By the time you finish this chapter, the quality of your Spanish connections should be excellent!

Reviewing Common Spanish Prepositions

Prepositions should be followed by objects to create prepositional phrases. Prepositions relate elements in a sentence: noun to noun, verb to verb, or verb to noun/pronoun. Prepositions also may contract with articles: **a** + **el** = **al** and **de** + **el** = **del** (see Chapter 4).

The following examples show how prepositions work in different sentences:

✔ Noun to noun: Necesito esa hoja **de** papel. (*I need that piece **of** paper.*)

✔ Verb to verb: El niño empieza **a** reír. (*The child begins **to** laugh.*)

✔ Verb to noun: Ella estudia **con** sus amigas. (*She studies **with** her friends.*)

✔ Verb to pronoun: ¿Qué piensas **de** ellos? (*What do you think **about** them?*)

You use prepositions before the names of geographical locations to refer to travel and location:

> Mi familia está **en** Puerto Rico. (*My family is **in** Puerto Rico.*)
>
> Voy **a** España. (*I'm going **to** Spain.*)

I list the Spanish prepositions that you'll find most useful in your sentences in Table 12-1.

Table 12-1	Common Spanish Prepositions		
Preposition	*Meaning*	*Preposition*	*Meaning*
a	to, at	detrás de	behind
a eso de (+ time)	about (time)	durante	during
a fuerza de	by persevering	en	in, on, by
a pesar de	in spite of	en cambio	on the other hand
a tiempo	on time	en casa de	at the house of
a través (de)	across, through	en lugar de	instead of
acerca de	about	en vez de	instead of
además de	besides	encima de	above, on top of
alrededor de	around	enfrente de	opposite, in front of
antes (de)	before	entre	between
cerca de	near	frente a	in front of
con	with	fuera de	outside of
contra	against	hacia	toward
de	of, from, about	hasta	until
de otro modo	otherwise	lejos de	far
debajo de	beneath, under	por	for, by
delante de	in front of	para	for
dentro de	inside, within	según	according to
desde	since	sin	without
después (de)	after	sobre	over, above, on, upon

Here are more examples to show you prepositions at work in Spanish:

> **La farmacia está cerca del supermercado.** (*The pharmacy is near the supermarket.*)
>
> **A fuerza de estudiar Ud. saldrá bien.** (*By studying you will succeed.*)

Manuel is writing an e-mail to a friend. In the e-mail, he states what he does when he leaves the office. Complete his e-mail with the missing prepositions, using each preposition only once:

a	al	antes de	cerca de	con	de
dentro de	después de	en	enfrente de	entre	para

New Message

File   Edit   View   Insert   Format   Tools   Message   Help

Send   Cut   Copy   Paste   Undo   abc✔
                                        Check

From: _____

📧 To: _____

📧 Cc: _____

Subject _____

No vivo _____ (1) mi oficina. Por eso, _____(2) ir_____(3) casa tomo el autobús. Afortunadamente, el autobús se para _____ (4) de mi casa. Cuando llego y_____(5) entrar, saco mis llaves_____ (6) mi bolsillo y abro la puerta._____(7) de entrar, pongo todo lo que llevo_____ (8) la mesa y hablo_____ (9) mi hermano. Entonces voy_____(10) comedor que está situado _____(11) la cocina y la sala. _____(12) cinco minutos ceno.

Distinguishing One Preposition from Another

Sometimes, selecting the correct preposition to use in a sentence can be tricky, because some prepositions have more than one meaning. Take **a,** for example, which can mean *to* or *at;* **en,** which can mean *at* or *in;* and **por** and **para,** which can both mean *for.* I'm sure you can see the dilemma. Fortunately, Spanish has some rules that will help you understand when the more common prepositions are appropriate.

A

I'll start with the preposition **a** (which contracts with the definite article **el** to become **al**). You use **a** to show

✔ Time: **Te llamo a las tres.** (*I'll call you at 3 o'clock.*)

✔ Movement: **Vamos a la playa.** (*We're going to the beach.*)

✔ Location: **Espere a la entrada.** (*Wait at the entrance.*)

✔ Means/manner: **Hágalo a mano.** (*Do it by hand.*) **Se prepara a la española.** (*It's prepared the Spanish way.*)

✔ Price: **Puede comprarlo a cien pesos.** (*You can buy it for 100 pesos.*)

✔ Speed: **Iba a cien kilómetros por hora.** (*He was going 1,000 km per hour.*)

You use the preposition **a** before a direct object alluding to a person; this is referred to as the *personal a* (see Chapter 10):

Buscamos al señor Nuñez. (*We are looking for Mr. Nuñez.*)

De

Another preposition with several meanings is **de** (which contracts with the definite article **el** to become **del**). You use **de,** which means *of, from,* or *about* to show:

✔ Possession: **Es el coche de Julio.** (*It's Julio's car.*)

✔ Origin: **Soy de Panamá.** (*I'm from Panama.*)

✔ Time: **No duerme de noche.** (*He doesn't sleep at night.*)

✔ Cause: **Fracasa de no estudiar.** (*He is failing from not studying.*)

✔ Material: **Es un anillo de oro.** (*It's a gold ring.*)

✔ Characteristics: **Es de buena calidad.** (*It's of a good quality.*)

✔ Contents: **Bebo una taza de café.** (*I'm drinking a cup of coffee.*)

✔ Relationship: **Madrid es la capital de España.** (*Madrid is the capital of Spain.*)

✔ Part of a whole: **Toma un trozo de pan.** (*She's taking a piece of bread.*)

✔ A subject: **No encuentro mi libro de arte.** (*I can't find my art book.*)

✔ A superlative: **Es el más alto de todos.** (*He's the tallest of them all.*)

En and hasta

The preposition **en** can mean *in, by,* or *on.* You use **en** to show

✔ Time: **Estamos en el otoño.** (*It's [We're in the] fall.*)

✔ Location: **Está en esa calle.** (*It's on that street.*)

✔ Means/manner: **Hable en voz baja.** (*Speak in a low voice.*) **Está escrita en español.** (*It's written in Spanish.*)

✔ Movement: **Entran en el banco.** (*They enter the bank.*)

✔ Means of transport: **Viajan en avión.** (*They are traveling by plane.*)

The preposition **hasta,** which means *until* (but which also can have the meaning *to*), shows the following:

✔ Place/location: **Conduzca hasta el semáforo.** (*Drive to the traffic light.*)

✔ Time: **Hasta luego.** (*See you later.* [*Until then.*])

Por and para

Now you come to two prepositions that can cause much confusion among students of Spanish. **Por** and **para** both mean *for* in English, which is what causes the problem. You study the explanations regarding their different uses in the following text, after which you should have a good idea of how to use each of these prepositions properly.

The preposition **para** shows the following:

- ✔ Destination/place: **Salimos para Madrid.** (*We are leaving for Madrid.*)
- ✔ Destination/person: **Esto es para Ud.** (*This is for you.*)
- ✔ A future time limit: **Es para mañana.** (*It's for tomorrow.*)
- ✔ Purpose/goal: **Nado para divertirme.** (*I swim to have fun.*)
- ✔ Use/function: **Es un cepillo para el pelo.** (*It's a hair brush.*)
- ✔ Comparisons: **Para su edad, lee bien.** (*For her age, she reads well.*)
- ✔ Opinion: **Para mí es demasiado crudo.** (*For me it's too rare.*)

The preposition **por** shows the following:

- ✔ Motion/place: **Caminan por las calles.** (*They walk through the streets.*)
- ✔ Means/manner: **Lo envío por correo aéreo.** (*I'm sending it by air-mail.*)
- ✔ In exchange for/substitution: **Voy a hacerlo por tí.** (*I'm going to do it for you.*)
- ✔ Duration of an action: **Trabajo por una hora.** (*I'm working for an hour.*)
- ✔ Indefinite time period: **Duerme por la tarde.** (*He sleeps in the afternoon.*)
- ✔ On behalf of: **La firmo por Ud.** (*I am signing it on your behalf.*)
- ✔ Per: **Me pagan por día.** (*They pay me per day.*)

If you're speaking about a means of transportation for a passenger, use **en** rather than **por** to express *by:*

> **Van a la capital en tren.** (*They are going to the capital by train.*)

You use **por** to express *for* after the verbs **enviar** (*to send*), **ir** (*to go*), **mandar** (*to order, send*), **preguntar** (*to ask*), **regresar** (*to return*), **venir** (*to come*), and **volver** (*to return*). Here are two examples:

> **Voy (Envío, Pregunto) por la factura.** (*I am going [sending, asking] for the bill.*)

> **Ven (Regresa, Vuelve) por tu libro.** (*Come [Return, Come back] for your book.*)

You also use **por** in the following adverbial expressions:

- ✔ **por eso** (*therefore, so*)

  Trabaja mucho y por eso gana mucho dinero. (*He works a lot and therefore he earns a lot of money.*)
- ✔ **por lo general** (*generally*)

  Por lo general me acuesto a las diez. (*Generally I go to bed at 10 o'clock.*)
- ✔ **por supuesto** (*of course*)

  ¿Puede Ud. ayudarme? ¡Por supuesto! (*Can you help me? Of course!*)

You're on vacation in Puerto Rico, and you're writing a postcard home to a friend. Complete the postcard with the correct proposition:

a (al)   de   en

hasta   para   por

This is a handmade post-card from the art studio of
Fernando

Postcard

Place
Stamp
Here

Rodrigo,

Estoy_____(13) San Juan. Es la capital
_____(14) Puerto Rico. Voy_____(15) la
playa todos los días._____(16)
divertirme hablo_____(17) todo el
mundo. No me quedo_____(18) sol
porque no quiero sufrir_____(19) una
quemadura de sol. Compré dos botellas_____
(20) bronceador_____(21) diez dólares
cada una. Nado_____(22) el mar
cada día_____(23) una hora_____
(24) hacer ejecicio. Cada noche salgo_____
(25) las nueve y no regreso_____(26) el
dos_____(27) la mañana. Voy_____
(28) quedarme aquí en San Juan_____
(29) el tres de junio._____(30) luego.

Fernando

Focusing on Prepositions Used with Infinitives

The only verb form in the Spanish language that may follow a preposition is an infinitive. Some Spanish verbs require the preposition **a, de, en,** or **con** before the infinitive. Other Spanish verbs are followed immediately by the infinitive and don't require a preposition. The following sections break down all the categories for you.

Spanish verbs requiring a

How can you tell which verbs require the preposition **a** before the infinitive? Generally, verbs that express beginning, motion, teaching, or learning take **a**. There are, however, many other verbs that use this preposition before an infinitive. So the best answer to the question is that you have to memorize these verbs. After you've used them often enough, however, you'll develop the instinctive feeling that **a** is the preposition of choice. Table 12-2 shows which Spanish verbs call for the use of **a** before the infinitive. (Stem changes are shown in parentheses.)

Table 12-2	Spanish Verbs Requiring a
Infinitive	*Meaning*
acercarse	*to approach*
acostumbrarse	*to become accustomed to*
aprender	*to learn to*
apresurarse	*to hurry to*
aspirar	*to aspire to*
atreverse	*to dare to*
ayudar	*to help to*
comenzar (ie)	*to begin to*
convidar	*to invite*
correr	*to run to*
decidirse	*to decide to*
dedicarse	*to devote oneself to*
disponerse	*to get ready to*
empezar (ie)	*to begin to*
enseñar	*to teach to*
ir	*to go*
llegar	*to succeed in*
negarse (ie)	*to refuse to*
obligar	*to force to*
ponerse	*to begin to*
regresar	*to return to*
resignarse	*to resign oneself to*
salir	*to go out to*
venir (ie)	*to come to*
volver (ue)	*to return (again) to*

Here are some examples that show how you use the preposition **a:**

> **Los niños se apresuran a llegar a tiempo.** (*The children hurry to arrive on time.*)

> **No empieza a llorar.** (*Don't start to cry.*)

Spanish verbs requiring de

The list of verbs requiring **de** before an infinitive is much shorter than the list for those verbs requiring **a.** I can't give you any hard and fast rules to help you with these. You simply have to memorize them and use them as much as possible. Table 12-3 lists the Spanish verbs that are followed by **de** before an infinitive.

Table 12-3	Spanish Verbs Requiring de
Infinitive	*Meaning*
acabar	*to have just done something*
acordarse (ue)	*to remember to*
alegarse	*to be glad*
cesar	*to stop*
dejar	*to stop*
encargarse	*to take charge of*
olvidarse	*to forget*
tratar	*to try to*

Examples showing you how to use **de** before an infinitive follow:

Mi mejor amiga dejó de fumar. (*My best friend stopped smoking.*)

Mi esposo siempre olivida de sacar la basura. (*My husband always forgets to take out the garbage.*)

Spanish verbs requiring en

The list of verbs that require **en** before an infinitive is even shorter than the others, thankfully! Again, you must commit them to memory to know when to use them. Table 12-4 lists the Spanish verbs that are followed by **en** before an infinitive.

Table 12-4	Spanish Verbs Requiring en
Infinitive	*Meaning*
consentir (ie)	*to agree to*
consistir	*to consist of*
convenir (ie)	*to agree to*
insistir	*to insist on*
tardar	*to delay in*

These examples illustrate how you use **en** before an infinitive:

> **Yo consiento en ir al teatro con Ramón.** (*I agree to go to the theater with Ramón.*)
>
> **¿Por qué insistes en partir ahora?** (*Why do you insist on leaving now?*)

Spanish verbs requiring con

The good news? As you move through all the preposition tables, your memorization duties get shorter and shorter! Table 12-5 shows the Spanish verbs that use **con** before an infinitive.

Table 12-5	Spanish Verbs Requiring con
Infinitive	*Meaning*
contar (ue)	*to count on*
soñar (ue)	*to dream of*
amenazar	*to threaten*

Here are examples with verbs that require **con** before the infinitive:

> **Él cuenta con trabajar con nosotros.** (*He is counting on working with us.*)
>
> **Yo sueño con salir con él.** (*I am dreaming about going out with him.*)

Spanish verbs requiring no preposition

What's that? You thought your memorization duties were over? Actually, you have one more important list that you need to study. Table 12-6 presents a list of verbs that don't require a preposition and are followed immediately by the infinitive.

Table 12-6	Verbs That Require No Preposition
Infinitive	*Meaning*
deber	*to must (have to)*
dejar	*to allow to*
desear	*to want, wish to*
esperar	*to hope to*
hacer	*to make (have something done)*
lograr	*to succeed in*
necesitar	*to need to*
oír	*to hear*
pensar (ie)	*to intend to*

(continued)

Table 12-6 (continued)

Infinitive	Meaning
poder (ue)	to be able to
preferir (ie)	to prefer to
pretender	to attempt to
prometer	to promise to
querer (ie)	to want, to wish to
saber	to know how to
ver	to see

Example sentences containing verbs that require no preposition before the infinitive follow:

> **Pensamos hacer un viaje pronto.** (*We plan to take a trip soon.*)

> **Sé tricotar.** (*I know how to knit.*)

You're conducting an interview with a famous Spanish actress for your Spanish club's newsletter. You've taken notes on her responses, but now you have to complete your sentences by conjugating the verbs and joining the elements with prepositions, if needed (for more on verb conjugation, see Chapter 4). Here are some examples:

Q. me/convenir/dar esta entrevista

A. Me **conviene en** dar esta entrevista. (*I agree to give this interview.*)

Q. querer/ser modelo para los jóvenes

A. **Quiero** ser modelo para los jóvenes. (*I want to be a model for young people.*)

31. insistir/dar muchas entrevistas

_____

32. acabar/hacer una nueva película

_____

33. pensar/hacer muchas películas

_____

34. consentir/leer todos los manuscritos que recibo

_____

35. aprender/bailar mejor

_____

36. saber/hablar tres idiomas extranjeros

_____

37. dedicarse/ayudar a todo el mundo

_____

38. llegar/ser famosa

_____

39. esperar/ganar mucho dinero

_____

40. tratar/contestar bien a sus preguntas

_____

Using Prepositional Pronouns

You must use certain special Spanish pronouns after prepositions. The prepositional pronoun is used as the object of a preposition and always follows the preposition. Table 12-7 presents these prepositional pronouns.

Table 12-7	Prepositional Pronouns
Singular	*Plural*
mí (*me*)	**nosotros** (**nosotras**) (*us;* polite)
ti (*you;* familiar)	**vosotros** (**vosotras**) (*you;* familiar)
él (*him, it;* masculine)	**ellos** (*them;* masculine)
ella (*her, it;* feminine)	**ellas** (*them;* feminine)
Ud. (*you;* formal/polite)	**Uds.** (*you;* formal/polite)
sí (*yourself, himself, herself, itself*)	**sí** (*yourselves, themselves*)

Here are some examples that show how you'll use these pronouns:

Esta carta es para mí, no es para ella. (*This letter is for me, not for her.*)

Juego al tenis con él, no con ella. (*I play tennis with him, not with her.*)

Perhaps you've noticed that the pronouns that follow prepositions are the same as the subject pronouns I discuss in Chapter 4, except for **mí, ti,** and **sí.** (Good for you!)

You use the reflexive prepositional pronoun **sí** both in the singular to express *yourself, himself, herself,* or *itself* and in the plural to express *themselves* or *yourselves:*

Puedes sentarte detrás de mí. (*You can sit behind me.*)

Yo no quiero salir sin ti. (*I don't want to leave without you.*)

Logró preparar la comida por sí sola. (*She was able to prepare the meal by herself.*)

The prepositional pronouns **mí, ti,** and **sí** combine with the preposition **con** as follows:

- ✔ **conmigo:** *with me*
- ✔ **contigo:** *with you*
- ✔ **consigo:** *with him/her/you/them*

The following list presents some examples of these words:

¿Puedes ir al cine conmigo? (*Can you go to the movies with me?*)

No puedo ir contigo. (*I can't go with you.*)

Siempre lleva una cartera consigo. (*She always carries a wallet with her.*)

To express *himself, herself, yourself, yourselves,* and *themselves,* you add the adjective **mismo** (**misma, mismos, mismas**) after **consigo:**

Él habla consigo mismo. (*He is talking with himself.*)

Your friend always annoyingly says the opposite of what you say. In the following exercise, write his sentences based upon what you said. Here's an example:

0. Nosotros vivimos cerca de Uds.

A. **Uds. viven cerca de nosotros.** (*You live near us.*)

41. Yo salgo con él.

_____

42. Ellas piensan en nosotros.

_____

43. Él compra un helado para ella.

_____

44. Vosotros habláis por mí.

_____

45. Nosotros recibimos un e-mail de él.

_____

46. Tú vas al estadio con ellas.

_____

Answer Key

1 cerca de

2 para

3 a

4 enfrente de

5 antes de

6 de

7 después de

8 en

9 con

10 al

11 entre

12 dentro de

13 en

14 de

15 a

16 para

17 a

18 al. A contracts with el to become al.

19 de

20 de

21 por

22 en

23 por

24 para

25 a

26 hasta

27   de

28   a

29   hasta

30   hasta

31   **Insisto en** dar muchas entrevistas. (*I insist on giving many interviews.*)

32   **Acabo de** hacer una película nueva. (*I just made a new film.*)

33   **Pienso en** hacer muchas películas. (*I intend to make many films.*)

34   **Consiento en** leer todos los manuscritos que recibo. (*I agree to read all the manuscripts that I receive.*)

35   **Aprendo a** bailar mejor. (*I am learning to dance better.*)

36   **Sé hablar** tres idiomas extranjeros. (*I know how to speak three foreign languages.*)

37   **Me dedico a** ayudar a todo el mundo. (*I am dedicated to helping everyone.*)

38   **Llego a** ser famosa. (*I am becoming famous.*)

39   **Espero** ganar mucho dinero. (*I hope to earn a lot of money.*)

40   **Trato de** contestar bien a sus preguntas. (*I am trying to answer your questions well.*)

41   **Él sale conmigo. Mí** joins with **con** to become **conmigo.** (*He goes out with me.*)

42   **Nosotros pensamos en ellas.** (*We are thinking about them.*)

43   **Ella compra un helado para él.** (*She buys an ice cream for him.*)

44   **Yo hablo por vosotros.** (*I speak for you.*)

45   **Él recibe un e-mail de nosotros.** (*He receives an e-mail from us.*)

46   **Ellas van al estadio contigo. Tí** joins with **con** to become **contigo.** (*They go to the stadium with you.*)

Part IV

Writing in the Past and in the Future

The 5th Wave   By Rich Tennant

@RICHTENNANT

I'm not sure what he's yelling about. It's all in Spanish. But I think he's calling you a monster.

In this part . . .

There's more to life than the present. Although the past is gone with the wind, I can think of many situations in which a student, a traveler, or a businessperson will have to use the past tense to express thoughts, ideas, or questions. This part presents the formation and use of the most commonly used past tenses in Spanish — from the preterit to the imperfect. And if you have hopes and dreams for the future, this part also helps you express them through the use of the present tense, expressions of the near future, and the future tense (for the distant future).

Chapter 13

Leaving It Completely in the Past

In This Chapter

▶ Forming the preterit of various types of verbs

▶ Using the preterit to express a past action

Some people look back on the past with fond memories. For others, however, the past is a time they'd like to forget! No matter how you feel about it, the past is a time that can help you learn and grow. In Spanish, several different tenses allow you to express past actions. One of them is the *preterit,* which expresses an action, event, or state of mind that occurred and was completed at a specific time in the past. (For example, *She closed her book* or *He caught the ball.*) In other words, if you had a digital camera, it would capture that moment instantly. If you remember that an action ended at a definite moment, you'll have no trouble using the preterit, and you won't get the preterit confused with another Spanish past tense you'll see in a later chapter.

In this chapter, I show you how to form the preterit of regular verbs, verbs with spelling changes, verb with stem changes, and irregular verbs. Along the way, I include helpful hints on how to remember the changes and irregularities you'll have to know and memorize. I also provide a detailed explanation on when to use the preterit so you won't make mistakes when the tense is called for and appropriate. By the end of this chapter, you'll be able to express what you did in the past — for better or for worse!

Forming the Preterit

Forming the preterit isn't as challenging as you may believe. All regular verbs and verbs with spelling and stem changes whose infinitives end in **-ar** have the same preterit endings. The same holds true for verbs whose infinitives end in **-er** and **-ir.** And all irregular verbs have the same endings, and most fall into categories that make them easy to digest. The following sections show you the way.

Regular verbs

Forming the preterit of regular verbs is rather easy, because although there are three different infinitive endings — **-ar, -er,** and **-ir** — you use only two different sets of endings for the preterit. Only **-ir** verbs with present tense stem changes undergo a change in the preterit, and there are just a few verbs with spelling changes.

To form the preterit of regular verbs, you drop the **-ar, -er,** or **-ir** infinitive ending and add the preterit endings. The following table shows the conjugation of an **-ar** verb:

mirar (*to look at*)	
yo mir**é**	nosotros mir**amos**
tú mir**aste**	vosotros mir**asteis**
él, ella, Ud. mir**ó**	ellos, ellas, Uds. mir**aron**
Yo miré la televisión. (*I watched television.*)	

Here's the conjugation of an **-er** verb:

beber (*to drink*)	
yo beb**í**	nosotros beb**imos**
tú beb**iste**	vosotros beb**isteis**
él, ella, Ud. beb**ió**	ellos, ellas, Uds. beb**ieron**
Él no bebió nada. (*He didn't drink anything.*)	

Finally, allow me to give you this **-ir** conjugation:

recibir (*to receive*)	
yo recib**í**	nosotros recib**imos**
tú recib**iste**	vosotros recib**isteis**
él, ella, Ud. recib**ió**	ellos, ellas, Uds. recib**ieron**
¿Qué recibiste? (*What did you receive?*)	

The **nosotros** preterit forms of **-ar** verbs and **-ir** verbs are the same as their present-tense forms:

> **Nosotros hablamos.** (*We speak; We spoke.*)

> **Nosotros subimos al ático.** (*We go up to the attic; We went up to the attic.*)

Here are some more examples that show you how to write a sentence by using the preterit tense:

- ✔ **Yo estudié el español.** (*I studied Spanish.*)
- ✔ **Todos los alumnos aprendieron mucho.** (*All the students learned a lot.*)
- ✔ **Mi amigo ecribió un poema en español.** (*My friend wrote a poem in Spanish.*)

You just got back from a vacation with a tour group. Express what different people did on the tour by giving the preterit of the verb indicated.

0. (beber) Tú _____ mucha agua y nosotros _____ mucho café.

A. Tú **bebiste** mucha agua y nosotros **bebimos** mucho café.

1. (comer) Yo _____ demasiado pero ella _____ poco.

2. (comprar) Vosotros _____ aretes y nosotros _____ relojes.

3. (correr) Nosotros _____ en el gimnasio y vosotros _____ en el campo.

4. (escribir) Tú _____ tarjetas postales y ellos _____ cartas.

5. (gastar) Tú _____ mucho dinero pero Juanita _____ poco.

6. (hablar) Yo _____ con todo el mundo pero ellos _____ con nadie.

Verbs with spelling changes

Only two categories of verbs have spelling changes in the preterit tense:

✔ Those with **-car, -gar,** and **-zar** endings (whose changes you see in Chapter 7 when dealing with the subjunctive)

✔ Those that have a vowel before their **-er** or **-ir** ending

The following sections dive into these changes.

Verbs ending in -car, -gar, and -zar

Verbs ending in **-car, -gar,** and **-zar** have the same change that they have in the subjunctive (see Chapter 7), but only in the **yo** form of the preterit. This is necessary to preserve the original sound of the verb. The following table presents a refresher course:

c changes to **qu**	**tocar** (*to touch*)	**yo toqué** (*I touched*)
g changes to **gu**	**jugar** (*to play*)	**yo jugué** (*I played*)
z changes to **c**	**empezar** (*to begin*)	**yo empecé** (*I began*)

Here are some example sentences that highlight these endings:

✔ **Yo expliqué el problema.** (*I explained the problem.*)

✔ **Yo llegué antes de ellos.** (*I arrived before them.*)

✔ **Yo almorcé con mis amigos.** (*I ate lunch with my friends.*)

Verbs that change i to y

Verbs that contain a vowel immediately preceding their **-er** or **-ir** ending change **i** to **y** in the third-person singular (**él, ella, Ud.**) and plural (**ellos, ellas, Uds.**) forms. All other forms have an accented i: **í.**

The **i** to **y** change doesn't hold true for the verb **traer** (*to bring*):

Él no trajó su pasaporte. (*He didn't bring his passport.*)

The tables that follow show high-frequency Spanish verbs that require the **i** to **y** change:

caer (*to fall*)	
yo caí	nosotros caí**mos**
tú caí**ste**	vosotros caí**steis**
él, ella, Ud. ca**yó**	ellos, ellas, Uds. ca**yeron**
El turista se cayó al lago. (*The tourist fell in the lake.*)	

creer (*to believe*)	
yo creí	nosotros creí**mos**
tú creí**ste**	vosotros creí**steis**
él, ella, Ud. cre**yó**	ellos, ellas, Uds. cre**yeron**
Ellos no me creyeron. (*They didn't believe me.*)	

leer (*to read*)	
yo leí	nosotros leí**mos**
tú leí**ste**	vosotros leí**steis**
él, ella, Ud. le**yó**	ellos, ellas, Uds. le**yeron**
¿Leyó Ud. este artículo? (*Did you read this article?*)	

oír (*to hear*)	
yo oí	nosotros oí**mos**
tú oí**ste**	vosotros oí**steis**
él, ella, Ud. o**yó**	ellos, ellas, Uds. o**yeron**
No oyeron nada. (*They didn't hear anything.*)	

Verbs ending in **-uir** (**concluir** [*to conclude*], **destruir** [*to destroy*], **sustituir** [*to substitute*], and so on) follow the **i** to **y** change, but they don't accent the **i** in the **tú**, **nosotros**, and **vosotros** forms. The following table presents an example:

concluir (*to conclude*)	
yo concluí	nosotros conclui**mos**
tú conclui**ste**	vosotros conclui**steis**
él, ella, Ud. conclu**yó**	ellos, ellas, Uds. conclu**yeron**
Ellos concluyeron sus estudios. (*They concluded their studies.*)	

Verbs with stem changes

The only verbs with stem changes in the preterit tense are **-ir** infinitive verbs that have a stem change in the present tense (see Chapter 4). Be careful, though! The change is different in the preterit tense than it is in the present. Here's how you form the preterit: Change **e** to **i** or **o** to **u** only in the third-person singular (**él, ella, Ud.**) and plural (**ellos, ellas, Uds.**) forms. The following tables show what these verbs look like in the preterit tense:

preferir (*to prefer*) — e **to** ie	
yo prefer**í**	nosotros prefer**imos**
tú prefer**iste**	vosotros prefer**isteis**
él, ella, Ud. pref**irió**	ellos, ellas, Uds. pref**irieron**
Ella prefirió quedarse en casa ese día. (*She preferred to stay home that day.*)	

pedir (*to ask*) — e **to** i	
yo ped**í**	nosotros ped**imos**
tú ped**iste**	vosotros ped**isteis**
él, ella, Ud. p**idió**	ellos, ellas, Uds. p**idieron**
Nosotros pedimos su ayuda. (*We asked for his help.*)	

dormir (*to sleep*) — o **to** u	
yo dorm**í**	nosotros dorm**imos**
tú dorm**iste**	vosotros dorm**isteis**
él, ella, Ud. d**urmió**	ellos, ellas, Uds. d**urmieron**
¿Dormiste bien? (*Did you sleep well?*)	

The verbs **reír** (*to laugh*) and **sonreír** (*to smile*) change **-e** to **-i** in the stem of the third-person singular (**él, ella, Ud.**) and third-person plural (**ellos, ellas, Uds.**) forms, and add accents in the **tú, nosotros,** and **vosotros** forms. Here's the conjugation:

reir (*to laugh*)	
yo re**í**	nosotros re**ímos**
tú re**íste**	vosotros re**ísteis**
él, ella, Ud. r**ió**	ellos, ellas, Uds. r**ieron**
Ellas rieron de él. (*They laughed at him.*)	

Here are some examples that use other verbs with these changes:

✔ **Él mintió.** (*He lied.*)

✔ **Ellos sirvieron vino.** (*They served wine.*)

✔ **El hombre murió.** (*The man died.*)

Express what happened yesterday by completing the conversations you had with and about friends and others. Change the verbs I provide from the infinitive to the preterit tense:

Q. (reírse) ¿_____ Ud. con los chistes de Luz? Sí, yo _____ de sus chistes.

A. **se río/me reí**

7. (jugar) ¿_____ tú al tenis? No, yo _____ al fútbol.

8. (caerse) ¿Quién _____? Nosotros _____.

9. (leer) ¿_____ Ud. este artículo? No, yo no lo _____.

10. (dormir) ¿_____ José una siesta? Sí, el y yo _____ una siesta.

11. (platicar) ¿_____ Ud. con sus amigos? Sí, yo _____ con ellos.

12. (sentirse) ¿_____ Uds. bien ayer? Sí, nosotros _____ bien.

13. (oír) ¿Qué chismes _____ Ud.? Yo no _____ ningunos.

14. (abrazar) ¿_____ tú a tus padres? Yo los _____.

15. (vestirse) ¿A qué hora _____ Uds. Nosotros _____ a las seis y media.

16. (distribuir) ¿Qué _____ Pablo y Juan. No sé pero yo _____ folletos.

Irregular verbs

Many verbs that are irregular in the present tense also are irregular in the preterit, which makes them easier to recognize as irregular verbs. Some of these irregular verbs may be grouped according to the changes they undergo. Unfortunately, a small number of verbs are completely irregular and must be memorized. I cover both in the sections that follow.

Most irregular verbs fall into categories, which makes them easier to remember. The irregular verbs in the categories in this section have the following endings in the preterit tense:

✔ yo: **-e**

✔ tú: **-iste**

✔ él, ella, Ud.: **-o**

- ✔ nosotros: **-imos**

- ✔ vosotros: **-isteis**

- ✔ ellos, ellas, Uds.: **-ieron** (or **-jeron** if the stem ends in **-j**)

Verbs with i in the preterit stem

Some Spanish verbs with an **e** or an **a** in their stem change the **e** or **a** to **i** in the preterit. The following tables present four such verbs:

decir (*to say*)	
yo **dije**	nosotros **dijimos**
tú **dijiste**	vosotros **dijisteis**
él, ella, Ud. **dijo**	ellos, ellas, Uds. **dijeron**
¿Qué dijo Ud.? (*What did you say?*)	

venir (*to come*)	
yo **vine**	nosotros **vinimos**
tú **viniste**	vosotros **vinisteis**
él, ella, Ud. **vino**	ellos, ellas, Uds. **vinieron**
¿A qué hora vinieron? (*At what time did they come?*)	

querer (*to want*)	
yo **quise**	nosotros **quisimos**
tú **quisiste**	vosotros **quisisteis**
él, ella, Ud. **quiso**	ellos, ellas, Uds. **quisieron**
Yo no quise salir anoche. (*I didn't want to go out last night.*)	

hacer (*to make, to do*)	
yo **hice**	nosotros **hicimos**
tú **hiciste**	vosotros **hicisteis**
él, ella, Ud. **hizo**	ellos, ellas, Uds. **hicieron**
Los muchachos no hicieron nada. (*The boys didn't do anything.*)	

In the third-person singular preterit of **hacer, -c** changes to **-z** to maintain the original sound of the verb.

Verbs with u in the preterit stem

Some irregular Spanish verbs with an **a** or an **o** in their stem change the **a** or the **o** to **u**. The following tables present examples of such verbs:

caber (*to fit*)	
yo **cupe**	nosotros **cupimos**
tú **cupiste**	vosotros **cupisteis**
él, ella, Ud. **cupo**	ellos, ellas, Uds. **cupieron**
Nosotros no cupimos todos en el coche. (*We didn't all fit in the car.*)	

saber (*to know*)	
yo **supe**	nosotros **supimos**
tú **supiste**	vosotros **supisteis**
él, ella, Ud. **supo**	ellos, ellas, Uds. **supieron**
¿Supo Ud. la respuesta? (*Did you know the answer?*)	

poner (*to put*)	
yo **puse**	nosotros **pusimos**
tú **pusiste**	vosotros **pusisteis**
él, ella, Ud. **puso**	ellos, ellas, Uds. **pusieron**
Lo puse en la mesa. (*I put it on the table.*)	

poder (*to be able*)	
yo **pude**	nosotros **pudimos**
tú **pudiste**	vosotros **pudisteis**
él, ella, Ud. **pudo**	ellos, ellas, Uds. **pudieron**
No pudieron hacerlo. (*They couldn't do it.*)	

Verbs with uv in the preterit stem

Three Spanish verbs use **uv** before their preterit endings. Be careful, though, because **tener** doesn't follow the same pattern as **andar** and **estar**:

andar (*to walk*)	
yo and**uve**	nosotros and**uvimos**
tú and**uviste**	vosotros and**uvisteis**
él, ella, Ud. and**uvo**	ellos, ellas, Uds. and**uvieron**
Nosotros anduvimos al teatro. (*We walked to the theater.*)	

estar (*to be*)	
yo est**uve**	nosotros est**uvimos**
tú est**uviste**	vosotros est**uvisteis**
él, ella, Ud. est**uvo**	ellos, ellas, Uds. est**uvieron**
Ayer yo estuve en casa. (*Yesterday I was at home.*)	

tener (*to have*)	
yo **tuve**	nosotros **tuvimos**
tú **tuviste**	vosotros **tuvisteis**
él, ella, Ud. **tuvo**	ellos, ellas, Uds. **tuvieron**
Ella tuvo un catarro. (*She had a cold.*)	

Verbs with j in the preterit stem

Some irregular Spanish verbs have a **j** in their preterit stem. This category includes all verbs that end in **-ducir** as well as the verb **decir** (*to say;* see the section "Verbs with i in the preterit stem"). Note that there's no **i** in the third-person singular or plural preterit endings. Here are some examples:

traer (*to bring*)	
yo tra**je**	nosotros tra**jimos**
tú tra**jiste**	vosotros tra**jisteis**
él, ella, Ud. tra**jo**	ellos, ellas, Uds. tra**jeron**
Ellos no trajeron sus libros en clase. (*They didn't bring their books to class.*)	

conducir (*to drive*)	
yo condu**je**	nosotros condu**jimos**
tú condu**jiste**	vosotros condu**jisteis**
él, ella, Ud. condu**jo**	ellos, ellas, Uds. condu**jeron**
¿Quién condujo? (*Who drove?*)	

The preterit of dar and ver

The Spanish verbs **dar** and **ver** have the same irregular preterit endings. You drop their respective **-ar** and **-er** infinitive endings and then add their preterit endings to **d-** and **v-**:

dar (*to give*)	
yo d**i**	nosotros d**imos**
tú d**iste**	vosotros d**isteis**
él, ella, Ud. d**io**	ellos, ellas, Uds. d**ieron**
Dimos un paseo por el parque. (*We took a walk in the park.*)	

ver (*to see*)	
yo v**i**	nosotros v**imos**
tú v**iste**	vosotros v**isteis**
él, ella, Ud. v**io**	ellos, ellas, Uds. v**ieron**
¿Qué vio Ud? (*What did you see?*)	

The preterit of ser and ir

The two irregular verbs **ser** (*to be*) and **ir** (*to go*) have the exact same preterit forms. How can you tell which verb is being used in a sentence? You have to look at the context of the sentence. The highly irregular conjugations of these two verbs are as follows:

ser (*to be*); ir (*to go*)	
yo **fui**	nosotros **fuimos**
tú **fuiste**	vosotros **fuisteis**
él, ella, Ud. **fue**	ellos, ellas, Uds. **fueron**

The following examples show these verbs in action:

> **ir: Yo fui al mercado.** (*I went to the market.*)

> **ser: Yo fui con él en el mercado.** (*I was with him in the market.*)

Write the story of your day with friends in your journal. Give the correct form of each verb by changing its infinitive to the preterit tense.

Hoy, yo (**hacer**) _____ [17] una cosa y mi hermano (**hacer**) _____ [18] otra. Yo (**ir**) _____ [19] de compras y él (**ir**) _____ [20] al estadio de fútbol. Mis amigos y yo (**querer**) _____ [21] comprar un regalo para Julia. Mis amigos (**venir**) _____ [22] a mi casa. Todos (**caber**) _____ [23] en mi coche. Yo (**conducir**) _____ [24] al centro. En una media hora nosotros (**estar**) _____ [25] allá. Nosotros (**andar**) _____ [26] por muchas tiendas y (**ver**) _____ [27] muchas cosas interesantes. Yo (**ponerse**) _____ [28] una camisa. Mis amigos me (**decir**) _____ [29]: "Cómprala!" Yo (**decidirse**) _____ [30] a comprarla. Desafortunadamente, yo no (**poder**) _____ [31] encontrar mi cartera. El dependiente no (**saber**) _____ [32] porque yo (**empezar**) _____ [33] a llorar. Yo (**traer**)

_____ (34) mi dinero en mi cartera. Luis (**tener**) _____ (35) un billete de cincuenta dólares. Él me (**dar**) _____ (36) su dinero. Yo (**ser**) _____ (37) optimisita. Finalmente, yo (**encontrar**) _____ (38) mi cartera en la guantera de mi coche.

Using the Preterit

You can use the preterit tense in many ways to convey past actions, events, or states of mind. You use the preterit to express the following:

- An action or event that began at a specific time in the past:

  El avión despegó a las seis. (*The plane took off at 6 o'clock.*)

- An action or event that was completed at a specific time in the past:

  Anoche fuimos a una fiesta. (*Last night we went to a party.*)

- An action or event that was completed in the past within a specific time period:

  Preparé la cena. (*I prepared dinner.*)

- A series of events that were completed within a definite time period in the past:

  Me desperté, me bañé y me vestí antes de desayunarme. (*I woke up, I bathed, and I got dressed before eating breakfast.*)

Strange as it may seem, some verbs can have special meanings when used in the preterit. The following verbs may have different meaning in the past tense from the usual meaning of their infinitive form:

- **Conocer,** which usually means *to know,* may mean *to meet* in the preterit:

  La conocimos en España. (*We met her in Spain.*)

- **Saber,** which usually means *to know,* may mean *to learn* in the preterit:

  ¿Cuándo supiste la verdad? (*When did you learn the truth?*)

- **Tener,** which usually means *to have,* may mean *to receive* in the preterit:

  Tuvo un regalo de mí. (*He received a gift from me.*)

- **Querer,** which usually means *to want,* may mean *to refuse* when negated in the preterit:

  No quisieron discutirlo. (*They refused to discuss it.*)

- **Poder,** which usually means *to be able to,* may mean *to manage* in the preterit:

  Pudimos hacerlo. (*We managed [finally were able] to do it.*)

Last night you had a date with your special someone. Write an e-mail to a friend to tell her all about it. Translate the following past tense sentences into Spanish, writing from your point of view.

Dear Luz,

39. He arrived at your house at 7 p.m. _____

40. You went to the movies. _____

41. You asked for a bag of popcorn and a drink. _____

42. He had a box of candy. _____

43. The movie was bad. _____

44. He almost fell asleep. _____

45. After the movie, you walked in the park. _____

46. Finally, you returned home. _____

47. He wanted to kiss you. _____

48. You said, "Of course!" _____

Sincerely, Pilar

Answer Key

1 comí/comió

2 comprasteis/compramos

3 corrimos/corristeis

4 escribiste/escribieron

5 gastaste/gastó

6 hablé/hablaron

7 jugaste/jugué. Verbs ending in **-gar** change **g** to **gu** only in the **yo** form of the preterit.

8 se cayó/nos caímos. Verbs that contain a vowel immediately preceding their **-er** or **-ir** endings change **i** to **y** in the third-person singular and plural forms. All other forms have an accented i: **í. Caerse** is a reflexive verb and requires the use of a reflexive pronoun before the verb (see Chapter 11).

9 leyó/leí

10 durmió/dormimos. Change **o** to **u** only in the third-person singular and plural forms.

11 platicó/platiqué. Verbs ending in **-car** change **c** to **qu** only in the **yo** form of the preterit.

12 se sintieron/nos sentimos. Change **e** to **i** only in the third-person singular and plural forms.

13 oyó/oí

14 abrazaste/abracé. Verbs ending in **-zar** change **z** to **c** only in the **yo** form of the preterit.

15 se vistieron/nos vestimos

16 distribuyeron/distribuí. Verbs ending in **-uir** change **i** to **y** but don't accent the **i** in the **tú, nosotros,** or **vosotros** forms.

17 hice. Some verbs with an **e** or an **a** in their stem change the **e** or **a** to **i** in the preterit.

18 hizo. Hacer has an irregular third-person singular preterit form.

19 fui. Ser and ir have the same irregular preterit forms.

20 fue

21 quisimos

22 vinieron

23 cupieron. Some verbs with an **a** or an **o** in their stem change the **a** or the **o** to **u** in the preterit.

24 conduje. Some verbs have a **j** in their preterit stem, including those that end in **-ducir,** as well as the verb **decir.**

25 **estuvimos. Estar** uses **uv** before its preterit stem.

26 **anduvimos. Andar** uses **uv** before its preterit stem.

27 **vimos. Ver** drops the **-er** infinitive ending and then adds the irregular preterit ending.

28 **me puse**

29 **dijeron**

30 **me decidí.**

31 **pude**

32 **supo**

33 **empecé**

34 **traje**

35 **tuvo.**

36 **dio**

37 **fui**

38 **encontré.**

39 **Llegó a mi casa a las siete de la noche.**

40 **Fuimos al cine.**

41 **Pedí un saco de palomitas y un refresco.**

42 **Él tuvo una caja de dulces.**

43 **La película fue mala.**

44 **Casi se durmió.**

45 **Después de la película anduvimos por el parque.**

46 **Finalmente regresamos a mi casa.**

47 **Él quise besarme.**

48 **Yo dije, "¡Por supuesto!"**

Chapter 14

Looking Back with the Imperfect

• •

In This Chapter

▶ Forming the imperfect of regular and irregular verbs

▶ Using the imperfect to express a past action

▶ Pitting the preterit against the imperfect

• •

*C*an you describe a beautiful place you once visited? Do you remember what you used to do when you were younger? Another past tense, the *imperfect,* allows you to give descriptions and to speak about what you were in the habit of doing in the past. Whereas the preterit tense allows you to express what you did in the past, the imperfect allows you to express what was happening or what used to happen previously. To put it in a visual sense, if the preterit tense captures a snapshot of a past action with the click of a button, the imperfect tense captures the motion of a past action with a video camera. For example, "He was swimming (used to/would swim) every day." If you recall that an action extended over an indefinite period of time, you'll have no trouble using the imperfect, and you won't confuse it with the preterit.

In this chapter, you see how to form the imperfect of regular and irregular verbs. (You'll be delighted to discover that there are no verbs with spelling or stem changes in this tense!) You also work on using the imperfect, and I include plenty of explanations and clues to help you decide when the imperfect, rather than the preterit, is the tense of choice. The various exercises in this chapter, along with those in Chapter 13, will give you the practice you need so that you can easily select the proper past tense for any situation.

Perfecting the Imperfect

Unless you've studied a romance language before, the imperfect is a tense you've never worked with. That's because we have no grammatical English equivalent for this past tense. If you're unfamiliar with the imperfect, you need to know, before you work on forming it, that it expresses a continuing state or action in the past — an action that was taking place or that used to happen repeatedly over an indefinite period of time. You also use the imperfect to describe scenes, settings, situations, or states in the past. (For more specific uses of the imperfect tense and examples of these uses, see the later section "Uses of the Imperfect.") In the imperfect, beginnings and endings are unimportant; only the events taking place have significance. Here are a few examples:

Durante el verano yo viajaba. (*During the summer I used to [would] travel.*)

¿Adónde iban? (*Where were they going?*)

La puerta estaba cerrada. (*The window was closed.*)

Here's a handy tip to remember: The imperfect expresses what the subject "would do" if "would" has the sense of "used to":

> **Generalmente, me despertaba a las seis.** (*Generally, I would wake up at six o'clock.*)

The following sections now work on helping you form the imperfect of both regular and irregular verbs (of which there are few).

Forming the imperfect of regular verbs

Just as with the preterit, forming the imperfect of regular verbs is rather easy. Although there are three different infinitive endings for regular verbs — **-ar**, **-er**, and **-ir** — you use only two different sets of endings to form the imperfect of these verbs.

You form the imperfect of a regular verb by dropping the **-ar**, **-er**, or **-ir** infinitive ending and adding the proper imperfect ending. The endings for **-er** and **-ir** verbs are the same, as you'll see in the following conjugation tables.

Here's the imperfect conjugation of **-ar** verbs:

mirar (*to look at*)	
yo mir**aba**	nosotros mir**ábamos**
tú mir**abas**	vosotros mir**abais**
él, ella, Ud. mir**aba**	ellos, ellas, Uds. mir**aban**

Here's the imperfect conjugation of **-er** and **-ir** verbs:

beber (*to drink*)	
yo beb**ía**	nosotros beb**íamos**
tú beb**ías**	vosotros beb**íais**
él, ella, Ud. beb**ía**	ellos, ellas, Uds. beb**ían**

recibir (*to receive*)	
yo recib**ía**	nosotros recib**íamos**
tú recib**ías**	vosotros recib**íais**
él, ella, Ud. recib**ía**	ellos, ellas, Uds. recib**ían**

Here are some examples of the imperfect in action, using regular verbs:

> **Los turistas admiraban a los animales.** (*The tourists were admiring the animals.*)
>
> **Los monos comían cacahuetes.** (*The monkeys were eating peanuts.*)
>
> **Los tigres preferían dormirse.** (*The tigers preferred to go to sleep.*)

Forming the imperfect of irregular verbs

It's your lucky day! You don't have to memorize any Spanish verbs with stem or spelling changes in the imperfect tense, because there are no changes in these verbs:

No conocía a ese hombre. (*I didn't know that man.*)

Ella no te entendía. (*She didn't understand you.*)

In fact, want some more good news? There are only three Spanish verbs that are irregular in the imperfect tense. I show these irregular verbs in the tables that follow:

ir (*to go*)	
yo **iba**	nosotros **íbamos**
tú **ibas**	vosotros **ibais**
él, ella, Ud. **iba**	ellos, ellas, Uds. **iban**
Nosotros íbamos al restaurante. (*We were going to the restaurant.*)	

ser (*to be*)	
yo **era**	nosotros **éramos**
tú **eras**	vosotros **erais**
él, ella, Ud. **era**	ellos, ellas, Uds. **eran**
Él era alto. (*He was tall.*)	

ver (*to see*)	
yo **veía**	nosotros **veíamos**
tú **veías**	vosotros **veíais**
él, ella, Ud. **veía**	ellos, ellas, Uds. **veían**
Ellas veían a sus amigos los viernes. (*They saw their friends on Fridays.*)	

In your journal, discuss what various people around you were doing during a black-out by using the imperfect tense. I include the infinitive of the verb and you must change it to the imperfect. Here's an example to get you started:

Q. nosotros/escuchar música.

A. Nosotros escuchábamos música. (We were listening to music.)

1. yo/leer una revista: _____
2. vosotros/dormir una siesta: _____
3. ellos/discutir con sus amigos: _____
4. tú/jugar al baloncesto: _____
5. mis hermanas/escribir sus tareas: _____
6. Ana/hacer ejercicios: _____
7. nosotros/preparar la cena: _____
8. Pablo y José/mirar la televisión: _____
9. Geraldo/telefonear a su novia: _____
10. mis padres/limpiar la casa: _____
11. Uds./comer al restaurante: _____
12. Ud./ir a la farmacia: _____

Uses of the Imperfect

You'll have no problem knowing when to use the imperfect tense if you can remember that the imperfect is a descriptive past tense. You use the imperfect in the following situations:

- To describe ongoing or continuous actions in the past (which may or may not have been completed):

    Yo lo veía todos los días. (*I saw him every day.*)

- To describe repeated or habitual actions that took place in the past:

    Ella viajaba mucho. (*She used to travel a lot.*)

- To describe an action that continued for an unspecified period of time:

    Vivíamos en México. (*We lived in Mexico.*)

- To describe a person, place, thing, weather condition, time, day of the week, state of mind, or emotion in the past:

    - **Estaba contento.** (*I was happy.*)

    - **La casa era muy grande.** (*The house was very big.*)

    - **Hacía frío.** (*It was cold.*)

    - **Eran las dos.** (*It was two o'clock.*)

    - **Era el lunes.** (*It was Monday.*)

    - **Quería comprenderlo.** (*I wanted to understand it.*)

    - **Creía que no era urgente.** (*He thought it wasn't urgent.*)

✔ To describe actions that took place simultaneously:

Yo escuchaba la radio mientras mi amiga miraba la televisión. (*I was listening to the radio while my friend was watching television.*)

✔ To describe a situation that was going on in the past when another action or event, expressed by the preterit (see Chapter 13), took place:

Yo escuchaba la radio cuando alguien sonó a la puerta. (*I was listening to the radio when someone rang the doorbell.*)

✔ To express an event or action that began in the past and continued in the past, using **hacía (que)** or **desde hacía** (*had been*):

• **¿Cuánto tiempo hacía que trabajas allá? ¿Desde hacía cuándo trabajas allá?** (*How long had you been working there?*)

• **Hacía tres años (que trabajaba allá). Trabajaba allá desde hacía tres años.** (*I'd been working there for three years.*)

For Spanish homework, your teacher asked you to write a description of a photo. Use the imperfect tense to describe what was happening in the picture you chose. I provide the verb, and you provide its imperfect conjugation.

(ser)_____(13) la primavera. (hacer)_____(14)

buen tiempo. No (haber)_____(15) nubes en el cielo. La familia

Cortés (ir) _____(16) al parque. Mi madre (empujar)

_____(17) un cochecito mientras mi padre (hablar)_____

(18) con mi hermano mayor, Fernando. Fernando (tener)_____

(19) un globo rojo en las manos. Él (estar)_____(20) muy

contento. Una muchacha (mirar) _____(21) a la familia.

Ella (llevar) _____(22) un vestido amarillo y negro y (comer)

_____(23) un helado. Ella (parecer)_____(24)

como una abeja. (ser) _____(25) evidente que (querer)

_____(26) ver al bebé porque ella (sonreír)_____(27).

Comparing the Preterit and the Imperfect

The preterit tense (see Chapter 13) expresses an action that was completed at a specific time in the past. You could represent such an event or action by drawing a dot. Boom! The action took place and was completed, and that's the end of it.

The imperfect tense, on the other hand, expresses a past action that continued over an indefinite period of time. You could represent such an action or event with a wavy line: It just kept moving and moving without an end in sight. The action continued over a period of time in the past: it *was* happening, *used to* happen, or *would* (meaning *used to*) happen.

In some instances, either the preterit *or* the imperfect is acceptable as a past tense. The tense you use may depend on the meaning you want to convey. For instance, if you want to convey that the action was completed, you can say

Ella estudió. (*She studied.*)

If you want to convey that the action was ongoing or continuous, you can say

Ella estudiaba. (*She was studying.*)

In the following list, I compare some examples of the preterit and the imperfect:

Preterit: **Ellos bailaron.** (*They danced.*)

Imperfect: **Ellos bailaban.** (*They were dancing.*)

Preterit: **Yo salí anoche.** (*I went out last night.*) **Yo salí dos veces.** (*I went out two times.*)

Imperfect: **Yo salía cada noche.** (*I went out each night.*)

One big difference is that you use the imperfect to describe a person, place, thing, state of mind, time, day, or weather condition in the past:

Ella era optimista. (*She was optimistic.*)

El viaje era agradable. (*The trip was nice.*)

Esperaba ganar. (*He was hoping to win.*)

Era la una. (*It was one o'clock.*)

Era martes. (*It was Tuesday.*)

Llovía. (*It was raining.*)

You recently wrote a composition for Spanish class in the present tense, but your teacher wanted it written in the past tense. Oops! Rewrite the composition, changing all the verbs in the present tense to the preterit or imperfect tense.

Es _____ (28) sábado. **Hace** _____ (29) frío. **Está** _____ (30) nevando. El sol no **brilla** _____ (31) y **hay** _____ (32) muchos nubes en el cielo. Los pájaros no **cantan** _____ (33) No **tengo** _____ (34) nada de particular a hacer. De repente el teléfono **suena** _____ (35) y yo **contesto** _____ (36). **Es** _____ (37) mi amigo, Manuel. Me **dice** _____ (38) que se **aburre** _____ (39) mirando la televisión. Me **pregunta** _____ (40) si **quiero** _____ (41) salir. Yo **creo** _____ (42) que **es** _____ (43) una buena idea. Yo **sugiero** _____ (44): "Nosotros **podemos** _____ (45) construir un muñeco de nieve." A Manuel no le **gusta** _____ (46) esa idea. Él **prefiere** _____ (47) construir una fortaleza de nieve. Yo **acepto** _____ (48) esa idea. Yo le **pido** _____ (49) permiso a mi madre para salir. Naturalmente, ella **dice** _____ (50) "Sí" inmediatamente. Nosotros nos **decidimos** _____ (51) a reunirnos a la una y nosotros **colgamos** _____ (52) el teléfono. El día **es** _____ (53) maravilloso.

Certain words in Spanish act as clues that you should use the preterit or the imperfect tense, because they show that an action occurred at a specific time or imply that an action was ongoing over a period of time. The sections that follow will help you determine which past tense you should use in a given situation.

Clues to the preterit

You often use the preterit tense along with words and expressions that specify a time period. Table 14-1 presents many of these common words and expressions.

Table 14-1	Clues to the Preterit Tense
Spanish	*Meaning*
anoche	last night
anteayer	day before yesterday
ayer	yesterday
ayer por la noche	last night
de repente	suddenly
el año pasado	last year
el otro día	the other day
el verano pasado	last summer
finalmente	finally
la semana pasada	last week
por fin	finally
primero	first
un día	one day
una vez	one time

Here are some example sentences that show how you use these words with the preterit:

> **Anoche me quedé en casa.** (*Last night I stayed home.*)
>
> **De repente, oímos un ruido fuerte.** (*Suddenly we heard a loud noise.*)
>
> **Finalmente, lo terminé.** (*Finally, I finished it.*)

Clues to the imperfect

You often use the imperfect tense with words and expressions that imply habitual action or repetition in the past. Table 14-2 lists many of these words and expressions.

Table 14-2	Clues to the Imperfect Tense
Spanish	*Meaning*
a menudo	*often*
a veces	*sometimes*
cada día	*each day, every day*
con frecuencia	*frequently*
de vez en cuando	*from time to time*
en general	*generally*
frecuentemente	*frequently*
generalmente	*generally*
habitualmente	*habitually*
normalmente	*normally*
siempre	*always*
todo el tiempo	*all the time*
todos los días	*every day*
usualmente	*usually*

Here are examples that show how you use the imperfect tense with some words and expressions from the previous table:

> **Normalmente regresaba a las seis.** (*You normally returned home at six o'clock.*)

> **Siempre jugaban al tenis.** (*They always played tennis.*)

You want to talk to a friend about why certain people acted in a particular way in the past by using the preterit and the imperfect tenses. I provide the infinitives and you provide the preterit of the first verb and the imperfect of the second verb. Here's an example to get you started:

Q. (ir/tener) Pablo _____ al dentista porque _____ un dolor de muelas.

A. Pablo **fue** al dentista porque **tenía** un dolor de muelas. (*Pablo went to the dentist because he had a toothache.*)

54. (comer/seguir) Yo no _____ chocolate porque _____ un régimen.

55. (quedarse/estar) Mi novio _____ en casa porque _____ enfermo.

56. (caerse/prestar) Tú _____ porque no _____ atención.

57. (comprar/querer) Los muchachos _____ billetes porque _____ ver el partido de fútbol.

58. (enviar/celebrar) Luisa _____ una carta a su amiga porque ella
_____ su cumpleaños.

59. (sacar/hacer) Nosotros _____ un traje de baño porque _____ sol.

PRACTICE

You're writing a composition for school about your friend, Eduardo, who received a sizable inheritance from his grandfather. Express what he did on one fine summer day by putting the verbs in parentheses in their proper tense: the preterit or the imperfect. Be on the lookout for the clue words I present earlier in this section.

(ser) _____ (60) el verano. (hacer) _____ (61) buen tiempo. (ser) _____ (62) el mediodía. Ayer Eduardo (recibir) _____ (63) una herencia de su abuela y (ir) _____ (64) al banco con el cheque que (querer) _____ (65) depositar en su cuenta. (pasar) _____ (66) por una concesión de coches. (llegar) _____ (67) al banco pero desafortunadamente (estar) _____ (68) cerrado porque (ser) _____ (69) la hora de almorzar. No (haber) _____ (70) otra cosa que hacer. En ese momento Eduardo (regresar) _____ (71) a la concesión y (mirar) _____ (72) por los escaparates. Él (escoger) _____ (73) un coche gris que le (gustar) _____ (74) enormamente. Él (tener) _____ (75) mucha curiosidad. Él (entrar) _____ (76) y (empezar) _____ (77) a hablar con el vendedor. Él le (hacer) _____ (78) muchas preguntas. El vendedor le (contestar) _____ (79) con mucha paciencia. Él le (explicar) _____ (80) todo. Ese coche (ser) _____ (81) muy deportivo. Eduardo (desear) _____ (82) comprarlo. Él le (pedir) _____ (83) el precio al vendedor. (ser) _____ (84) veinte mil dólares. Eduardo (tener) _____ (85) suficiente dinero y (comprar) _____ (86) el coche. (estar) _____ (87) tan contento. Ese día, Eduardo no (ir) _____ (88) otra vez al banco. En vez de hacer eso, él (ir) _____ (89) al campo en su coche nuevo.

PRACTICE

Your teacher has asked you to write a composition for your Spanish class in which you tell how you celebrated Christmas. Express what you did in the past by using the preterit or the imperfect as needed. Here's an example to get you started:

Q. You left your house at 10 am.

A. **Yo salí de mi casa a las diez de la mañana.**

90. You celebrated Christmas at your sister's house.

_____

91. There was a lot of snow.

_____

92. You arrived safely.

_____

93. Your sister prepared a delicious dinner.

_____

94. While you were all eating, your uncle called.

_____

95. He wanted to say "Merry Christmas."

_____

96. After dinner all of you opened your gifts.

_____

97. You gave your sister a gold bracelet.

_____

98. She liked it a lot.

_____

99. You received a beautiful wool sweater.

_____

100. You put it on immediately.

_____

101. Everybody had a good time.

_____

Answer Key

1 Yo **leía** una revista. (*I was reading a magazine.*)

2 Vosotros **dormíais** una siesta. (*You were taking a nap.*)

3 Ellos **discutían** con sus amigos. (*They were arguing with their friends.*)

4 Tú **jugabas** al baloncesto. (*You were playing basketball.*)

5 Mis hermanas **escribían** sus tareas. (*My sisters were writing their homework.*)

6 Ana **hacía** ejercicios. (*Ana was doing exercises.*)

7 Nosotros **preparábamos** la cena. (*We were preparing the dinner.*)

8 Pablo y José **miraban** la televisión. (*Pablo and José were watching television.*)

9 Geraldo **telefoneaba** a su novia. (*Geraldo was calling his girlfriend on the phone.*)

10 Mis padres **limpiaban** la casa. (*My parents were cleaning the house.*)

11 Uds. **comían** al restaurante. (*You were eating at a restaurant.*)

12 Ud. **iba** a la farmacia. (*You were going to the drugstore.*)

13 **era**

14 **hacía**

15 **había**

16 **iba**

17 **empujaba**

18 **hablaba**

19 **tenía**

20 **estaba**

21 **miraba**

22 **llevaba**

23 **comía**

24 **parecía**

25 **era**

26 **quería**

27 **sonreía**

28 **era** (imperfect)

29 **hacía** (imperfect)

30 **estaba** (imperfect)

31 **brillaba** (imperfect)

32 **había** (imperfect)

33 **cantaban** (imperfect)

34 **tenía** (imperfect)

35 **sonó** (preterit)

36 **contesté** (preterit)

37 **era** (imperfect)

38 **dijo** (preterit)

39 **aburría** (imperfect)

40 **preguntó** (preterit)

41 **quería** (imperfect)

42 **creía** (imperfect)

43 **era** (imperfect)

44 **sugerí** (preterit)

45 **podíamos** (imperfect)

46 **gustaba** (imperfect)

47 **prefería** (imperfect)

48 **acepté** (preterit)

49 **pedí** (preterit)

50 **dijo** (preterit)

51 **decidimos** (preterit)

52 **colgamos** (preterit)

53 **era** (imperfect)

54 **comí/seguía**

55 **se quedó/estaba**

56 **te caíste/prestabas**

57 **compraron/querían**

58 **envió/celebraba**

59 **sacamos/hacía**

60 **era** (imperfect)

61 **hacía** (imperfect)

62 **era** (imperfect)

63 **recibió** (preterit)

64 **iba** (imperfect)

65 **quería** (imperfect)

66 **pasó** (preterit)

67 **llegó** (preterit)

68 **estaba** (imperfect)

69 **era** (imperfect)

70 **había** (imperfect)

71 **regresó** (preterit)

72 **miró** (preterit)

73 **escogió** (preterit)

74 **gustaba** (imperfect)

75 **tenía** (imperfect)

76 **entró** (preterit)

77 **empezó** (preterit)

`78` **hizo** (preterit)

`79` **contestó** (preterit)

`80` **explicó** (preterit)

`81` **era** (imperfect)

`82` **deseaba** (imperfect)

`83` **pidió** (preterit)

`84` **era** (imperfect)

`85` **tenía** (imperfect)

`86` **compró** (preterit)

`87` **estaba** (imperfect)

`88` **fue** (preterit)

`89` **fue** (preterit)

`90` **Celebré** la Navidad en casa de mi hermana.

`91` **Había** mucha nieve.

`92` Yo **llegué** sin incidentes.

`93` Mi hermana **preparó** una comida deliciosa.

`94` Mientras nosotros **comíamos** mi tió **telefoneó (llamó).**

`95` **Quería** decirnos "Feliz Navidad."

`96` Después de la cena nosotros **abrimos** nuestros regalos.

`97` Yo le **di** a mi hermana una pulsera de oro.

`98` Le **gustaba** mucho.

`99` Yo **recibí** un suéter de lana muy bello.

`100` Me lo **pusé** inmediatamente.

`101` Todo el mundo **se divirtió.**

Chapter 15

Seeing into the Future

. . . .

In This Chapter

▶ Using the present and **ir** + **a** to form the future

▶ Putting regular and irregular verbs into the future

▶ Reviewing the uses of the future

. . . .

*A*t one time or another, every person thinks about the future and makes plans based on hopes and dreams. For some dreamers, "preparing for the future" means getting an education. For others, it means getting a job, saving money, and starting a family. And then there are those who, each week without fail, proceed to the nearest candy store to purchase lottery tickets with the fantasy of becoming an instant millionaire! What unites everyone is the fact that the future is a time you look toward. In Spanish, you have three different ways to express future actions. One of them, believe it or not, is using the present tense. Another is to state what you're "going to do." Finally, you can use the future tense, which expresses what you "will do."

This chapter covers these topics to allow you to look toward the future. You discover how to use the present tense to express a future action. You practice using the Spanish verb **ir** (*to go*) + the preposition **a** to say what a subject is going to do. I also teach you how to form the future of regular and irregular verbs. You'll like this tense because there are no verbs with spelling or stem changes! Finally, you review the functions of this tense so that you can comfortably use it when you speak or write — in the future!

Forming and Expressing the Future

In Spanish, you can express the future in three ways. One way is to use the present. If that's your method of choice, look back to Chapter 4 for all the details on proper usage. Another way is to use the verb **ir** (*to go*) and the preposition **a**. You use this method to express what's going to be done by the subject in the near future. For this, you need to know the present-tense conjugation of **ir.** These are the two methods I cover in the following sections. (For info on using the future tense, which requires some new stems and some new endings, see the future sections of this chapter.)

Discussing the future by using the present

You use the present tense to imply the future when asking for instructions or when the proposed action will take place in the not-so-distant or near future. Here are two examples of these usages:

¿**Dejo de hablar?** (*Shall I stop talking?*)

Ellos pasan por nuestra casa. (*They'll be stopping by our house.*)

Using ir + a to express the near future

You use the present tense of the verb **ir** (*to go*) + the preposition **a** (which, in this case, has no meaning) + the infinitive of the verb to express an action that will be taking place rather soon or that's imminent. Here are some examples that express what the subject is going to do:

Voy a salir. (*I'm going to go out.*)

Vamos a esperarlos. (*We are going to wait for them.*)

The present tense of **ir** is irregular, and you conjugate it as follows:

ir (*to go*)	
yo **voy**	nosotros **vamos**
tú **vas**	vosotros **vais**
él, ella, Ud. **va**	ellos, ellas, Uds. **van**

The parents in a family have decided to assign chores for everyone so the house stays clean. In Spanish, write the chores the family members must execute by using **ir** + **a.** Here's an example:

Q. Marta/lavar la ropa

A. Marta **va a** lavar la ropa. (*Marta is going to wash the clothing.*)

1. yo/pasar la aspiradora

   _____

2. nosotros/preparar la comida

   _____

3. Alejandro/arreglar su cuarto

   _____

4. vosotros/limpiar el coche

   _____

5. tú/cortar el césped

   _____

6. Cristina y Blanca/quitar el polvo de los muebles

   _____

Sending regular verbs to the future

The future tense explains what a subject will do or what action or event will take place in future time. Want some good news? The future tense in Spanish is just about as easy to form as possible, because there is only one set of endings. *All* verbs — that's right, every single one of them: regular verbs, verbs with spelling and stem changes, and irregular verbs — have the same future endings. Well, some verbs do have irregular future stems, but these are limited in number (see the following section for more on these verbs).

To form the future tense of a regular verb, you add the appropriate future ending (dependent on the subject) to the infinitive of the verb:

Future Endings for All Verbs	
yo -**é**	nosotros -**emos**
tú -**ás**	vosotros -**éis**
él, ella, Ud. -**á**	ellos, ellas, Uds. -**án**

Time for some examples. The tables that follow show how you form the future of some regular verbs with the endings from the previous table:

- ✔ **-ar** verbs:

trabajar (*to work*)	
yo trabajar**é**	nosotros trabajar**emos**
tú trabajar**ás**	vosotros trabajar**éis**
él, ella, Ud. trabajar**á**	ellos, ellas, Uds. trabajar**án**

- ✔ **-er** verbs:

vender (*to sell*)	
yo vender**é**	nosotros vender**emos**
tú vender**ás**	vosotros vender**éis**
él, ella, Ud. vender**á**	ellos, ellas, Uds. vender**án**

- ✔ **-ir** verbs:

discutir (*to discuss, argue*)	
yo discutir**é**	nosotros discutir**emos**
tú discutir**ás**	vosotros discutir**éis**
él, ella, Ud. discutir**á**	ellos, ellas, Uds. discutir**án**

Now check out some example sentences utilizing the future tense:

> **Yo no los invitaré a mi fiesta.** (*I won't invite them to my party.*)
>
> **Ellos no beberán alcohol.** (*They won't drink alcohol.*)
>
> **¿Abrirás una cuenta bancaria pronto?** (*Will you open a bank account soon?*)

Verbs such as **oír** (*to listen*) and **reír** (*to laugh*) — whose infinitives contain an accent mark over the "i" — drop their accent in the future tense:

> **Yo no oiré esas mentiras.** (*I won't listen to those lies.*)
>
> **Ellos no reirán de él.** (*They won't laugh at him.*)

In the following exercise, express what different students both will and won't do in a study-abroad program. The first section provides the subject. The second section provides the verb that states what the subject will do. The final section provides the verb that, when preceded by the word **no,** states what the subject won't do. Follow this example:

Q. Elena/escribir notas/jugar

A. Elena **escribirá** notas. No **jugará.** (*Elena will write notes. She won't play.*)

7. tú/estudiar/mirar la television

_____

8. Carolina/asistir a todas las clases/visitar a sus amigas

_____

9. Luz y yo/leer todos los libros/escuchar música

_____

10. vosotros/aprender el vocabulario/descansar

_____

11. yo/prestar atención/pensar en otras cosas

_____

12. Jaime y Luis/correr a las clases/andar por el parque

_____

Sending irregular verbs to the future

Certain Spanish verbs are irregular in the future tense. These verbs have irregular future stems, which always end in **-r** or **-rr** — an easy way to remember them! To form the future of these irregular verbs, you do one of three things:

✔ Drop **e** from the infinitive ending before adding the proper future ending I list in the section "Sending regular verbs to the future":

Infinitive	Meaning	Future Stem
caber	to fit	**cabr-**
poder	to be able	**podr-**
querer	to want	**querr-**
saber	to know	**sabr-**

Here are some example sentences:

¿Cabrá esa máquina en el gabinete? (*Will that machine fit in the cabinet?*)

No podremos venir. (*We will not be able to come.*)

Querré verlo. (*I will want to see it.*)

¿Sabrá hacerlo? (*Will he know how to do it?*)

✔ Drop **e** or **i** from the infinitive ending and replace the vowel with a **d** before adding the proper future ending:

Infinitive	Meaning	Future Stem
poner	to put	**pondr-**
salir	to leave	**saldr-**
tener	to have	**tendr-**
valer	to be worth	**valdr-**
venir	to come	**vendr-**

These verbs are illustrated in the following example sentences:

Yo pondré los papeles en la mesa. (*I will put the papers on the table.*)

¿Cuándo saldrán? (*When will they leave?*)

Ella no tendrá bastante dinero. (*She will not have enough money.*)

¿Cuánto valdrá ese coche? (*How much will that car be worth?*)

¿No vendrás mañana? (*Won't you be coming tomorrow?*)

✔ Memorize the irregular stems and add the proper future endings. At this level, you need to know only two high-frequency verbs in Spanish that are irregular in the future:

Infinitive	Meaning	Future Stem
decir	to say	**dir-**
hacer	to make, to do	**har-**

Observe these verbs in action:

Yo diré lo que pienso. (*I will say what I think.*)

¿Qué harán para resolver el problema? (*What will they do to solve the problem?*)

In the following exercise, use the future tense of the verb provided to express what will happen at the next business conference you attend. Here's an example:

Q. (escuchar) Yo _____ atentamente.

A. Yo **escucharé** atentamente. (*I will listen attentively.*)

MEMO

TO:			
FROM:			

13. (valer)_____la pena asistir a la conferencia.
14. (querer) Todos _____venir a la conferencia en tren.
15. (venir) Todos los participantes_____mañana.
16. (hacer) Nosotros _____todo lo posible para todos.
17. (saber) Nosotros no_____con antelación si el presidente
    (venir)_____.
18. (poder) Nosotros_____ hospedar a todos.
19. (poner) Nosotros_____ carros a las órdenes de todos.
20. (tener) Todos _____que reservar lo más antes posible.
21. (decir) Todo el mundo_____que es una conferencia importante.
22. (salir) Todos_____ contentos.

Using the Future Tense to Foretell, Predict, and Wonder

It seems kind of obvious that you should use the future to express future time. However, you must be aware of other instances in Spanish when you may use the future, too. For instance, you use the future

✔ To express what will happen:

Yo te ayudaré. (*I will help you.*)

✔ To predict a future action or event:

Lloverá pronto. (*It will rain soon.*)

✔ To express wonder, probability, conjecture, or uncertainty in the present.

The Spanish future, in this case, is equivalent to the following English phrases:

"I wonder," "probably," or "must be."

¿Cuánto dinero tendrán? (*I wonder how much money they have.*)

Serán las seis. (*It's probably [It must be] six o'clock.*)

Alguien viene. ¿Quién será? (*Someone is coming. I wonder who it is.*)

¿Será mi esposo? (*I wonder if it's my husband.*)

¿Irá a darme un anillo mi novio? (*I wonder if my boyfriend is going to give me a ring.*)

✔ To express something that you expect and that's due to or caused by a present action or event:

Si viene a tiempo el jefe no se quejará. (*If you come on time, the boss will not complain.*)

Si sigues la receta prepararás una buena comida. (*If you follow the recipe, you will prepare a good meal.*)

It's your job to write Spanish horoscopes for your club's newsletter. I provide the English version of the horoscope; you translate it into Spanish, using your mastery of the future.

23. ARIES (marzo 21–abril 19): You will meet an important person. He will present an incredible opportunity to you.

_____

24. TAURO (abril 20–mayo 20): You will have good luck. You will buy a lottery ticket, and you will win a lot of money.

_____

25. GÉMINIS (mayo 21–junio 21): You will receive an important letter in the mail. It will give you good news.

_____

26. CÁNCER (junio 22–julio 21): Your friend will give you advice. You will listen to it, and you will be able to get a better job.

_____

27. LEO (julio 22–agosto 21): You will take a trip, and you will meet many influential people.

_____

28. VIRGO (agosto 22–septiembre 22): Very soon your house will be worth a million dollars. You will sell it and take a cruise around the world.

_____

29. LIBRA (septiembre 23–octubre 22): You will go out with a friend, and you will have a lot of fun.

_____

30. ESCORPIÓN (octubre 23–noviembre 21): You will lose some important documents. A stranger will return them to you.

_____

31. SAGITARIO (noviembre 22–diciembre 21): You will lie to a friend. Your friend will forgive you.

_____

32. CAPRICORNIO (diciembre 22–enero 20): You will earn a lot of money. You will put that money in the bank for the future.

_____

33. ACUARIO (enero 21–febrero 19): You will go to Spain, and you will learn to speak Spanish fluently.

_____

34. PISCIS (febrero 20–marzo 20): You will leave your office, and you will find a $100 bill in the street.

_____

Answer Key

1 Yo **voy a** pasar la aspiradora. (*I am going to vacuum.*)

2 Nosotros **vamos a** preparar la comida. (*We are going to prepare the meal.*)

3 Alejandro **va a** arreglar su cuarto. (*Alejandro is going to tidy his room.*)

4 Vosotros **vais a** limpiar el coche. (*You are going to clean the car.*)

5 Tú **vas a** cortar el césped. (*You are going to mow the lawn.*)

6 Cristina y Blanca **van a** quitar el polvo de los muebles. (*Cristina and Blanca are going to dust the furniture.*)

7 Tú **estudiarás.** No **mirarás** la televisión.

8 Carolina **asisitirá** a todas las clases. No **visitará** a sus amigas.

9 Luz y yo **leeremos** todos los libros. No **escucharemos** música.

10 Vosotros **aprenderéis** el vocabulario. No **descansaréis.**

11 Yo **prestaré** atención. No **pensaré** en otras cosas.

12 Jaime y Luis **correrán** a las clases. No **andarán** por el parque.

13 **Valdrá** la pena asistir a la conferencia. (*It will be worthwhile to attend the conference.*)

14 Todos **querrán** venir a la conferencia en tren. (*Everyone will want to come to the conference by train.*)

15 Todos los participantes **vendrán** mañana. (*All the participants will come tomorrow.*)

16 Nosotros **haremos** todo lo posible para todos. (*We will do everything possible for everyone.*)

17 Nosotros no **sabremos** con antelación si el presidente **vendrá.** (*We will not know in advance if the president will come.*)

18 Nosotros **podremos** hospedar a todos. (*We will be able to give a room to everyone.*)

19 Nosotros **pondremos** carros a las órdenes de todos. (*We will have cars available for everyone.*)

20 Todos **tendrán** que reservar lo más antes posible. (*Everyone will have to make a reservation as soon as possible.*)

21 Todo el mundo **dirá** que es una conferencia importante. (*Everyone will say that it is an important conference.*)

22 Todos **saldrán** contentos. (*Everyone will leave happy.*)

23 **Conocerá** a una persona importante. Le **dará** una oportunidad increíble.

24 **Tendrá** buena suerte. **Comprará** un billete de lotería y **ganará** mucho dinero.

25 **Recibirá** una carta importante en el correo. Le **dará** buenas noticias.

26 Su amigo le **dará** consejos. Los **escuchará** y **podrá** conseguir un mejor puesto.

27 **Hará** un viaje y **conocerá** a muchas personas influyentes.

28 Pronto su casa **valdrá** un millón de dólares. La **venderá** y **hará** un crucero por mundo.

29 **Saldrá** con un amigo y se **divertirán** mucho.

30 **Perdrá** documentos importantes. Un desconocido se los **devolverá** a Ud.

31 **Mentirá** a un amigo. Su amigo le **perdonará** a Ud.

32 **Ganará** mucho dinero. **Pondrá** ese dinero en el banco para el futuro.

33 **Irá** en España y **aprenderá** a hablar español con fluidez.

34 **Saldrá** de su oficina y **encontrará** un billete de cien dólares en la calle.

Part V
The Part of Tens

The 5th Wave   By Rich Tennant

BOB'S FIRST TRIP TO SPAIN

@RICHTENNANT

"Please stop yelling 'Olé' every time the bartender spears an olive for a martini."

In this part . . .

The Part of Tens is an integral part of every For Dummies book. It contains special tips and information that somehow didn't make it or fit into the other chapters. In this part, you get the top ten common writing mistakes in Spanish. Avoid them if you want others to believe you've acquired native writing skills. You review the ten skills you need in order to polish your writing so that it has a professional quality about it. Finally, I introduce you to ten pairs of verbs. The verbs in each pair have distinctive meanings that require more detailed explanations.

Chapter 16

Ten Most Common Writing Mistakes in Spanish

In This Chapter

▶ Applying English rules to Spanish grammar

▶ Using parts of speech improperly

*I*nfants learn their native language by listening and internalizing the sounds, vocabulary, and structures they hear. They eventually start to mimic what the people around them are saying. Watch out! Perhaps you've had an embarrassing moment when your little tyke innocently blurted out a colorful four-letter word.

After a child has achieved a reasonable grasp of the language, he or she then learns to read. At this time, parents can breathe a sigh of relief, because when little junior(ette) is engrossed in a story, he (she) may manage to avoid those verbal difficulties mentioned previously. Finally, a child uses all that he (she) has been exposed to in order to put original thoughts down on paper. This ability may be scary to adults, who may stumble upon diaries or journals containing the intimate thoughts of teenage sons or daughters.

Writing — in any language — is, by far, the most advanced skill you can learn. Writing is, well, an art. Mastering your native language is difficult enough, with all its rules and exceptions. But when you want to acquire a second language — especially after you've already reached the ripe old age of 12 or 13, when the rules of your first language are deeply rooted into your subconscious — you really have to work *hard* at memorizing and internalizing a whole new set of sounds, vocabulary, structures, and rules. This is quite a daunting task; I commend you for undertaking it!

As a token of my admiration, allow me to attempt to help you perfect your Spanish writing skills. In this chapter, I present the ten most common writing mistakes people make when learning Spanish. You need to avoid these if you want to write well.

Confusing Gender Differences

In English, a noun is a noun and an adjective is an adjective. Yes, gender counts, but only when English speakers are speaking about a male or female person. You can use adjectives, which you place in front of the nouns, to describe anyone or anything without regard to gender or to the number of people or things you're speaking about.

In Spanish, however, every noun — no matter who or what it is — is either masculine or feminine. The gender of the noun determines whether you must use a masculine or feminine adjective to describe that noun. Also, if the noun is singular, the adjective you use to describe it must also be singular. Likewise for plural nouns: They require plural adjectives.

And to complicate matters further, unlike in English, Spanish adjectives generally follow the nouns they describe.

To perfect your writing in Spanish, make sure your adjectives agree with your nouns and that they're in the right position (see Chapter 8). Here's an example sentence:

Los vestidos rojos son bonitos. (*The red dresses are pretty.*)

Insisting on Word for Word Translations

Whatever you do, don't try to translate your English thoughts word for word into Spanish. It simply won't work, and you may sound quite foolish if you make an unwise word selection.

Every language has its own set of idiomatic phrases that just don't translate well. Imagine how impossible it would be to translate and capture the true flavor of this English sentence: "She fell head over heels for him." Here's a Spanish example: **Él se ahogó en un vaso de agua.** The literal translation is *He drowned in a glass of water.* The Spanish idiomatic expression **ahogarse en un vaso de agua** means *To make a mountain out of a molehill.* A computer language translator or even the best bilingual dictionary won't help you write Spanish properly unless you take idioms into consideration.

Forgetting the Personal a

English has no equivalent for the Spanish personal **a**. It's something so foreign and so unusual to English speakers that many of us tend to forget all about it when writing in Spanish. No doubt, if you omit the personal **a,** you'll be marked as a gringo (foreigner)!

Use the personal **a** when the direct object in a sentence refers to a person. And don't forget that the preposition **a** contracts with the definite article **el** to become **al** before a masculine singular noun. Here are some examples:

Busco los libros. (*I'm looking for the books.*)

Busco a Ana. (*I'm looking for Ana.*)

Busco al muchacho. (*I'm looking for the boy.*)

Busco a las muchachas. (*I'm looking for the girls.*)

Using the Indefinite Article with an Unqualified Profession

"What do you do for a living?" "Well, I'm a teacher and my husband is an artist." In English, you use the indefinite article *a* or *an* when referring to a person's profession. In Spanish, the only time you use the indefinite article with a career is when the career is qualified or described. If you're mentioning only the profession, omit the indefinite article:

Es ingeniero y su esposa es dentista. (*He's an engineer and his wife is a dentist.*)

Es un buen ingeniero y su esposa es una dentista popular. (*He's a good engineer and his wife is a popular dentist.*)

Mixing Up Por and Para

The two prepositions **por** and **para** usually mean *for*, but in a few cases may have other meanings. This has puzzled and frustrated Spanish students forever. Even advanced students have a tendency to confuse them sometimes. Here's a rundown of the most common rules for their usage:

You use **por**

✔ To express the preposition *through:*

   Anduve por el bosque. (*I walked through the forest.*)

✔ To express the duration of an action:

   Estudié por dos horas. (*I studied for two hours.*)

✔ To express a means of transportation:

   Viajaron por avión. (*They traveled by airplane.*)

✔ To express doing something for someone:

   Lo hizo por su mejor amigo. (*He did it for his best friend.*)

✔ To perform multiplication:

   Dos por dos son cuatro. (*Two times two is four.*)

You use **para** to express

✔ A recipient:

   Esta carta es para Ud. (*This letter is for you.*)

✔ A purpose or a goal:

   Leo para relajarme. (*I read [in order] to relax.*)

✔ A time in the future:

   Es el horario para mañana. (*It's tomorrow's schedule.*)

✔ An opinion:

   Para mí, esta casa es perfecta. (*For me, this house is perfect.*)

✔ A destination:

   Ella va para la oficina. (*She's heading for the office.*)

Confusing Direct and Indirect Objects

Direct object nouns and the pronouns that replace them answer *whom* or *what* the subject is acting upon. *Indirect object nouns* and the pronouns that replace them answer *to/for whom* the subject is doing something. Indirect objects refer only to people. The pronouns **me, te, nos,** and **os** can be both direct and indirect object pronouns and generally present no problems (see Chapter 10).

The difficulty lies in distinguishing the direct object pronouns

> **lo** (*him, you, it*), **le** (*him, you* in Spain), **la** (*her, you, it*), **los** (*you, them*), and **las** (*you, them*)

from the indirect object pronouns

> **le** (*to/for him her, you, it*) and **les** (*to/for you, them*)

Certain verbs in Spanish require a direct object (because the *to* or *for* actually is part of the verb) even though they require an indirect object in English. This can cause quite a bit of confusion when you're trying to select the correct pronoun for a sentence. Allow me to provide some lists to help out! The following verbs require a direct object in Spanish:

- ✔ **buscar** (*to look for*)
- ✔ **escuchar** (*to listen to*)
- ✔ **esperar** (*to wait for, to hope for*)
- ✔ **llamar** (*to call*)
- ✔ **pagar** (*to pay for [something]*)
- ✔ **mirar** (*to look at, to watch*)

Here's an example using **mirar:**

> **¿La televisión? Yo la miro todos los días.** (*The television? I watch it every day.*)

The following verbs are some that take an indirect object pronoun where the *to* isn't obvious:

- ✔ **aconsejar** (*to advise*)
- ✔ **contestar** (*to answer*)
- ✔ **preguntar** (*to ask*)
- ✔ **prohibir** (*to forbid, prohibit*)
- ✔ **telefonear** (*to phone*)

Here's an example using **telefonear:**

> **Le telefoneé anoche.** (*I called him last night.*)

English sentences may omit *to,* which could trick you into using the incorrect object pronoun. Here's a rule: If *to* or *for* makes sense in the sentence — even though it may not be used in English — use the indirect object pronoun.

> **Le leyó el poema.** (*He read her the poem. [He read the poem to her.]*)

Note, too, that you must use an indirect object pronoun in Spanish even if you explicitly express *to* or *for* whom the action was done:

> **Le dio a ella el regalo.** (*He gave her the gift. [He gave the gift to her.]*)

Lost in music translation

In a term paper about rock music, one of my students made the mistake of trying to translate literally. Unfortunately, he used a computer language translator and consistently referred to rock music as **la música piedra.** I had tears rolling down from my eyes after I read that one. Are you currently laughing as hard as I was?

Una piedra is, indeed, *a rock.* But it's a rock that you find on the ground when digging in your garden. Had this student taken the time to use his bilingual dictionary, he would've found that Spanish borrowed the word "rock" from English, and that the correct expression in Spanish is **la música rock.**

Misusing Gustar and Similar Verbs

English speakers often misuse **gustar** (*like*) because they forget that in the **gustar** construction, an indirect object precedes the verb and the subject follows the verb. Because a verb must agree with its subject, **gustar** must agree with the noun that comes after it. In most instances, you use only the third person singular form (**gusta**) and the third person plural form (**gustan**). Only the **gusta** form may be used before infinitives. The following examples highlight these points:

> **Me gusta el postre.** (*I like the dessert.*)
>
> **Me gustan las frutas.** (*I like fruits.*)
>
> **Me gusta bailar.** (*I like to dance.*)
>
> **Me gusta bailar y cantar.** (*I like to dance and sing.*)

You can study other high-frequency verbs like **gustar** in Chapter 10.

Forgetting about Idioms with Tener

Although **tener** literally means *to have,* there are certain very commonly used idiomatic expressions in which **tener** means *to be* or in which it may have another, unexpected meaning. Be careful, when writing, not to use the verbs **ser** or **estar** (*to be*) in these idiomatic expressions. Improper verb selection for common phrases will mark you as a novice. These idiomatic expressions include the following:

tener calor	(*to be warm, hot*)	**tener sed**	(*to be thirsty*)
tener frío	(*to be cool, cold*)	**tener lugar**	(*to take place*)
tener celos de	(*to be jealous of*)	**tener miedo de**	(*to be afraid of*)
tener cuidado	(*to be careful*)	**tener prisa**	(*to be in a hurry*)
tener dolor de . . .	(*to have a . . . ache*)	**tener razón**	(*to be right*)
tener éxito	(*to succeed*)	**tener sueño**	(*to be sleepy*)
tener ganas de	(*to feel like*)	**tener suerte**	(*to be lucky*)
tener hambre	(*to be hungry*)		

The following example uses **tener suerte:**

Tienes mucha suerte. (*You are very lucky.*)

Using the Incorrect Past Tense (Preterit or the Imperfect)

Because English features only one past tense, Spanish having the preterit and the imperfect (the former to state a completed action and the latter to describe what was happening in the past) confuses English speakers and can cause a tremendous amount of mistakes. Time and again, I've had students perfectly memorize the uses of the preterit and the imperfect only to use them improperly when they had to write compositions (see Chapter 13).

When writing in the past, always double check the verbs you've used and make sure of the following:

- ✔ Any verb that states a completed action at a particular moment in the past is in the preterit.
- ✔ Any verb that describes a scene or that expresses what "used to be" or "was" happening is in the imperfect.

Certain verbs that describe a state of mind — such as **querer** (*to want*), **poder** (*to be able to*), **saber** (*to know*), **pensar** (*to think*), and so on — are generally, but not always, used in the imperfect. The correct tense often depends on whether the writer perceives the action as completed at a specific time.

Ignoring the Subjunctive

Because English speakers are so unaware of the use of the subjunctive in English, we tend to have difficulty with its use in Spanish. If, however, you want to write like a native Spanish speaker, and if you want to do more than create simple, one-clause sentences, you must have a good command of the subjunctive. The subjunctive helps you to express, among other things, your wishes, emotions, needs, and doubts.

Using the subjunctive properly will help you avoid the common mistakes associated with word-for-word translations. Here's an example:

I want you to go to the supermarket. (*Quiero que vayas al supermercado.*)

Although the English "I want you to go" is perfectly acceptable, in Spanish you can't say "I want you . . ." without being very fresh, if you know what I mean. You must join your two thoughts with **que,** and you must put your dependent clause (the one following the clause showing the wishing, emotion, doubt, need, and so on) in the subjunctive. I cover the subjunctive in detail in Chapter 7 so you can raise your level of speaking and writing.

Chapter 17

Ten Tips for Writing Well in Spanish

In This Chapter

▶ Applying good English writing skills to Spanish

▶ Avoiding common mistakes that ruin writing

▶ Using helpful resources to write well

*1*f you know how to avoid errors when writing in English, you have a head start on avoiding errors when you write in Spanish. You can apply the tools you picked up in English 101 as you write down your thoughts in Spanish. But just in case you need a little extra help, this chapter presents ten tips that will allow you to express yourself correctly in Spanish. When it comes to grammar, there are mistakes, and then there are *mistakes!* If you can avoid the big ones by following the rules and tips I present in Chapter 16, and if you can apply the skills I list here, your writing will be clear, concise, and easily understood.

Some of the tips in this chapter may seem a bit obvious, but you'd be surprised at how many papers I've corrected where the students knew the work but gave very poor, sloppy presentations. Students who follow these tips always wind up with better grades because they put in the extra effort that makes the difference between well-written work and substandard rambling.

Write in Complete Sentences

I've had many students whose writing was inconsistent. What do I mean by this? In one part of a student's paper, a paragraph would consist of one sentence that rambled on and on for five to ten lines — what grammarians refer to as a *run-on*. Unfortunately, the thought at the beginning often had very little to do with what went on at the end. I got lost somewhere around the middle! And in the next paragraph, the student would have a series of words that didn't constitute a complete thought. Some sentences didn't even have verbs! Sadly, I had only *sentence fragments* to contend with.

Don't let yourself fall into the run-on or fragment trap when writing in Spanish. It's better to write one short, well-constructed sentence than to try to prove that you're the next Spanish Shakespeare. The same writing principles that you learned in your English classes also apply to your Spanish writing: Use complete sentences.

Use Correct Punctuation

Spanish uses the same punctuation marks as English, but it features some variations in the rules of usage. The following list presents the major differences:

- ✔ In numerals, you use a comma rather than a period, and vice versa:

  English: $7,537.26

  Spanish: $7.537, 26

- ✔ In lists, you don't put a comma between the last item and **y** (*and*), whereas in English some writers use a comma before *and:*

  Necesito un lápiz, una regla y una hoja de papel. (*I need a pencil, a ruler, and a piece of paper.*)

- ✔ For quotation marks, the main difference is that sentence punctuation in Spanish goes outside the quotation marks. In English, the punctuation goes inside the quotation marks:

  Él dijo, "Te quiero". (*He said, "I love you."*)

- ✔ In Spanish, you use an upside-down question mark at the beginning of a question and a regular question mark at the end of the question. If a sentence contains more parts than just the question, you place the question marks around the question only:

  Si estás cansada, ¿por qué vas al cine? (*If you are tired, why are you going to the movies?*)

- ✔ In Spanish, you use an upside-down exclamation point at the beginning of the exclamation and a regular exclamation point at the end of the exclamation. If a sentence contains both a question and an exclamation, you must use one of the marks at the beginning of the sentence and the other at the end:

  ¡Qué lastima, encontraste tu cartera? (*What a shame, did you find your wallet?*)

  Note that you can also separate the previous sentence:

  ¡Qué lástima! ¿Encontraste tu cartera? (*What a shame! Did you find your wallet?*)

Avoid Slang

An *idiom* is a phrase that's an acceptable grammatical peculiarity used in oral and written expression. You can't deduce the meaning of an idiom from the combined meaning of the words it contains. The idiom is simply understood by those in the know. Native speakers customarily use idioms, and they may be suitable for your written work. Here are some examples of idioms in English:

That dress cost me **a pretty penny.**

His comments only **added fuel to the fire.**

The ball is in your court.

I discuss some Spanish idioms in Chapter 4.

Slang, on the other hand, is very informal, non-standard language that's generally spoken rather than written. Slang is considered unconventional street language. It's often off-color; in some instances, it's plain rude and offensive. Slang has no place in formal writing. You should never use it in Spanish compositions, letters, term papers, or any written material viewed by a teacher, boss, or other person of authority. Here are some examples of mild English slang:

> I want to **veg out** today.

> She's so **wired** because she drank too much coffee.

> He makes **megabucks.**

Steer Clear of False Assumptions

In order to write well in Spanish, you must avoid some common incorrect assumptions English speakers make:

- ✔ Don't assume that every English word has an equivalent Spanish cognate that you can form simply by adding **-o.** I've heard many intelligent, professional English speakers try to express that everything is just fine by exclaiming **¡No problemo!** Even if you gently try to correct them with **"No hay problema",** they persist in using the incorrect phrase. Don't allow yourself to fall into this trap. If you're unsure of a word, consult your bilingual dictionary. In most instances, adding a final **-o** won't create a Spanish word, but it will make your work appear sloppy.

- ✔ Be careful with the gender of nouns. Just because a Spanish noun ends in **-o** doesn't mean it's masculine: **la mano** (*the hand*). And Spanish nouns ending in **-a** aren't necessarily feminine: **el mapa** (*the map*). If you're unsure about nouns ending in other letters, look them up. You want your writing to look polished; your bilingual dictionary will help you achieve that goal. (For more on gender, see Chapter 3.)

- ✔ Don't assume that all Spanish words that look like English words have the same meaning in both languages. For instance, you'll wind up with egg on your face if you try to express that a man is **embarazado.** Although it appears, from your knowledge of English, that you're saying he's embarrassed, in actuality you use **embarazada** only for females — and to describe them as being *pregnant,* no less! Watch out for these "false friends" that can trick you into writing something you don't mean.

Watch Out for Subject/Verb Agreement

If you want to produce quality writing, take all the time you need to ensure that your verbs agree with the subjects you use. For instance, be aware that collective nouns, such as **la familia** (*the family*) and **el grupo** (*the group*), require singular verb forms. If necessary, use the verb charts in Appendix A or consult *Spanish Verbs For Dummies,* by Cecie Kraynak (Wiley). If you use a trusted source, your verb endings will always be correct and you'll internalize the forms as you're exposed to them and as you use them more frequently.

Watch out for verbs that have spelling and stem changes. Stem changes usually are indicated in parentheses next to the verbs: **mostrar (ue)** — (*to show*). Know the verbs that have irregular forms so that you can write them correctly (for more information on verb changes and verb agreement, check out Chapter 4).

Select the Appropriate Verb Tense/Mood

Always bear in mind that the tense of a verb reflects the time period in which the action is taking place. The key words that are followed by verbs should jump out at you as requiring specific tenses:

- *Am, are, is, do,* and *does* usually indicate the present. *Am*, *are*, and *is* may also indicate the present progressive.
- *Did* or an English past participle generally indicates the preterit.
- *Was, were,* and *used to* indicate the imperfect.
- *Will* indicates the future.

The indicative mood, the most commonly used, states a fact and requires the present, past, or future tense. The imperative mood requires a command. The subjunctive is a mood that shows wishing, wanting, emotion, need, or doubt (among other things) and requires special verb forms. Finally, the infinitive is a mood that shows the verb in its "to" form, before it's conjugated: *to dance,* for instance.

Avoid switching tenses and moods unnecessarily in mid-sentence or mid-paragraph because this will make your work seem choppy. If you want your work to flow smoothly, watch the tense and the mood you select. For more on these verb forms, check out various chapters in this book (such as the chapters in Part IV for the past and future).

Correct Dangling Prepositions

You've probably heard this one before in one of your English classes: Don't let a preposition dangle at the end of a sentence. Colloquial English usage, however, has become more tolerant of those pesky prepositions that finish off sentences. It seems far less awkward to say "That's what I'm accustomed to" than to give the correct version: "It is that to which I'm accustomed." Face it, very few people speak in this manner — perhaps only the most pedantic grammarian. It just sounds too stuffy and too clumsy.

Spanish, however, is less forgiving. Although English lets you get away with the dangling preposition "to" in the previous example, Spanish does not. You may not end a sentence with a preposition. Here's the proper Spanish equivalent of the previous English example: **Estoy acostumbrado a eso.** (For more on prepositions, head to Chapter 12.)

Select the Proper Pronoun

Before selecting a pronoun for a Spanish sentence, you must know the purpose it serves so that you can choose wisely. Spanish features many different types of pronouns, and they can become very confusing. Here are some rules and examples (for more pronoun information, refer to Chapters 2, 3, 4, 10, 11, and 12):

- ✔ **yo** is a subject pronoun meaning *I:*

  Yo vengo. (*I'm coming.*)

- ✔ **me** can be a direct object pronoun meaning *me:*

  Él me mira. (*He's looking at me.*)

- ✔ **me** can be an indirect object pronoun meaning *to/for me:*

  Él me escribió. (*He wrote to me.*)

- ✔ **me** can be a reflexive pronoun meaning *myself:*

  Me lavo. (*I wash myself.*)

- ✔ **mi** (**mis**) are possessive pronouns meaning *my:*

  Es mi casa. (*This is my house.*) **¿Dónde están mis llaves?** (*Where are my keys?*)

- ✔ **mí** (note the accent) is a prepositional pronoun meaning *me* — **No es para mí.** (*That's not for me.*) **Mí** becomes **migo** after the preposition **con** (*with*):

  ¿Puedes ir conmigo? (*Can you go with me?*)

- ✔ **mío** (**mía, míos, mías**) are possessive pronouns meaning *mine:*

  Tu hermana es alta. La mía es baja. (*You sister is tall. Mine is short.*)

Rely on the Net and Your Computer

If you need some information when writing in Spanish, you can rely on your computer for help. Don't feel bad! You're not cheating. You can find some wonderful online bilingual dictionaries that are easy to use, have up-to-the-minute translations, and allow you to post queries when the dictionaries aren't quite specific enough to respond to your questions. Using the Internet as a resource is certainly more time-effective and pleasant than thumbing through a heavy dictionary that's balanced on your knees as you type.

You also can find some very informative Web sites if you need specialized vocabulary lists, help with grammar questions, or information about a specific country. One caveat, however, is that you must verify that the information you receive online is up-to-date and correct. Know the Web site before you trust its contents.

Computer spelling checks, grammar checks, and Internet translation programs — in any language — are notoriously unreliable. Your computer may miss a mistake or point one out where none exists because it doesn't take parts of speech into account. Here's a real-life example that I recently read on a student's paper:

Ella canta quiere un ruiseñor. (*She sings like a nightingale.*)

Quiere is a form of the verb **querer** (*to wish/want/like*). What's needed in this sentence, however, is the adverb **como** (*like*):

Ella canta como un ruiseñor.

Another student, writing a Spanish paper about music, mentioned Bill Haley. His translator program gave him this: **Cuenta Haley. Cuenta,** indeed, is the translation for *bill* — the bill you get at the restaurant at the end of your meal! So much for word-by-word translations. (Stop laughing so loud! It was an honest mistake!) The moral of the story? Be extremely cautious when you use your computer.

Proofread Your Work

I can't say this enough: Proofread your work! And after you finish checking your writing, give your work to a second pair of eyes: a friend, a classmate, a relative — anyone who's available! It's hard for one person to catch every mistake; it's even harder for that person to recognize every mistake. You've probably read the paper so many times that the errors have become unnoticeable. Different eyes will read your work in a different way than you did, and a new reader will notice things that you missed.

To produce really exceptional work, you must give your writing a once-over before submitting it. Proofreading takes so little time but makes all the difference in the world with your finished product.

Chapter 18

Ten Important Verb Distinctions

In This Chapter
▶ Avoiding verb mixups and selecting the proper verb
▶ Understanding different verb connotations

Have you used a thesaurus lately? A thesaurus is a wonderful tool that helps you write and speak without having to constantly repeat words. When your vocabulary varies, your prose tends to flow instead of dragging along. In some instances, if you're lucky, you'll find a word that has the exact meaning you're looking for. But more often than not, the words you must choose from are very close in meaning to the word you want to replace, but don't communicate the precise idea you want to get across. You make your selection by trying to preserve, as much as possible, the thought or idea you want to express.

Just like in English, you can describe actions or situations in Spanish by using different verbs, depending on the exact meaning you want to convey. When you're learning a foreign language, picking up a good bilingual dictionary and reading the examples that show the subtle nuances in meaning will ensure that you select the verbs best suited to your needs. In this chapter, I present 20 verbs in Spanish but only 10 English meanings. These verbs are often misused because they have the same English meanings but different English connotations. But not to worry. I explain how you can determine which to use in any given situation.

Ser versus Estar

The verbs **ser** and **estar** always cause considerable confusion, because both verbs mean *to be*. You use each of these verbs differently, however.

You use **ser** to express the following:

- ✔ An inherent characteristic or quality (one that probably won't change any time soon):

  Mi abuela es vieja. (*My grandmother is old.*)

- ✔ The identity of the subject:

  Mi padre es abogado. (*My father is a lawyer.*)

- ✔ The date, time, or place of an event:

  Es jueves. (*It's Thursday.*)

  Son las once. (*It's eleven o'clock.*)

  ¿Dónde es el concierto? (*Where is the concert?*)

✔ Origin and nationality:

Ella es de Cuba. (*She is from Cuba.*)

Ella es cubana. (*She is Cuban.*)

✔ Ownership:

Es mi perro. (*It's my dog.*)

✔ Material:

Es de oro. (*It's made of gold.*)

✔ An impersonal idea:

Es fácil escribir en español. (*It's easy to write in Spanish.*)

On the other hand, you use **estar** to express

✔ Heatlh:

¿Cómo estás? Estoy bien. (*How are you? I'm fine.*)

✔ Location, situation, or position:

El diccionario está en la mesa. (*The dictionary is on the table.*)

✔ Temporary conditions or states:

Ella está ocupada. (*She is busy.*)

✔ The present progressive tense (see Chapter 6):

El niño está durmiendo. (*The child is sleeping.*)

Saber versus Conocer

Both **saber** and **conocer** mean *to know*. **Saber** expresses knowing how to do something or knowing a fact. **Conocer** expresses knowing in the sense of being acquainted with a person, place, thing, or idea. Note the differences in the following examples:

Yo sé hablar español. (*I know how to speak Spanish.*)

Ella sabe mi nombre. (*She knows my name.*)

Sabemos el poema. (*We know the poem [by heart].*)

Yo conozco al señor López. (*I know Mr. López.*)

¿Conoces este libro? (*Do you know [Are you acquainted with] this book?*)

Conocemos el poema. (*We know [are acquainted with] the poem.*)

Tomar versus Llevar

Determining the correct usage for **tomar** and **llevar** can be a bit tricky. Both verbs mean *to take*. You use **tomar** when the subject picks up something in his or her hands in order to physically carry it to another location. You use **llevar** when the subject is taking or leading a person/thing somewhere, is leading a person/thing to a place, or is carrying or transporting an item.

In most instances, if you can substitute the word "lead" or "carry" for "take," you should use the verb **llevar**. If you can't substitute one of those words, you should use **tomar**.

Here are some examples to help clarify:

Tomo tu lápiz. (*I'm taking your pencil.*)

Tomó el niño de la mano. (*He took the child by the hand.*)

Llevo a mi hermano a la playa. (*I'm taking my brother to the beach.*)

Llevaron su coche al garaje. (*They took their car to the garage.*)

You can compare the two verbs at work in this example sentence:

Tomé mi libro y lo llevé a la escuela. (*I took my book and I brought it to school.*)

Deber versus Tener Que

You use both **deber** and **tener que** to express what a subject *must* or *has* to do. You generally use **deber** to express a moral obligation, whereas **tener que** expresses what has to be done:

Debes pedir permiso antes de salir. (*You must ask for permission before going out.*)

Tengo que ir al dentista porque tengo un dolor de las muelas. (*I have to go to the dentist because I have a toothache.*)

Preguntar versus Pedir

Preguntar and **pedir** both mean *to ask*. You use **preguntar** to show that the subject is asking a question or inquiring about someone or something. You use **pedir** to show that the subject is asking for or requesting something in particular:

Quiero preguntarle si quiere acompañarme. (*I want to ask him if he wants to go with me.*)

¿Van a pedirles permiso? (*Are you going to ask them permission?*)

Yo le pregunté por qué me pidió tu dirección. (*I asked him why he asked me for your address.*)

The word **porqué** doesn't exist in Spanish. It's either **¿por qué . . . ?** (two separate words that together mean *why?* — or **porque,** one word that means *because*).

Jugar versus Tocar

Jugar and **tocar** both mean *to play*. You use **jugar** (generally followed by the preposition **a;** see Chapter 12) when the subject is engaging in a sport or game. You use **tocar** when the subject is playing a musical instrument:

Ellos jugaban a los naipes mientras yo tocaba el piano. (*They were playing cards while I was playing the piano.*)

Gastar versus Pasar

If you're into *spending,* **gastar** and **pasar** are the verbs you need to discuss your passions. Those of us who love to spend money use **gastar,** while people who spend time engaging in an activity should use **pasar:**

Pasé dos semanas en México. (*I spent two weeks in Mexico.*)

Gasté mucho dinero allí. (*I spent a lot of money there.*)

Dejar versus Salir

Dejar expresses that the subject has left something behind, whereas **salir** expresses that the subject has left a place:

Voy a dejar mis gafas en casa. (*I am going to leave my glasses home.*)

Ella no puede salir sin ellos. (*She can't leave without them.*)

Volver versus Devolver

Volver(ue) and **devolver(ue)** both have the same meaning — *to return* — and you conjugate them in the same way. Use **volver** when the subject is physically returning to a place. Use **devolver** when the subject is returning an item to its owner:

Siempre le devuelvo a ella sus llaves cuando vuelve a casa. (*I always return her keys to her when she returns home.*)

Poder versus Saber

Poder and **saber** can be a tricky pair of verbs. Both verbs mean *can,* but here's how they differ: **Poder** shows that the subject has the ability to perform an action, and **saber** shows that the subject actually knows how to perform the action.

If you can substitute the words "knows how to" for "can," you should use **saber.** Otherwise, use **poder.** Here are some examples:

Yo puedo cocinar. (*I can cook.*)

Here you're saying that you have the ability to cook, but that doesn't necessarily mean that you know *how* to cook.

Yo sé cocinar. (*I can cook.*)

Now you're saying that, yes, you know how to cook!

Part VI
Appendixes

The 5th Wave   By Rich Tennant

@RICHTENNANT

"Joe's pest control? Can you put me on hold again? I was really enjoying that snappy rendition of 'La Cucaracha!'"

In this part . . .

Have you forgotten a verb conjugation and you don't have the patience to scan the Table of Contents and then search for the proper table in the book? Have you forgotten a word and now you don't feel like leafing through the book to find the page you need? If so, you've come to the right part. Appendix A contains verb charts that help you quickly find the conjugations for all the verbs you need in many Spanish tenses and moods. If you know the word you're looking for but can't recall it in Spanish, just consult the English-to-Spanish dictionary in Appendix B. And if I've used a word you don't recognize, or if you've simply forgotten the meaning of a Spanish word, you can turn to Appendix C, the Spanish-to-English dictionary.

Appendix A
Verb Charts

Regular Verbs

The three families of Spanish verbs are those that end in **-ar, -er,** and **-ir.** Regular verbs within those categories follow the same rules for conjugation, no matter the tense (present, past, future) or mood (imperative, subjunctive). The regular verbs I list in this section drop their respective infinitive ending (**-ar, -er,** or **-ir**) and add the endings I have in bold.

-ar verbs

trabajar (to work)

Gerund: trabaj**ando**

Commands: ¡Trabaj**e** Ud.! ¡Trabaj**en** Uds.! ¡Trabaj**emos!** ¡Trabaj**a** tú! ¡No trabaj**es** tú! ¡Trabaj**ad** vosotros! ¡Trabaj**éis** vosotros!

Person	Present	Preterit	Imperfect	Future	Subjunctive
yo	trabaj**o**	trabaj**é**	trabaj**aba**	trabajar**é**	trabaj**e**
tú	trabaj**as**	trabaj**aste**	trabaj**abas**	trabajar**ás**	trabaj**es**
él, ella, Ud.	trabaj**a**	trabaj**ó**	trabaj**aba**	trabajar**á**	trabaj**e**
nosotros	trabaj**amos**	trabaj**amos**	trabaj**ábamos**	trabajar**emos**	trabaj**emos**
vosotros	trabaj**áis**	trabaj**asteis**	trabaj**abais**	trabajar**éis**	trabaj**éis**
ellos, ellas, Uds.	trabaj**an**	trabaj**aron**	trabaj**aban**	trabajar**án**	trabaj**en**

-er verbs

comer (to eat)

Gerund: com**iendo**

Commands: ¡Com**a** Ud.! ¡Com**an** Uds.! ¡Com**amos!** ¡Com**e** tú! ¡No com**as** tú! ¡Com**ed** vosotros! ¡No com**áis** vosotros!

Person	Present	Preterit	Imperfect	Future	Subjunctive
yo	com**o**	com**í**	com**ía**	comer**é**	com**a**
tú	com**es**	com**iste**	com**ías**	comer**ás**	com**as**
él, ella, Ud.	com**e**	com**ió**	com**ía**	comer**á**	com**a**
nosotros	com**emos**	com**imos**	com**íamos**	comer**emos**	com**amos**
vosotros	com**éis**	com**isteis**	com**íais**	comer**éis**	com**áis**
ellos, ellas, Uds.	com**en**	com**ieron**	com**ían**	comer**án**	com**an**

-ir verbs

abrir (to open)

Gerund: abr**iendo**

Commands: ¡Abr**a** Ud.! ¡Abr**an** Uds.! ¡Abr**amos**! ¡Abr**e** tú! ¡No abr**as** tú! ¡Abr**id** vosotros! No abr**áis** vosotros!

Person	Present	Preterit	Imperfect	Future	Subjunctive
yo	abr**o**	abr**í**	abr**ía**	abrir**é**	abr**a**
tú	abr**es**	abr**iste**	abr**ías**	abrir**ás**	abr**as**
él, ella, Ud.	abr**e**	abr**ió**	abr**ía**	abrir**á**	abr**a**
nosotros	abr**imos**	abr**imos**	abr**íamos**	abrir**emos**	abr**amos**
vosotros	abr**ís**	abr**isteis**	abr**íais**	abrir**éis**	abr**áis**
ellos, ellas, Uds.	abr**en**	abr**ieron**	abr**ían**	abrir**án**	abr**an**

Stem-Changing Verbs

Stem-changing verbs require an internal change in the *stem vowel* (the vowel before the **-ar, -er,** or **-ir** infinitive ending) in the **yo, tú, él, (ella, Ud.),** and **ellos (ellas, Uds.)** forms of certain tenses. In all other tenses, stem-changing verbs don't require any change; they follow the examples given in the "Regular Verbs" section according to their infinitive ending.

-ar verbs

pensar (e to ie) (to think)

Present: pienso, piensas, piensa, pensamos, pensáis, piensan

Subjunctive: piense, pienses, piense, pensemos, penséis, piensen

Other verbs like **pensar** include: **cerrar** (*to close*), **comenzar** (*to begin*), **despertarse** (*to wake up*), **empezar** (*to begin*), and **sentarse** (*to sit down*).

mostrar (o to ue) (to show)

Present: muestro, muestras, muestra, mostramos, mostráis, muestran

Subjunctive: muestre, muestres, muestre, mostremos, mostréis, muestren

Other verbs like **mostrar** include: **acordarse de** (*to remember*), **almorzar** (*to eat lunch*), **acostarse** (*to go to bed*), **contar** (*to tell*), **costar** (*to cost*), **encontrar** (*to find*), **probar** (*to prove, to try*), and **recordar** (*to remember*).

jugar (u to ue) (to play [a sport or game])

Present: juego, juegas, juega, jugamos, jugáis, juegan

Preterit: jugué, jugaste, jugó, jugamos, jugasteis, jugaron

Subjunctive: juegue, juegues, juegue, juguemos, juguéis, jueguen

-er verbs

querer (e to ie) (to wish, want)

Present: quiero, quieres, quiere, queremos, queréis, quieren

Subjunctive: quiera, quieras, quiera, queramos, queráis, quieran

Other verbs like **querer** include **defender** (*to defend, to forbid*), **descender** (*to descend*), **entender** (*to understand, to hear*), and **perder** (*to lose*)

volver (o to ue) (to return)

Present: vuelvo, vuelves, vuelve, volvemos, volvéis, vuelven

Subjunctive: vuelva, vuelvas, vuelve, volvamos, volváis, vuelvan

Other verbs like **volver** include: **devolver** (*to return*), **envolver** (*to wrap*), **llover** (*to rain*), **morder** (*to bite*), **mover** (*to move*), and **poder** (*to be able to, can*).

-ir verbs

pedir (e to i) (to measure)

Gerund: pidiendo

Present: pido, pides, pide, pedimos, pedís, piden

Preterit: pedí, pediste, pidió, pedimos, pedisteis, pidieron

Subjunctive: pida, pidas, pida, pidamos, pidáis, pidan

Other verbs like **pedir** include: **impedir** (_to prevent_), **medir** (_to measure_), **repetir** (_to repeat_), and **servir** (_to serve_).

sentir (e to ie/i) (to feel)

Gerund: sintiendo

Present: siento sientes, siente, sentimos, sentís, sienten

Preterit: sentí, sentiste, sintió, sentimos, sentisteis, sintieron

Subjunctive: sienta, sientas, sienta, sintamos, sintáis, sientan

Other verbs like **sentir** include: **advertir** (_to warn, to notify_), **consentir** (_to consent_), **mentir** (_to lie_), **preferir** (_to prefer_), and **referir** (_to refer_).

dormir (o to ue/u) (to sleep)

Gerund: durmiendo

Present: duermo, duermes, duerme, dormimos, dormís, duermen

Preterit: dormí, dormiste, durmió, dormimos, dormisteis, durmieron

Subjunctive: duerma, duermas, duerma, dormamos, dormáis, duerman

Another verb like **dormir** is **morir** (_to die_).

-uir verbs (except -guir)

construir (add y) (to construct, build)

Gerund: construyendo

Present: construyo, construyes, construye, construimos, construís, construyen

Preterit: construí, construiste, construyó, construimos, construisteis, construyeron

Subjunctive: construya, construyas, construya, construyamos, construyáis, construyan

Other verbs like **construir** include: **concluir** (_to conclude_), **contribuir** (_to contribute_), **destruir** (_to destroy_), **incluir** (_to include_), and **sustituir** (_to substitue_).

-eer verbs

creer (add y) (to believe)

Preterit: creí, creíste, creyó, creímos, creísteis, creyeron

Other verbs like **creer** include: **leer** (*to read*), **poseer** (*to possess*), and **proveer** (*to provide*).

-iar verbs

guiar (i to í) (to guide)

Present: guío, guías, guía, guiamos, guiáis, guían

Subjunctive: guíe, guíes, guíe, guiemos, guiéis, guíen

Other verbs like **guiar** include: **confiar + en** (*to confide in*), **enviar** (*to send*), **esquiar** (*to ski*), and **variar** (*to vary*).

-uar verbs

continuar (u to ú) (to continue)

Present: continúo, continúas, continúa, continuamos, continuáis, continúan

Subjunctive: continúe, continúes, continúe, continuemos, continuéis, continúen

Another verb like **continuar** is **actuar** (*to act*).

Spelling-Change Verbs

Some verbs require a spelling change in certain tenses to preserve proper pronunciation. In all the tenses I don't list in this section, verbs with spelling changes don't require the changes; they follow the examples given in the "Regular Verbs" section according to their infinitive ending.

-car verbs

buscar (c to qu) (to look for)

Preterit: bus**qu**é, buscaste, buscó, buscamos, buscasteis, buscaron

Subjunctive: bus**qu**e, bus**qu**es, bus**qu**e, bus**qu**emos, bus**qu**éis, bus**qu**en

Other verbs like **buscar** include: **acercar** (*to bring near*), **aplicar** (*to apply*), **criticar** (*to criticize*), **educar** (*to educate*), **explicar** (*to explain*), **identificar** (*to identify*), **pescar** (*to fish*), **practicar** (*to practice*), **sacar** (*to take out*), and **significar** (*to mean*).

-gar verbs

llegar (g to gu) (to arrive)

Preterit: lle**gu**é, llegaste, llegó, llegamos, llegasteis, llegaron

Subjunctive: lle**gue**, lle**gu**es, lle**gu**e, lle**gu**emos, lle**gu**éis, lle**gu**en

Other verbs like **llegar** include: **apagar** (*to extinguish*), **castigar** (*to punish*), and **pagar** (*to pay*).

-zar verbs

lanzar (z to c) (to throw)

Preterit: lan**c**é, lanzaste, lanzó, lanzamos, lanzasteis, lanzaron

Subjunctive: lan**c**e, lan**c**es, lan**c**e, lan**c**emos, lan**c**éis, lan**c**en

Other verbs like **lanzar** include: **avanzar** (*to advance*), **gozar** (*to enjoy*), **memorizar** (*to memorize*), **organizar** (*to organize*), and **utilizar** (*to use*).

Consonant + -cer or -cir verbs

ejercer (c to z) (to exercise)

Present: ejer**z**o, ejerces, ejerce, ejercemos, ejercéis, ejercen

Subjunctive: ejer**z**a, ejer**z**as, ejer**z**a, ejer**z**amos, ejer**z**áis, ejer**z**an

Other verbs like **ejercer** include: **convencer** (*to convince*) and **vencer** (*to conquer*).

esparcir (c to z) (to spread out)

Present: espar**z**o, esparces, esparce, esparcimos, esparcéis, esparcen

Subjunctive: espar**z**a, espar**z**as, espar**z**a, espar**z**amos, espar**z**áis, espar**z**an

Vowel + -cer or -cir verbs

conocer (c to zc) (to know)

Present: cono**zc**o, conoces, conoce, conocemos, conocéis, conocen

Subjunctive: cono**zc**a, cono**zc**as, cono**zc**a, cono**zc**amos, cono**zc**áis, cono**zc**an

Other verbs like **conocer** include: **crecer** (*to grow*), **desobedecer** (*to disobey*), **desaparacer** (*to disappear*), **establecer** (*to establish*), **obedecer** (*to obey*), **ofrecer** (*to offer*), and **parecer** (*to seem*).

traducir (*c to zc*) (*to translate*)

> Present: tradu**zc**o, traduces, traduce, traducimos, traducéis, traducen

> Subjunctive: tradu**zc**a, tradu**zc**as, tradu**zc**a, tradu**zc**amos, tradu**zc**áis, tradu**zc**an

Other verbs like **traducir** include: **conducir** (*to drive*), **deducir** (*to deduce*), **inducir** (*to induce*), and **traducir** (*to translate*).

-ger or -gir verbs

escoger (*g to j*) (*to choose*)

> Present: esco**j**o, escoges, escoge, escogimos, escogís, escogen

> Subjunctive: esco**j**a, esco**j**as, esco**j**a, esco**j**amos, esco**j**áis, esco**j**an

Other verbs like **escoger** include: **coger** (*to take, to pick up*), **proteger** (*to protect*), and **recoger** (*to pick up*).

dirigir (*g to j*) (*to direct*)

> Present: diri**j**o, diriges, dirige, dirigimos, dirigís, dirigen

> Subjunctive: diri**j**a, diri**j**as, diri**j**a, diri**j**amos, diri**j**áis, diri**j**an

Another verb like **dirigir** is **exigir** (*to demand*).

-uir verbs

distinguir (*gu to g*) (*to distinguish*)

> Present: distin**g**o, distingues, distingue, distinguimos, distinguís, distinguen

> Subjunctive: distin**g**a, distin**g**as, distin**g**a, distin**g**amos, distin**g**áis, distin**g**an

Irregular Verbs

Irregular verbs may undergo changes in some or all tenses and moods and for some or all subjects. You must memorize the irregular forms because they follow no specific rules. For all the tenses I don't list in this section, the irregular verb follows the examples given in the "Regular Verbs" section according to its infinitive ending.

dar (*to give*)

> Present: **doy**, das, da, damos, dáis, dan

> Preterit: **di, diste, dió, dimos, disteis, dieron**

> Subjunctive: **dé,** des, **dé,** demos, déis, den

decir (to say, tell)

Gerund: **diciendo**

Affirmative Familiar Singular Command: **di**

Present: **digo, dices, dice,** decimos, decís, **dicen**

Preterit: **dije, dijiste, dijo, dijmos, dijisteis, dijeron**

Future: **diré, dirás, dirá, diremos, diréis, dirán**

Subjunctive: **diga, digas, diga, digamos, digáis, digan**

estar (to be)

Present: **estoy, estás, está,** estamos, estáis, **están**

Preterit: **estuve, estuviste, estuvo, estuvimos, estuvisteis, estuvieron**

Subjunctive: **esté, estés, esté,** estemos, estéis, **estén**

hacer (to make, do)

Affirmative Familiar Singular Command: **haz**

Present: **hago,** haces, hace, hacemos, hacéis, hacen

Preterit: **hice, hiciste, hizo, hicimos, hicisteis, hicieron**

Future: **haré, harás, hará, haremos, haréis, harán**

Subjunctive: **haga, hagas, haga, hagamos, hagáis, hagan**

ir (to go)

Gerund: **yendo**

Affirmative Familiar Command: **ve**

Present: **voy, vas, va, vamos, vais, van**

Preterit: **fui, fuiste, fue, fuimos, fuisteis, fueron**

Subjunctive: **vaya, vayas, vaya, vayamos, vayáis, vayan**

oír (to hear)

Gerund: **oyendo**

Affirmative Informal Singular Command: **oye**

Affirmative Informal Plural Command: **oíd**

Present: **oigo, oyes, oye,** oímos, oís, **oyen**

Preterit: oí, oíste, **oyó,** oímos, oísteis, **oyeron**

Subjunctive: **oiga, oigas, oiga, oigamos, oigáis, oigan**

poder (o to ue) (to be able to, can)

Gerund: **pudiendo**

Present: **puedo, puedes, puede,** podemos, podéis, **pueden**

Preterit: **pude, pudiste, pudo, pudimos, pudisteis, pudieron**

Future: **podré, podrás, podrá, podremos, podréis, podrán**

Subjunctive: **pueda, puedas, pueda,** podamos, podáis, **puedan**

poner (to put)

Past Participle: **puesto**

Affirmative Familiar Singular Command: **pon**

Present: **pongo,** pones, pone, ponemos, ponéis, ponen

Preterit: **puse, pusiste, puso, pusimos, pusisteis, pusieron**

Future: **pondré, pondrás, pondrá, pondremos, pondréis, pondrán**

Subjunctive: **ponga, pongas, ponga, pongamos, pongáis, pongan**

querer (to want, wish)

Present: **quiero, quieres, quiere,** queremos, queréis, **quieren**

Preterit: **quise, quisiste, quiso, quisimos, quisisteis, quisieron**

Future: **querré, querrás, querrá, querremos, querréis, querrán**

Subjunctive: **quiera, quieras, quiera,** queramos, queráis, **quieran**

saber (to know)

Present: **sé,** sabes, sabe, sabemos, sabéis, saben

Preterit: **supe, supiste, supo, supimos, supisteis, supieron**

Future: **sabré, sabrás, sabrá, sabremos, sabréis, sabrán**

Subjunctive: **sepa, sepas, sepa, sepamos, sepáis, sepan**

salir (to go out, leave)

Affirmative Familiar Singular Command: **sal**

Present: **salgo,** sales, sale, salimos, salís, salen

Future: **saldré, saldrás, saldrá, saldremos, saldréis, saldrán**

Subjunctive: **salga, salgas, salga, salgamos, salgáis, salgan**

ser (to be)

Affirmative Familiar Singular Command: **sé**

Present: **soy, eres, es, somos, sois, son**

Preterit: **fui, fuiste, fue, fuimos, fuisteis, fueron**

Imperfect: **era, eras, era, éramos, erais, eran**

Subjunctive: **sea, seas, sea, seamos, seáis, sean**

278 Part VI: Appendixes

tener (to have)

Affirmative Familiar Singular Command: **ten**

Present: **tengo, tienes, tiene,** tenemos, tenéis, **tienen**

Preterit: **tuve, tuviste, tuvo, tuvimos, tuvisteis, tuvieron**

Future: **tendré, tendrás, tendrá, tendremos, tendréis, tendrán**

Subjunctive: **tenga, tengas, tenga, tengamos, tengáis, tengan**

traer (to bring)

Present: **traigo,** traes, trae, traemos, traéis, traen

Preterit: **traje, trajiste, trajo, trajimos, trajisteis trajeron**

Subjunctive: **traiga, traigas, traiga, traigamos, traigáis, traigan**

venir (to come)

Gerund: **viniendo**

Affirmative Familiar Singular Command: **ven**

Present: **vengo, vienes, viene,** venimos, **venís, vienen**

Preterit: **vine, viniste, vino, vinimos, vinisteis, vinieron**

Future: **vendré, vendrás, vendrá, vendremos, vendréis, vendrán**

Subjunctive: **venga, vengas, venga, vengamos, vengáis, vengan**

ver (to see)

Present: **veo,** ves, ve, vemos, veis, ven

Preterit: **vi,** viste, **vio,** vimos, visteis, vieron

Imperfect: **veía, veías, veía, veíamos, veíais, veían**

Subjunctive: **vea, veas, vea, veamos, veáis, vean**

Appendix B

English-to-Spanish Dictionary

The English-to-Spanish Dictionary includes words that you need to complete the English-to-Spanish exercises contained in this book. Where gender isn't obvious, **(m.)** or **(f.)** indicate masculine or feminine, respectively. I show feminine forms of adjectives by a bolded **(a)**. Irregular plurals are shown in parenthesis. A bolded **(se)** at the end of a verb indicates that the verb may or may not be used reflexively. Stem changes (**ie, ue,** and so on) appear in parentheses after verbs that require them. (For further information on the tenses that require stem changes, see Appendix A.)

abolish, to: **abolir**

accompany, to: **acompañar**

act, to: **actuar**

advice: **consejo**

Africa: **África**

after: **después**

afternoon (PM): **tarde**

afterwards: **después**

all: **todo (a) (s)**

almost: **casi**

answer: **respuesta**

April: **abril**

around: **alrededor de**

arrive, to: **llegar**

as: **tan**

ask, to: **pedir (i), preguntar**

August: **agosto**

autumn: **otoño**

bad: **mal (o, a)**

bag: **saco**

bank: **banco**

be able to, to: **poder (ue)**

be, to: **ser, estar**

beach: **playa**

beautiful: **bello (a)**

because: **porque**

best: **mejor**

better: **mejor**

bill: **billete m.**

boat: **barco**

book: **libro**

box: **caja**

bracelet: **pulsera**

bring, to: **traer**

brother: **hermano**

bull: **toro**

bus: **autobús m.**

but: **pero**

call, to: **llamar, telefonear**

calmly: **calmamente**

candy: **dulces m. pl.**

car, race: **un auto de carreras**

cathedral: **catedral m.**

celebrate, to: **celebrar**

chicken: **pollo**

choose, to: **escoger**

Christmas: **Navidad f.**

church: **iglesia**

class: **clase f.**

climb, to: **subir**

color: **color m.**

come, to: **venir**

conscientiously: **conscienzudamente**

correct, to: **corregir (i)**

cruise: **crucero**

cure, to: **curar**

date: **fecha**

day: **día m.**

December: **diciembre**

delicious: **delicioso (a)**

deserve, to: **merecer**

dinner: **cena**

disease: **enfermedad f.**

do, to: **hacer**

doctor: **doctor m.**

document: **documento**

dollar: **dólar m.**

downtown: **centro**

dress oneself, to: **vestirse (i)**

drive, to: **conducir**

driver: **chófer m.**

dry oneself, to: **secarse**

early: **temprano**

earn, to: **ganar**

eat breakfast, to: **desayunarse**

eat, to: **comer**

educate, to: **educar**

eight: **ocho**

eighteen: **dieciocho (diez y ocho)**

eighth: **octavo (a)**

eighty: **ochenta**

eleven: **once**

end, to: **poner fin a**

every: **cada**

everybody: **todo el mundo**

fall asleep: **dormirse (ue)**

family: **familia**

far (from): **lejos (de)**

fast: **rápido (a)**

February: **febrero**

feed, to: **alimentar**

fifteen: **quince**

fifth: **quinto (a)**

fifty: **cincuenta**

film: **película**

find, to: **encontrar (ue)**

firefighter: **bombero**

first: **primero (a)**

five: **cinco**

flower: **flor f.**

fluently: **fluidamente**

follow, to: **seguir (i)**

for: **por, para**

forgive, to: **perdonar**

forty: **cuarenta**

four: **cuatro**

fourteen: **catorce**

fourth: **cuarto (a)**

Friday: **viernes m.**

friend: **amigo (a)**

fun, to have: **divertirse (ie)**

future: **futuro**

game: **juego**

get, to: **conseguir (i)**

get up, to: **levantarse**

gift: **regalo**

give, to: **dar, presentar**

go, to: **ir**

go out, to: **salir**

gold: **oro**

good: **buen (o, a)**

government: **gobierno**

governor: **gobernador m.**

grade: **nota**

he: **él**

help (to): **ayuda (ayudar)**

her: **su(s)**

here: **aquí**

his: **su(s)**

home: **casa**

homeless: **los sin techo**

homework: **tarea**

honesty: **honestidad f.**

honeymoon: **luna de miel**

house: **casa**

hundred: **cien(to)**

I: **yo**

immediately: **inmediatamente**

important: **importante**

impulsively: **impulsivamente**

in: **en**

in front of: **enfrente de**

incident: **incidente m.**

incredible: **increíble**

influential: **influyente**

insist, to: **insistir en**

inspire: **inspirar**

instructions: **instrucciones f. pl.**

invite, to: **invitar**

January: **enero**

job: **puesto**

July: **julio**

June: **junio**

kiss, to: **besar**

know, to: **conocer, saber**

law: **ley f.**

learn, to: **aprender**

least, at: **por lo menos**

leave, to: **salir de**

less: **menos**

letter: **carta**

lie, to: **mentir (ie)**

listen (to), to: **escuchar**

little: **poco**

lose, to: **perder (ie)**

lot, a: **mucho**

lottery: **lotería**

luck: **suerte f.**

lucky, to be: **tener suerte**

magazine: **revista**

mail: **correo**

mall: **centro comercial**

marathon: **maratón m.**

March: **marzo**

masses: **masas**

May: **mayo**

me: **me, mí**

meal: **comida**

meet, to: **encontrar (ue)**

memorize, to: **aprender de memoria**

merchant: **comerciante m./f.**

merry: **feliz (felices)**

midnight: **medianoche f.**

million: **millón m.**

mistake: **error m., falta**

Monday: **lunes m.**

money: **dinero**

more: **más**

morning (AM): **mañana**

movies: **cine m.**

much: **mucho (a)**

my: **mi(s)**

necessary: **necesario (a)**

neither . . . nor: **ni . . . ni**

news: **noticias**

nine: **nueve**

nineteen: **diecinueve (diez y nueve)**

ninety: **noventa**

ninth: **noveno (a)**

noon: **mediodía m.**

November: **noviembre**

October: **octubre**

of: **de**

of course: **por supuesto**

office: **oficina**

Olympic: **Olímpico**

one: **un (o), una**

open, to: **abrir**

opportunity: **oportunidad f.**

other: **otro (a)**

our: **nuestro(a)(s)**

park: **parque m.**

participate(in), to: **participar (en)**

pay, to: **pagar**

peace: **paz f.**

person: **persona**

pilot, to: **pilotar**

please, to: **gustar**

police officer: **policía m.**

poor: **pobre**

popcorn: **palomitas de maíz**

prepare (oneself), to: **preparar(se)**

present: **regalo**

president: **presidente m.**

put, to: **poner**

put (on), to: **poner(se)**

question: **pregunta**

quickly: **rápidamente**

react, to: **reaccionar**

receive, to: **recibir**

reception: **recepción f.**

record, to: **grabar**

regret, to: **sentir (ie)**

remain, to: **quedarse**

repeat, to: **repetir (i)**

research: **investigación f.**

respectfully: **respetuosamente**

responsible: **responsable**

restaurant: **restaurante m.**

return, to: **regresar, volver (ue), devolver (ue)**

run, to: **correr**

safari: **safari m.**

sail, to: **navegar**

salesperson: **dependiente m./f.**

Saturday: **sábado**

say, to: **decir**

school: **escuela**

scientific: **científico (a)**

second: **segundo (a)**

sell, to: **vender**

September: **septiembre**

serve, to: **servir (i)**

seven: **siete**

seventeen: **diecisiete (diez y siete)**

seventh: **séptimo (a)**

seventy: **setenta**

she: **ella**

shelter, to: **abrigar**

shower, to: **ducharse**

sister: **hermana**

six: **seis**

sixteen: **dieciséis (diez y seis)**

sixth: **sexto (a)**

sixty: **sesenta**

soft drink: **refresco**

some: **algunos (algunas)**

soon: **pronto**

Spain: **España**

Spanish: **español m.**

speak, to: **hablar**

spring: **primavera**

steak: **bistec m.**

stranger: **desconocido (a)**

street: **calle f.**

study, to: **estudiar**

summer: **verano**

sunbathe, to: **tomar sol**

Sunday: **domingo**

surf, to: **hacer el surf**

sweater: **suéter m.**

take, to: **tomar**

take a cruise, to: **hacer un crucero**

take a trip, to: **hacer un viaje**

taxi: **taxi m.**

tell, to: **decir**

ten: **diez**

tenth: **décimo (a)**

theater: **teatro**

their: **su(s)**

there is, are: **hay**

they: **ellos, ellas**

third: **tercer (a)**

thirteen: **trece**

thirty: **treinta**

thousand: **mil m.**

three: **tres**

through: **por**

Thursday: **jueves m.**

ticket: **billete m.**

time: **hora, tiempo**

to: **a**

train: **tren m.**

trip: **viaje m.**

truth: **verdad f.**

Tuesday: **martes m.**

twelve: **doce**

twenty: **veinte**

two: **dos**

uncle: **tío**

unjust: **injusto (a)**

until: **hasta**

us: **nosotros**

very: **muy**

vocabulary: **vocabulario**

volleyball: **voleibol, volibol m.**

wake up, to: **despertarse (ie)**

walk, to: **andar**

want, to: **querer (ie)**

war: **guerra**

watch, to: **mirar**

we: **nosotros**

wedding: **boda**

Wednesday: **miércoles m.**

well: **bien**

what: **¿qué?, ¿cuál?**

where (to): **¿dónde? (¿adónde?)**

while: **mientras**

why: **¿por qué?**

wide: **ancho (a)**

win, to: **ganar**

winter: **invierno**

with: **con**

without: **sin**

wool: **lana**

word: **palabra**

work, to: **trabajar**

world: **mundo**

worth, to be: **valer**

write, to: **escribir**

you: **tú, Ud., vosotros, Uds.**

your: **tu(s), su(s), vuestro(a)(s)**

zero: **cero**

Appendix C
Spanish-to-English Dictionary

∙ ∙

*T*he Spanish-to-English Dictionary includes words that you need to complete the Spanish-to-English exercises contained in this book. Where gender isn't obvious, I include (**m.**) or (**f.**) to indicate masculine or feminine, respectively. I show feminine adjectives and nouns by a bolded (**a**). Irregular plurals are shown in parentheses. A bolded (**se**) at the end of a verb indicates that the verb may or may not be used reflexively. Stem changes (**ie, ue,** and so on) are shown in parentheses after verbs that require them. (For further information on the tenses that require stem changes, see Appendix A.)

a las órdenes: *at the disposition*

a menudo: *often*

a veces: *sometimes*

abeja: *bee*

abogado (a): *lawyer*

abrazarse: *to hug each other*

abrigo: *coat*

abril: *April*

abrocharse: *to fasten*

absurdo (a): *absurd that*

abuelo (a): *grandfather (grandmother)*

aburrido (a): *boring*

aburrir: *to bore*

aburrirse: *to become bored*

acabar de: *to have just*

aconsejar: *to advise*

acordar (ue): *to agree*

acostar (ue): *to put to bed*

acostarse (ue): *to go to bed*

actuar: *to act*

adiós: *good-bye*

afeitarse: *to shave*

afortunado (a): *fortunate*

afuera: *outside*

agosto: *August*

agua: *water*

ahora: *now*

ahora mismo: *right now*

ahorrar: *to save*

al fin: *finally*

almacenes m. pl.: *department stores*

alcalde m./f.: *mayor*

alegrarse (de): *to be glad, to be happy*

alegre: *happy*

alegremente: *happily*

alemán (alemana): *German*

algún (alguna): *some*

allá: *there*

almorzar (ue): *to eat lunch*

almuerzo: *lunch*

alto (a): *tall*

amable: *nice*

amar: *to love*

amarillo (a): *yellow*

añadir: *to add*

andar: *to walk*

año: *year*

antelación f.: *beforehand, in advance*

antes (de): *before*

apagar: *to turn off*

aparecer: *to appear*

aplaudir: *to applaud*

aplicar(se): *to apply (oneself)*

aprender: *to learn*

aprender de memoria: *to memorize*

apresurarse: *to hurry*

aquel: *that*

aquél: *that one*

aquella: *that*

aquélla: *that one*

aquellas: *those*

aquéllas: *those ones*

aquellos: *those*

aquéllos: *those ones*

aquí: *here*

aretes m. pl.: *earrings*

arreglar: *to tidy*

asegurarse de: *to make sure*

asesor (a): *consultant*

asistir: *to attend*

asombrado (a): *astonished, surprised, amazed*

aspiradora: *vacuum cleaner*

asustado (a): *afraid*

atentamente: *sincerely yours*

atractivo (a): *attractive*

atroz (atroces): *atrocious*

aumento: *raise*

avergonzado (a): *embarrassed, ashamed*

avergonzarse de: *to be ashamed of*

ayer: *yesterday*

ayudar: *to help*

azul: *blue*

bailar: *to dance*

bajado (a): *low*

bajo (a): *short, below*

baloncesto: *basketball*

bañar: *to bathe (someone)*

bañarse: *to bathe oneself*

bañera: *bathtub*

baño: *bathroom*

banquero (a): *banker*

barco: *boat*

basta: *enough*

bastante: *quite, rather, enough*

basura: *garbage*

bate m.: *bat*

batir: *to hit*

beber: *to drink*

bebida: *drink*

besar: *to kiss*

biblioteca: *library*

billete m.: *ticket, bill*

bolsillo: *pocket*

bonito (a): *pretty*

botella: *bottle*

brevemente: *briefly*

brillar: *to shine*

broma: *joke*

bronceador m.: *suntan lotion*

broncearse: *to tan*

bueno (a): *good, nice*

burlarse (de): *to make fun of*

caballito balancín: *rocking horse*

caber: *to fit*

caer: *to fall*

caja: *box*

cajero (a): *cashier*

callarse: *to be silent*

calle f.: *street*

cama: *bed*

camarero (a): *waiter (waitress)*

camarote m.: *cabin (stateroom))*

cambiar: *to change*

camisa: *shirt*

camiseta: *tee shirt*

campo: *countryside, field*

canción f.: *song*

cansado (a): *tired*

cansarse: *to become tired*

cantar: *to sing*

cariño: *affection*

carro: *car*

carta: *letter*

cartel m.: *sign*

cartera: *wallet*

cartero (a): *postal worker*

casarse: *to get married*

cascada: *waterfall*

casi: *almost*

cebolla: *onion*

cena: *dinner*

cepillarse: *to brush (hair, teeth)*

cerca: *near*

cero: *zero*

cerrado (a): *closed*

cerrar (ie): *to close*

cerveza: *beer*

césped m.: *lawn*

champán m.: *champagne*

chaqueta: *jacket*

cheque m.: *check*

chiste m.: *joke*

chófer m.: *driver*

cielo: *sky*

ciencia: *science*

cierto (a): *certain, sure*

cirujano (a): *surgeon*

cita: *appointment, date*

ciudad f.: *city*

claro: *clear*

coche m.: *car*

cochecito: *baby carriage*

cocinar: *to cook*

cocinero (a): *cook*

coger: *to catch*

colgar (ue): *to hang up*

collar m.: *necklace*

colocar: *to place (something)*

colocarse: *to place oneself; to get a job*

comedor m.: *dining room*

comenzar (ie): *to begin*

comer: *to eat*

comida: *meal, food*

cómo: *how*

compañero (a): *friend*

compartir: *to share*

completamente: *completely*

comportamiento: *behavior*

comprar: *to buy*

concesión f.: *dealership*

concienzudo (a): *conscientious*

concluir: *to conclude*

confianza: *confidence*

conocer: *to know (to be acquainted with)*

conseguir (i): *to get, obtain*

consejo: *advice*

consentir (ie): *to consent*

construir: *to build*

contar (ue): *to tell*

contento (a): *happy*

contestar: *to answer*

continuar: *to continue*

contribuir: *to contribute*

convencer: *to convince*

conveniente: *fitting*

conviene: *it is advisable that*

copiar: *to copy*

corregir (i): *to correct*

correo: *mail*

correr: *to run*

corrida de toros: *bullfight*

cortar: *to cut*

cortés (cortesa): *courteous*

cortesía: *courtesy*

cosa: *thing*

costar (ue): *to cost*

creer: *to disbelieve*

crucero: *cruise*

cuál(es): *which, what*

cuándo: *when*

cuánto(-a, -s): *how much, many*

cuarto: *room*

cuarto (a): *fourth, quarter*

cubrir: *to cover*

cuenta: *account*

cuenta bancaria: *bank account*

cuerpo: *body*

cuidado: *care*

cumpleaños m.: *birthday*

curioso(a): *curious*

dar: *to give*

dar un paseo: *to take a walk*

dato: *data*

de buena gana: *willingly*

de nuevo: *again*

de repente: *suddenly*

de retraso: *late (in arriving)*

de vez en cuando: *from time to time*

deber: *to have to*

débil: *weak*

decidir: *to decide*

décimo (a): *tenth*

decir: *to tell, say*

dedo: *finger*

defender: *to defend*

dejar: *to leave, allow*

delante (de): *in front of*

delgado (a): *thin*

delicioso: *delicious*

demasiado: *rather, too, too much*

demostrar: *to demonstrate*

dentro (de): *inside (of)*

deporte m.: *sport*

deportivo (a): *sporty*

derecha: *right*

derramar: *to spill*

desafortunadamente: *unfortunately*

desayunarse: *to have breakfast*

descansar: *to rest*

desconocido (a): *stranger*

describir: *to describe*

descubrir: *to discover*

descuidado (a): *untidy*

desde: *from, since*

desear: *to desire, to wish, to want*

desfile m.: *parade*

despacio: *slowly*

despedir(se) (i): *to say goodbye*

despertar(se) (ie): *to wake up*

después: *after*

destruir: *to destroy*

desvestirse (i): *to get undressed*

devolver (ue): *to return*

día m.: *day*

diciembre: *December*

diente m.: *tooth*

difícil: *difficult*

dinero: *money*

discutir: *to argue*

distinguir: *to distinguish*

distribuir: *to distribute*

divertido (a): *fun*

divertirse (ie): *to have fun*

doce: *twelve*

doler (ue): *to hurt*

dolor m.: *pain*

domingo: *Sunday*

dónde: *where*

dormir (ue): *to sleep*

dormirse (ue): *to fall asleep*

dos: *two*

ducharse: *to take a shower*

duda: *doubt*

dudar: *to doubt*

dudoso(a): *doubtful*

dulce m.: *sweet*

durante: *during*

edificio: *building*

eficiente: *efficient*

egoísta: *selfish*

ejercerse: *to exercise*

el: *the*

él: *he*

elegante: *elegant*

elegir (i): *to elect*

ella: *she*

ellas: *they*

ellos: *they*

empezar (ie): *to begin, start*

empujar: *to push*

en: *in, on, at*

en seguida: *immediately*

en vez de: *instead of*

encantado (a): *delighted*

encantador (a): *enchanting*

encender (ie): *to light*

encontrar (ue): *to meet, find*

encontrarse (ue): *to be located, meet*

encuesta: *survey*

enemigo (a): *enemy*

enero: *January*

enfadado (a): *displeased*

enfadar: *to anger, irritate*

enfadarse (con): *to get angry, annoyed*

enfermo (a): *sick*

enfrente (de): *in front (of)*

engañar: *to deceive*

engañarse: *to be mistaken*

enojado (a): *angry*

enojarse: *to become angry*

enseñar: *to teach, show*

entender (ie): *to understand*

entonces: *then*

entre: *between*

entrenador (a): *trainer*

entrevista: *interview*

enviar: *to send*

envolver (ue): *to wrap up*

equipaje m.: *baggage*

equivocarse: *to make a mistake, to be mistaken*

esa: *that*

ésa: *that one*

esas: *those*

ésas: *those ones*

escaparate m.: *store window*

escena: *scene*

escoger: *to choose*

esconder: *to hide (something)*

esconder(se): *to hide (oneself)*

escribir: *to write*

ese: *that*

ése: *that one*

esencial: *essential*

esos: *those*

ésos: *those ones*

español (a): *Spanish*

esparcir: *to spread out*

especialmente: *especially*

espectáculo: *show*

esperar: *to hope, to wait for*

esposo (a): *spouse*

esquiar: *to ski*

esta: *this*

ésta: *this one*

estadio: *stadium*

estallar: *to break out*

estar: *to be*

estas: *those*

éstas: *those ones*

este: *this*

éste: *this one*

estómago: *stomach*

estos: *those*

éstos: *those ones*

estrecho (a): *narrow*

estupendo (a): *stupendous*

evidente: *evident*

exacto (a): *exact*

excelente: *excellent*

exigir: *to require, to demand*

expedir (i): *to send*

explicación f.: *explanation*

explicar: *to explain*

extraer: *to extract*

extranjero (a): *foreign*

extraño (a): *strange*

fácil: *easy*

familia: *family*

famoso (a): *famous*

fastidiado (a): *bothered*

favor de: *please*

fe f.: *faith*

febrero: *February*

felicidad f.: *happiness*

feliz (felices): *happy*

feo (a): *ugly*

feroz (feroces): *ferocious*

ferozmente: *ferociously*

fiarse en: *to trust*

fiel: *loyal*

fiesta: *party*

fijarse (en): *to notice*

finalmente: *finally*

firmar: *to sign*

físico (a): *physical*

flaco (a): *thin*

folleto: *brochure*

fortaleza: *fort*

fotografiar: *to photograph*

fraqueza: *frankness*

frecuentemente: *frequently*

frío (a): *cold*

furioso (a): *furious*

gabinete m.: *cabinet*

ganar: *to earn, win*

ganga: *bargain*

gato: *cat*

generoso (a): *generous*

genial: *pleasant*

gerente m./f.: *manager*

globo: *balloon*

gordo (a): *fat*

grande: *big*

gris: *grey*

gritar: *to scream*

guantera: *glove compartment*

guapo (a): *pretty, good-looking*

guía m./f.: *guide*

guiar: *to guide*

guisantes m. pl.: *peas*

gustar: *to like*

habituar: *to accustom someone to*

hablador (a): *talkative*

hablar: *to speak, talk*

hace + time: *ago*

hacer: *to make, to do*

hacerse: *to become*

hambre f.: *hunger*

hay: *there is, are*

helado: *ice cream*

helar (ie): *to freeze*

herencia: *inheritance*

hija: *daughter*

hijo: *son*

hijos: *children*

hora: *hour*

horrible: *horrible*

hospedar: *to house*

hoy: *today*

hoy día: *nowadays*

idioma m.: *language*

imperativo (a): *imperative*

impermeable m.: *raincoat*

importante: *important*

imposible: *impossible*

improbable: *improbable*

impuesto: *tax*

incluir: *to include*

increíble: *incredible*

indispensable: *indispensable*

infeliz (infelices): *unhappy*

ingeniero: *engineer*

inglés (inglesa): *English*

ingresar: *to deposit*

injusto (a): *unfair*

inodoro: *without a smell*

insistir: *to insist*

inteligente: *intelligent*

interesante: *interesting*

invierno: *winter*

ir: *to go*

irónico (a): *ironic*

irritado (a): *irritated*

irse: *to go away*

isla: *island*

jamás: *never*

jardín m.: *garden, backyard*

jarrón m.: *vase*

jefe m.: *boss*

joven: *young*

jueves m.: *Thursday*

juez m.: *judge*

jugar (ue): *to play*

jugar (ue) a las damas: *to play checkers*

jugo: *juice*

juguete m.: *toy*

julio: *July*

junio: *June*

justo (a): *fair*

la: *the; to him, her, you, it*

ladrar: *to bark*

lago: *lake*

lamentable: *regrettable*

lamentar: *to regret*

largo (a): *wide*

las: *the, them*

lástima: *pity*

lavar: *to wash*

lavarse: *to wash oneself*

le: *to him, him, to her*

leal: *loyal*

leer: *to read*

lejos: *far*

lentamente: *slowly*

les: *to them*

levantar: *to raise (something)*

levantarse: *to get up*

ley f.: *law*

libra: *pound*

libre: *free*

ligero (a): *light*

limpiar: *to clean*

lisonjeado (a): *flattered*

listo (a): *ready*

llamar: *to call*

llamarse: *to be called, to call oneself*

llave f.: *key*

llegar: *to arrive*

llevar: *to take, wear*

llorar: *to cry*

llover (ue): *to rain*

lo: *him, it*

lodo: *mud*

los: *the, them*

luego: *then*

lujoso (a): *luxurious*

lunes m.: *Monday*

madera: *wood*

magnífico (a): *magnificent*

maleta: *suitcase*

malo (a): *bad*

mañana: *tomorrow, morning*

mandar: *to command, to order. to send*

mantel m.: *tablecloth*

mantequilla: *butter*

maquillarse: *to put on makeup*

máquina: *machine*

mar m.: *sea*

maravilloso (a): *marvelous*

marcharse: *to go away*

maridos m. pl.: *married couple*

martes m.: *Tuesday*

marzo: *March*

más: *more*

más tarde: *later*

masticar: *to chew*

materialista: *materialistic*

mayo: *May*

me: *me, to me*

mediodía m.: *noon*

medir (i): *to measure*

mejor: *better*

menos: *less*

mensajero (a): *messenger*

mentir: *to lie*

merecer: *to deserve, merit*

mes m.: *month*

mesa: *table*

metro: *subway*

mezclar: *to mix*

mi(s): *my*

mientras: *while*

miércoles m.: *Wednesday*

mil m.: *one thousand*

millón m.: *one million*

minuto: *minute*

mío(a)(s): *mine*

mirar: *to look at*

mismo (a): *same*

moderno (a): *modern*

moda: *style*

mojado (a): *wet*

montaña: *mountain*

moreno (a): *dark-haired, dark haired*

morir (ue): *to die*

mostaza: *mustard*

mostrar (ue): *to show*

mucho (a): *much, many*

muebles m. pl.: *furniture*

mujer f.: *woman*

muñeca: *wrist*

muñeco de nieve: *snowman*

muy: *very*

nacer: *to be born*

nada: *nothing*

nadar: *to swim*

nadie: *nobody, no one*

naipe m.: *card (playing)*

natación f.: *swimming*

natural: *natural*

necesario (a): *necessary*

necesitar: *to need*

negar (ie): *to deny*

negro (a): *black*

nevar (ie): *to snow*

ni . . . ni: *neither . . . nor*

ningún (ninguno, ninguna): *none, not any*

no: *no, not*

noche f.: *evening*

nos: *us, to us, ourselves*

nosotros: *we, us*

noticias: *news*

noveno (a): *nineth*

noviembre: *November*

novio (a): *boyfriend (girlfriend)*

nube f.: *cloud*

nuera: *daughter-in-law*

nuestro (a)(s): *our, ours*

nuevo (a): *new*

nunca: *never*

o: *or*

obedecer: *to obey*

obvio (a): *obvious*

octavo (a): *eighth*

octubre: *October*

ocupado (a): *busy*

ofrecer: *to offer, give*

oír: *to hear*

ojalá que . . .: *if only . . .*

ojo: *eye*

oler: *to smell*

olvidar: *to forget*

olvidarse (de): *to forget*

optimista: *optimistic*

ordenar: *to order*

ordinario (a): *ordinary*

orgulloso (a): *proud*

oro: *gold*

os: *you, to you, yourselves*

otoño: autumn

otro (a): *other, another*

paciencia: *patience*

pagar en efectivo: *to pay in cash*

país m.: *country (nation)*

pájaro: *bird*

palabra: *word*

palomitas de maíz: *popcorn*

panadero (a): *baker*

pantalla: *screen*

papel m.: *paper, role*

para: *for*

parar: *to stop (something)*

pararse: *to stop oneself*

pardo (a): *brown*

parecer: *to seem*

partido: *match*

partir: *to leave*

pasado (a): *last*

pasar: *to spend (time)*

pase m.: *showing*

pasearse: *to go for a walk*

pastel m.: *cake*

pedir (i): *to ask for*

peinarse: *to comb one's hair*

pelar: *to peel*

película: *film*

peligroso (a): *dangerous*

pelo: *hair*

pensar (ie): *to think*

peor: *worse*

pequeño (a): *small*

perder (ie): *to lose*

perezoso (a): *lazy*

perfeccionar: *to perfect*

perfecto (a): *perfect*

perla: *pearl*

permitir: *to permit*

pero: *but*

perro: *dog*

pescado: *fish*

pesimista: *pessimistic*

peso: *weight*

pierna: *leg*

piscina: *swimming pool*

piso: *floor*

planchar: *to iron*

plato: *plate*

playa: *beach*

pobre: *poor*

poco (a): *little*

poder (ue): *to be able to, can*

pollo: *chicken*

polvo: *dust*

poner: *to put*

ponerse: *to put (something on) to become, to place oneself*

popular: *popular*

por: *for, per*

por consiguiente: *consequently*

por qué: *why*

por supuesto: *of course*

porción f.: *portion*

porque: *because*

posible: *possible*

precio: *price*

preferible: *preferable*

preferir (ie): *to prefer*

preocuparse (de): *to worry (about)*

prestar: *to borrow*

prestar atención: *to pay attention*

primavera: *spring*

primero (a): *first*

primo (a): *cousin*

probable: *probable*

probar (ue): *to try (on)*

producir: *to produce*

producto lácteo: *dairy product*

profundamente: *deeply*

prohibir: *to forbid*

prometer: *to promise*

pronto: *soon*

pronunciar: *to pronounce*

propietario: *proprietor*

próximo (a): *next*

proyecto: *project*

puerto: *port*

puesto: *job*

quedar(se): *to remain*

quejarse (de): *to complain*

quemadura: *burn*

queso: *cheese*

quién(es): *who, whom*

quitar(se): *to remove, to take off*

rato: *while*

receta: *recipe*

reclamar: *to demand*

refresco: *soft drink*

refriarse: *to catch a cold*

regalo: *gift*

régimen m.: *diet*

regla: *rule*

regresar: *to return*

reino: *kingdom*

reír: *to laugh*

relámpagos: *lightening*

reunirse: *to meet*

romper: *to break*

rótulo: *sign*

ruido: *noise*

ruta: *road, route*

sábado: *Saturday*

saco: *bag*

sagaz (sagaces): *astute, wise*

salir: *to go out*

saltar: *to jump*

saludable: *healthy*

secar(se): *to dry (oneself)*

seda: *silk*

seguir (i): *to follow*

selva: *rainforest*

sentir (ie): *to be sorry, to regret*

ser: *to be*

siempre: *always*

sol m.: *sun*

sonar (ue): *to ring*

sorprendido (a): *surprised*

suelo: *ground*

suerte f.: *luck*

sugerir (ie): *to suggest*

tal vez: *perhaps*

también: *also, too*

tampoco: *neither/not . . . either*

tempestad f.: *storm*

temprano: *early*

tener (ie): *to have*

timbre m.: *bell*

tintorería: *dry cleaner*

torpe: *clumsy*

trabajador (a): *hard-working*

traducir: *to translate*

traer: *to bring*

traje m. de baño: *bathing suit*

tratar de: *to try to*

tronar (ue): *to thunder*

trozo: *piece*

truenos: *thunder*

uva: *grape*

vaciar: *to empty*

valer: *to be worth*

venir: *to come*

venta: *sale*

ver: *to see*

vestir (i): *to clothe*

viernes m.: *Friday*

víspera: *eve*

volver (ue): *to return*

voz f.: *voice*

vuestro (a)(s): *your, yours*

ya: *already*

zanahoria: *carrot*

Index

present subjunctive, 107, 111
present tense, 73–78
preterit past tense, 216–220

• J •

jamás (never), 88–90
jugar (to play)
 chart, 271
 imperative mood/command form
  formal, 149
  informal plural, 158
  informal singular, 154
 present subjunctive, 110
 present tense, 69
 preterit past tense, 213
 versus **tocar**, 265–266

• K •

know (**conocer**)
 chart, 274
 preterit past tense, 221
 versus **saber**, 264
know (**saber**)
 chart, 277
 versus **conocer**, 264
 future tense, 243
 imperative mood/command form, 150
 imperfect past tense, 256
 present subjunctive, 111
 preterit past tense, 218, 221

• L •

leave (**dejar**). *See also* **salir**
 expressions with, 78
 prepositions and, 202–203
 versus **salir**, 266
le/les, 174
like (**gustar**), 176–177, 255
llevar (to take), 264–265
lo
 neuter article, 42
 use in Spain, 166–167
 when placed with **le/les**, 174

• M •

make (**hacer**)
 chart, 276
 expressions with, 77–78
 imperative mood/command form, 148, 154, 159
 prepositions and, 203–204
 present tense, 73
 preterit past tense, 217
 with **que**, 65
maybe (**quizás**, **tal vez**), 120
months, 17–18
moods. *See also* tenses
 imperative/command form
  formal, 146–150
  informal, 151–161
  overview, 145–146
  pronoun placement, 173, 175, 192
 indicative
  defined, 105, 260
  expressing wishing, emotion, need, doubt, 117–118
  impersonal expressions, 116
  with **tal vez** and **quizás**, 120
 infinitive
  consecutive verbs, 65
  defined, 30, 260
  with **gustar**, 177, 255
  with **ir** + **a**, 240
  negative words before, 89
  with **ni . . . ni** construction, 89
  with **pensar**, 78
  prepositions and, 200–204
  pronoun placement, 172, 174–175, 190
  used as nouns, 41, 95–96
 selecting, 260
 subjunctive
  imperfect, 105
  past, 105
  pluperfect, 105
  present, 105–111, 113–121, 256
must (**deber**)
 prepositions and, 203
 versus **tener que**, 265

• W •

• Y •

• Z •

BUSINESS, CAREERS & PERSONAL FINANCE

0-7645-9847-3

0-7645-2431-3

Also available:

- Business Plans Kit For Dummies
  0-7645-9794-9
- Economics For Dummies
  0-7645-5726-2
- Grant Writing For Dummies
  0-7645-8416-2
- Home Buying For Dummies
  0-7645-5331-3
- Managing For Dummies
  0-7645-1771-6
- Marketing For Dummies
  0-7645-5600-2

- Personal Finance For Dummies
  0-7645-2590-5*
- Resumes For Dummies
  0-7645-5471-9
- Selling For Dummies
  0-7645-5363-1
- Six Sigma For Dummies
  0-7645-6798-5
- Small Business Kit For Dummies
  0-7645-5984-2
- Starting an eBay Business For Dummies
  0-7645-6924-4
- Your Dream Career For Dummies
  0-7645-9795-7

HOME & BUSINESS COMPUTER BASICS

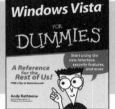

0-470-05432-8

0-471-75421-8

Also available:

- Cleaning Windows Vista For Dummies
  0-471-78293-9
- Excel 2007 For Dummies
  0-470-03737-7
- Mac OS X Tiger For Dummies
  0-7645-7675-5
- MacBook For Dummies
  0-470-04859-X
- Macs For Dummies
  0-470-04849-2
- Office 2007 For Dummies
  0-470-00923-3

- Outlook 2007 For Dummies
  0-470-03830-6
- PCs For Dummies
  0-7645-8958-X
- Salesforce.com For Dummies
  0-470-04893-X
- Upgrading & Fixing Laptops For Dummies
  0-7645-8959-8
- Word 2007 For Dummies
  0-470-03658-3
- Quicken 2007 For Dummies
  0-470-04600-7

FOOD, HOME, GARDEN, HOBBIES, MUSIC & PETS

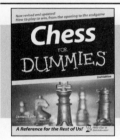

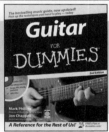

0-7645-8404-9

0-7645-9904-6

Also available:

- Candy Making For Dummies
  0-7645-9734-5
- Card Games For Dummies
  0-7645-9910-0
- Crocheting For Dummies
  0-7645-4151-X
- Dog Training For Dummies
  0-7645-8418-9
- Healthy Carb Cookbook For Dummies
  0-7645-8476-6
- Home Maintenance For Dummies
  0-7645-5215-5

- Horses For Dummies
  0-7645-9797-3
- Jewelry Making & Beading For Dummies
  0-7645-2571-9
- Orchids For Dummies
  0-7645-6759-4
- Puppies For Dummies
  0-7645-5255-4
- Rock Guitar For Dummies
  0-7645-5356-9
- Sewing For Dummies
  0-7645-6847-7
- Singing For Dummies
  0-7645-2475-5

INTERNET & DIGITAL MEDIA

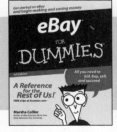

0-470-04529-9

0-470-04894-8

Also available:

- Blogging For Dummies
  0-471-77084-1
- Digital Photography For Dummies
  0-7645-9802-3
- Digital Photography All-in-One Desk Reference For Dummies
  0-470-03743-1
- Digital SLR Cameras and Photography For Dummies
  0-7645-9803-1
- eBay Business All-in-One Desk Reference For Dummies
  0-7645-8438-3
- HDTV For Dummies
  0-470-09673-X

- Home Entertainment PCs For Dummies
  0-470-05523-5
- MySpace For Dummies
  0-470-09529-6
- Search Engine Optimization For Dummies
  0-471-97998-8
- Skype For Dummies
  0-470-04891-3
- The Internet For Dummies
  0-7645-8996-2
- Wiring Your Digital Home For Dummies
  0-471-91830-X

* Separate Canadian edition also available
† Separate U.K. edition also available

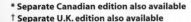

Available wherever books are sold. For more information or to order direct: U.S. customers visit www.dummies.com or call 1-877-762-2974.
U.K. customers visit www.wileyeurope.com or call 0800 243407. Canadian customers visit www.wiley.ca or call 1-800-567-4797.

SPORTS, FITNESS, PARENTING, RELIGION & SPIRITUALITY

0-471-76871-5

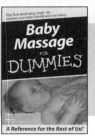

0-7645-7841-3

Also available:
- Catholicism For Dummies
  0-7645-5391-7
- Exercise Balls For Dummies
  0-7645-5623-1
- Fitness For Dummies
  0-7645-7851-0
- Football For Dummies
  0-7645-3936-1
- Judaism For Dummies
  0-7645-5299-6
- Potty Training For Dummies
  0-7645-5417-4
- Buddhism For Dummies
  0-7645-5359-3

- Pregnancy For Dummies
  0-7645-4483-7 †
- Ten Minute Tone-Ups For Dummies
  0-7645-7207-5
- NASCAR For Dummies
  0-7645-7681-X
- Religion For Dummies
  0-7645-5264-3
- Soccer For Dummies
  0-7645-5229-5
- Women in the Bible For Dummies
  0-7645-8475-8

TRAVEL

0-7645-7749-2

0-7645-6945-7

Also available:
- Alaska For Dummies
  0-7645-7746-8
- Cruise Vacations For Dummies
  0-7645-6941-4
- England For Dummies
  0-7645-4276-1
- Europe For Dummies
  0-7645-7529-5
- Germany For Dummies
  0-7645-7823-5
- Hawaii For Dummies
  0-7645-7402-7

- Italy For Dummies
  0-7645-7386-1
- Las Vegas For Dummies
  0-7645-7382-9
- London For Dummies
  0-7645-4277-X
- Paris For Dummies
  0-7645-7630-5
- RV Vacations For Dummies
  0-7645-4442-X
- Walt Disney World & Orlando
  For Dummies
  0-7645-9660-8

GRAPHICS, DESIGN & WEB DEVELOPMENT

0-7645-8815-X

0-7645-9571-7

Also available:
- 3D Game Animation For Dummies
  0-7645-8789-7
- AutoCAD 2006 For Dummies
  0-7645-8925-3
- Building a Web Site For Dummies
  0-7645-7144-3
- Creating Web Pages For Dummies
  0-470-08030-2
- Creating Web Pages All-in-One Desk
  Reference For Dummies
  0-7645-4345-8
- Dreamweaver 8 For Dummies
  0-7645-9649-7

- InDesign CS2 For Dummies
  0-7645-9572-5
- Macromedia Flash 8 For Dummies
  0-7645-9691-8
- Photoshop CS2 and Digital
  Photography For Dummies
  0-7645-9580-6
- Photoshop Elements 4 For Dummies
  0-471-77483-9
- Syndicating Web Sites with RSS Feeds
  For Dummies
  0-7645-8848-6
- Yahoo! SiteBuilder For Dummies
  0-7645-9800-7

NETWORKING, SECURITY, PROGRAMMING & DATABASES

0-7645-7728-X

0-471-74940-0

Also available:
- Access 2007 For Dummies
  0-470-04612-0
- ASP.NET 2 For Dummies
  0-7645-7907-X
- C# 2005 For Dummies
  0-7645-9704-3
- Hacking For Dummies
  0-470-05235-X
- Hacking Wireless Networks
  For Dummies
  0-7645-9730-2
- Java For Dummies
  0-470-08716-1

- Microsoft SQL Server 2005 For Dummies
  0-7645-7755-7
- Networking All-in-One Desk Reference
  For Dummies
  0-7645-9939-9
- Preventing Identity Theft For Dummies
  0-7645-7336-5
- Telecom For Dummies
  0-471-77085-X
- Visual Studio 2005 All-in-One Desk
  Reference For Dummies
  0-7645-9775-2
- XML For Dummies
  0-7645-8845-1